The Still Divided Academy

The Still Divided Academy

How Competing Visions of Power, Politics, and Diversity Complicate the Mission of Higher Education

Stanley Rothman, April Kelly-Woessner,
and Matthew Woessner

ROWMAN & LITTLEFIELD PUBLISHERS, INC.
Lanham • Boulder • New York • Toronto • Plymouth, UK

Published by Rowman & Littlefield Publishers, Inc.
A wholly owned subsidiary of The Rowman & Littlefield Publishing Group, Inc.
4501 Forbes Boulevard, Suite 200, Lanham, Maryland 20706
http://www.rowmanlittlefield.com

Estover Road, Plymouth PL6 7PY, United Kingdom

British Library Cataloguing in Publication Information Available

Library of Congress Cataloging-in-Publication Data

Rothman, Stanley, 1927–
The still divided academy : how competing visions of power, politics, and diversity complicate the mission of higher education / Stanley Rothman, April Kelly-Woessner, and Matthew Woessner.
p. cm.
Includes bibliographical references and index.
ISBN 978-1-4422-0806-3 (cloth : alk. paper) — ISBN 978-1-4422-0808-7 (electronic)
1. Education, Higher—Aims and objectives—United States. 2. Education, Higher—Political aspects—United States. 3. Education, Higher—Social aspects—United States. 4. Universities and colleges—United States—Administration. 5. Academic freedom—United States. I. Kelly-Woessner, April. II. Woessner, Matthew. III. Title.
LA227.4.R675 2011
378.73—dc22

2010029031

∞™ The paper used in this publication meets the minimum requirements of American National Standard for Information Sciences—Permanence of Paper for Printed Library Materials, ANSI/NISO Z39.48-1992.

Printed in the United States of America

To
Seymour Martin Lipset
for his groundbreaking work in the empirical study of conflict in the American university

To our children,
Isaac Woessner and
Rachel Woessner

Contents

Preface

This book, as well as the survey on which it is based, was first proposed by Professor Stanley Rothman in the fall of 1998. As the director for the Center for Social and Political Change at Smith College, Rothman teamed with Seymour Martin Lipset of George Mason University, Everett Ladd of the University of Connecticut, and Neil Nevitte of the University of Toronto to conduct a study of higher education in the United States and Canada.

The North American Academic Study Survey (NAASS) was conducted by The Angus Reid Group in 1999 and included surveys of professors, administrators, and students. In part, the study was a follow-up to Ladd and Lipset's earlier work in *The Divided Academy* and Rothman's earlier work in *American Elites*. Rothman, Lipset, and Nevitte published some findings from the survey in 2002 and 2003 with articles in *The Public Interest*, the *International Journal of Public Opinion Research*, and *Academic Questions*. These articles explored the impact of racial diversity on college and university campuses. Following the deaths of Ladd and Lipset, Rothman invited his former coauthor, S. Robert Lichter, president of the Center for Media and Public Affairs, to join the research project. Together, Rothman, Lichter, and Nevitte published an article in *The Forum* in 2005 that investigated the relationship between political views and professional advancement among college faculty. Rothman and Lichter continued this line of research with a book chapter in *The Politically Correct University: Problems, Scopes, and Reforms* (Maranto, Redding, and Hess 2009).

While Rothman was successful in publishing some significant findings from the survey, the deaths of Ladd and Lipset, along with Rothman's own illness, delayed further work on the project. Both Nevitte and Lichter, while instrumental in the earlier articles, were constrained by long-standing professional responsibilities that prevented them from devoting the time required to complete the project. As such, important findings from the NAASS remained unpublished. Renewed efforts to write a book based on the NAASS findings began in earnest in November 2007 when, at an American Enterprise Institute research conference, Professor Robert Maranto introduced Stanley Rothman and Robert Lichter to April Kelly-Woessner and Matthew Woessner. Like Rothman and Lichter, the Woessners had been charged with writing a chapter for Maranto's edited volume, *The Politically Correct University*. Noting their prior work on politics in academia, Stanley Rothman invited the Woessners to join the project. By January 2008, the newly constituted research team of Rothman, Kelly-Woessner, and Woessner began work on a comprehensive examination of the NAASS data set.

In light of Professor Rothman's illness, the team agreed that the Woessners would take the lead in continuing the analysis of the NAASS survey data, based largely on the manuscript proposal first drawn up by the original research team of Rothman, Lipset, Ladd, and Nevitte. Matthew Woessner took the primary responsibility for organizing, analyzing, and presenting the study's findings. April Kelly-Woessner, charged with the integration of theory and literature, wrote the majority of the book's preliminary drafts. On completion of each draft chapter, Stanley Rothman offered detailed input on both the style and the substance of the manuscript, giving considerable attention to making the book both technically precise and accessible to a nonacademic audience.

Undoubtedly, a book that examines public opinion on American college campuses will, first and foremost, interest academics. An analysis of the competing views of professors, students, and administrators will understandably appeal to a unique class of Americans whose professional lives are tied to university politics. Nevertheless, throughout the book, the authors took great care to avoid a highly technical presentation of the findings, showing most of the results with straightforward figures and tables. On a few occasions, where the discussion required the introduction of more sophisticated statistical modeling, the research team made every effort to explain the meaning of the results clearly and unobtrusively. The more complicated statistical models are included in the appendices for those readers who wish to delve further into the analysis. Consequently, while the results of this study may be of interest primarily to academics, the findings are designed to reach a broader audience. The topics we address in the book (educational policy, academic power, politics, diversity, academic freedom, and so on) have great societal consequence. Some of our findings challenge conventional wisdom and long-standing norms in higher education. We have no doubt that some of our conclusions will be controversial. Yet it is the authors' hope that this research will help to facilitate thoughtful discussion on a range of controversies facing higher education in the twenty-first century.

Acknowledgments

The authors of this book owe a debt of gratitude to friends, colleagues, and contributors whose expertise in academia span four generations. Without a doubt, we owe our most profound thanks to three members of the original research team, the late Seymour Martin Lipset, the late Everett Carll Ladd, and Neil Nevitte, who, in the early stages of the undertaking, helped to conceive of the project, design the survey, and complete some early analyses of the results. It is with profound sadness that Seymour Lipset and Everett Ladd did not live long enough to see this project through to its completion.

The authors are especially grateful to S. Robert Lichter, professor of communication at George Mason University and president of the Center for Media and Public Affairs. In addition to his contributions as coauthor on some of the first studies of the NAASS dataset, Dr. Lichter provided extremely thoughtful and constructive comments on some of the preliminary drafts of the manuscript. His suggestions helped to elucidate some of the book's more important findings.

We also owe a great debt to Robert Maranto, the 21st Century Chair in Leadership at the Department of Education Reform at the University of Arkansas. As one of the leading figures in the field of educational reform, Dr. Maranto provided valuable feedback on several drafts of the manuscript, as well as offered us guidance and advice in the publishing process.

The authors are also grateful for the advice they received from Fredrick M. Hess, director of education policy studies at the American Enterprise Institute. Dr. Hess and his staff offered invaluable assistance as the authors navigated the publishing process.

The authors would also like to offer thanks to an eclectic array of additional contributors, who helped us navigate around some of the difficult obstacles often associated with a project of this scale and complexity. We are grateful to Dr. Ivan Katchanovski, formerly with University of Toronto, who served as the project statistician in the early stages of the research. Once the research team began the comprehensive analysis of the survey results, Dr. Katchanovski patiently answered their many questions about the organization and construction of the NAASS dataset. Theresa Harkless Woods was considerate enough to read through some of the earliest drafts of the manuscript, offering advice on style and clarity. Dr. Allyson M. Lowe of Carlow University was kind enough to advise us on student participation in faculty governance. Our research assistants, Tyler Loeb, Jade Kira Herbst, Kida Salley, and Jenna Shank were enormously supportive in helping to construct the bibliography and appendices and also assisted in some initial data analysis and chapter editing.

Finally, the NAASS research project would not have been possible without the generous support of the Sarah Scaife Foundation, The Randolph Foundation, and The Earhart Foundation. Scientific investigations, rooted in large-scale survey research, are enormously difficult and costly. It is thanks to their efforts on behalf of the Center for the Study of Social and Political Change, which is directed by Stanley Rothman, that such complex and far-reaching studies are possible.

Given the scope of this work and the sensitivity of the issues covered, we have no doubt that our findings will generate some controversy. While we are grateful for the assistance of those individuals and foundations listed above, our analysis may not reflect their own perspectives or understanding of these issues.

Chapter One

Introduction

The American system of higher education is still widely regarded as the best educational system in the world. Americans place a great deal of confidence in their colleges and universities, viewing them as the path to success and prosperity. Foreign students flock to American colleges and universities to earn both undergraduate and advanced degrees. Overall, colleges and universities have seen increased enrollments, albeit with significant changes in the demographics and skill levels of incoming students. In many ways, higher education is in a period of growth. Yet recent news coverage reveals some deep underlying anxieties about the future of American higher education. Students and their parents express considerable concern about the rising cost of higher education, a concern that is echoed by elected officials. College professors express concern about the changing nature of their work, the decline of the tenure system, the increasing reliance on adjunct professors, the lack of student preparedness, and the declining status of the faculty. Administrators lament cuts in public funding, pressures from accreditation agencies, increased government interference, and the ineffectiveness of shared governance. Underlying many of these concerns is the question of what higher education actually produces. A growing assessment movement requires colleges and universities to demonstrate that students actually accomplish clear learning objectives in the course of four years. Students expect even more, holding colleges and universities responsible for their ability—or inability—to find desirable employment opportunities.

While these anxieties appear to have little effect on overall enrollment rates or the general belief that college education is worthwhile, there appears to be a clear recognition from all quarters that change is on the horizon. We argue throughout the book that there are competing demands on higher education and incompatible visions of the university and its core mission. Hence, calls for education reform are bound to meet resistance from one sector or another, as academics, students, and the public disagree about the purpose of higher education, the problems facing the university, and the direction and scope of institutional reform. As a result, attempts to prescribe a course of treatment from outside the academy will continue to be met with suspicion, distrust, and resistance. This is already evident, as the higher-education community has launched a vigorous defense of its practices in light of both the Spellings Commission report and court challenges to college admissions practices. While this may suggest that the academic community is simply at odds with the demands of the public, we also find that academics themselves are divided on many of the issues facing the academy. In this sense, external pressures and demands for accountability serve to reveal and exacerbate these internal tensions, as calls for change force constituencies to grapple with incompatible goals and visions.

PREVIOUS STUDIES OF THE ACADEMY

Although the higher-education community is facing some new challenges, this is not the first time that it has been forced to respond to external economic, social, and political pressures. Recognizing the complex relationship between academia and the outside world, three generations of scholars have sought to understand how American higher education influences and is, in turn, influenced by society at large.

Although the sociological examinations of higher education stretch as far back as the early twentieth century (Ladd and Lipset 1975, 17), the most ambitious systematic studies of academia were rooted in the social and political unrest of the McCarthy era. In the years following World War II, the public was relatively unconcerned with either the threat of communism or the erosion of American civil liberties (Stouffer 1992, 59). At the same time, however, some members of the academic elite were concerned with the possible erosion of civil liberties, not just in academia but in society at large. Investigations into professors' political loyalties, especially at the nation's elite institutions, had a measurable effect on the campus climate. Prominent academics argued that high-profile investigations into the political loyalties of university professors undermined the foundation of American higher education. Robert M. Hutchins, former president and chancellor of the University of Chicago, wrote extensively on the topic. Hutchins argued that government interference with higher education compromised the underlying purpose of the university as a center for independent thought and criticism (Hutchins 1951). In his role as president of the

Fund for the Republic, Hutchins commissioned Paul Lazarsfeld to conduct the first major, systematic study of professors' values, political beliefs, and behaviors, with the goal of investigating the impact of the McCarthy era on academic culture.

In 1958, Paul Lazarsfeld and coauthor Wagner Thielens Jr. published their findings in *The Academic Mind.* Based on their surveys of over 2,400 social scientists, the researchers made some important discoveries about academic culture in the decade following World War II. While the authors demonstrate that the experiences and values of academics varied considerably in the post-war years, they also found that a significant portion of academics expressed some apprehension that their political opinions would have consequences for their academic careers. More than a third of professors expressed some fear that students would take what they said out of context or misquote them in a way that would raise questions about their political views. Yet the authors discovered that, for most professors, this apprehension did not prevent them from taking strong political positions. In fact, apprehensive professors were more likely to protest against administrative censorship of student activities. While most professors did not report substantial changes in their professional activities, Lazarsfeld and Thielens found that a sizable minority of professors did alter their behavior. For example, some professors reported that they avoided discussion of controversial topics in the classroom, while others admitted to slanting the material in a way as to make it less offensive to conservative students.

Although professors reported some apprehension about expressing their viewpoints to their students, it is clear from Lazarsfeld and Thielens's research that the general concern was not rooted in sensitivity to students' beliefs. Rather, professors were concerned that students would misrepresent their views in a manner that would expose them to public scrutiny and hostile forces from outside the university. In fact, professors routinely drew a distinction between the environment of the university, which allowed them to express controversial political ideas, and the hostile political environment outside the university. Thus, the apparent contradiction between professors' apprehension and their continued activism could be attributed to "a separation between the attitudes and behavior appropriate to the campus and those befitting the larger community" (Lazarsfeld and Thielens 1958, 99).

This is not to say that the university environment was free of political pressure. Lazarsfeld and Thielens note that many professors faced competing pressures. Fearing a backlash from their colleagues on the one hand and the administration on the other, many professors would often avoid contentious faculty meetings by claiming that they were "called away from campus on unavoidable business" (Lazarsfeld and Thielens 1958, 104). Nevertheless, professors were more willing to take political positions if those positions remained within the protective confines of the university.

Three decades after *The Academic Mind*, in response to the campus protests and upheaval of the Vietnam war years, Everett Carll Ladd Jr. and Seymour Martin Lipset published another comprehensive study of academic politics, based on a large-scale survey conducted by the Carnegie Commission on Higher Education. However, the political pressures on higher education during this time assumed a different form. Ladd and Lipset explained in *The Divided Academy* (1975),

> The contemporary context obviously differs in many ways from that which prompted *The Academic Mind*. In the McCarthy era, for one thing, internal divisions in the social sciences were not prominent as they now are. It was much more simply a case of hostile intrusions from without. The one parallel between the McCarthy and the Vietnam years . . . is the presence in both periods of deep tensions and conflicts in the polity which necessarily made both eras particularly stressful for the political sciences. (102)

Ladd and Lipset's analysis demonstrates that the campus protests and student activism of the late 1960s created division and tension between various groups on campus. Yet the politicization of the university in this period did not merely split the faculty along predictable ideological lines. Rather, the professoriate was deeply divided on the issue of student activism per se. A fair number of liberal Democrats formed alliances with conservatives in order to defend the university from the disruption of campus protests and the threat of student power movements that potentially undermined the authority of the faculty. In fact, even the majority of left-leaning faculty agreed with the position that campus disruptions were a threat to academic freedom and that students who disrupted the functioning of the college should be expelled (Ladd and Lipset 1975).

Similarly, the issue of affirmative action created strange alliances among faculty members. While some liberal Democrats favored affirmative action policies for the purpose of advancing racial equality, others saw preferential hiring for women and minorities as an attack on meritocracy. As a result, the highest-achieving liberal academics were more likely to split with their ideological brethren on issues of preferential hiring and admissions policies because of their commitment to "the competitive emphasis on originality and creativity" (Ladd and Lipset 1975, 305). This commitment to meritocracy and competitive rewards among the more elite faculty also translated into lower levels of support for faculty unionization among this group, which otherwise tended to be quite liberal on social issues.

The divisions among faculty in the Vietnam era raised questions and provoked debate about the general purpose of the university. In this way, political pressures from within the university had similar effects as the external pressures of the McCarthy era. Our analysis in the chapters to follow examines these themes in the post–Cold War era. We argue that new external pressures have come to bear on the university, once again raising questions about the mission of higher education. While familiar political divisions continue to be a source of tension between the academy and the public, modern pressures go well beyond the social and political culture wars. New debates about higher education have taken on a more practical bent, focusing on issues of cost, accessibility, and accountability. Yet these practical considerations have important theoretical implications and, again, force the academy to consider and explain its central mission and priorities.

Yet the university's internal constituents often hold contrary views on these modern debates. Our analysis of these divisions expands on previous studies by extending the scope of the research. In addition to examining divisions within the faculty, we also consider the perspectives of students and administrators, both of whom play an important role in defining the mission of the university. Arguably, the role of administrators and students has grown since earlier studies of the academy, at least in particular areas.

For example, in the period since Ladd and Lipset penned *The Divided Academy*, universities have seen a steady growth in administrative offices and costs (Leslie and Rhoades 1995). Some of this growth represents an extension of the role of the administration in shaping students' college experiences. Administrative offices are now involved in a number of activities designed to produce various student outcomes, many of which have a political bent. For example, most colleges have an administrative office designed to foster an appreciation for diversity. Other administrative offices aim to advance global awareness, sustainability, citizenship, or a commitment to social justice. Some long-standing administrative offices have redefined their functions to include activities designed to foster students' social and moral development. In fact, many of the campus programs that have been criticized for politicizing the campus in recent years have been run by administrative offices rather than the faculty.

One of the more controversial of these programs was initiated at the University of Delaware, whose residence life program required students to undergo various forms of diversity training (Kissel 2008a). After widespread public attention and an inquiry by the Foundation for Individual Rights in Education (FIRE), the university suspended the program (Hoover 2007). Whatever one's perspective on the value of the program, it is clear that residence life officials at the University of Delaware saw their role as an educational one. According to the revised 2008–2009 plan, "The Residence Life program encourages students to become engaged and active citizens on campus by understanding how their thoughts, values, beliefs, and actions affect the people with whom they live and by recognizing their citizenship responsibilities" (as quoted in Kissel 2008b). The proposal included a number of learning goals, including recognition of how history, background, and culture affect one's perspectives. In this respect, the University of Delaware is not alone. Residence life officers and other campus administrators now commonly tread into educational territory in defining their missions. For this reason, any analysis on perspectives within the academy, as they relate to student learning and the educational mission of the university, would be incomplete without some consideration of the campus administrators who oversee the large web of institutional offices and programs.

Likewise, it is important to recognize how students' roles in the university have changed over the past several decades. Even since the Ladd and Lipset study, student organizations have grown in power and influence, participating both directly and indirectly in important university decisions. Students' access to university decision makers has grown, in many instances, with student representatives often serving on university committees. Additionally, some institutions, such as Ohio public universities (e.g., Ohio State,[1] Miami University of Ohio, and Bowling Green University), now seat gubernatorially appointed student members on the board of trustees. Even at institutions that have not recognized a formal role for students in the governance process, students' influence over instruction and faculty practices has grown as a result of the rise in student evaluations of teaching. Student course evaluations have become an important part of the promotion and tenure process, providing some of the most tangible and heavily weighted evidence of a professor's skills as an instructor.

Students frequently place their own demands on the university. In his overview of the history of American higher education, John Thelin (2004) argues that student movements of the 1960s promoted a culture of student activism that extends to the current era. Whereas the activities of the late 1960s and early 1970s included student walkouts and protests over political issues like the war in Vietnam, contemporary student demonstrations often focus on more immediate and tangible concerns, such as better living conditions, enhanced student services, and, in the case of graduate students, better compensation for their service to the university. Even academic freedom itself has become a focus of student attention as some conservative student organizations petition their institutions to adopt an "Academic Bill of Rights" aimed at protecting students from political coercion by members of the faculty. While the Academic Bill of Rights has an obvious appeal to students, many faculty look on such proposals with great suspicion, believing that it places potentially problematic limitations on their freedom to run their classrooms as they see fit. The fact that many campuses give serious consideration to demands that potentially benefit students at the cost of faculty discretion provides additional evidence for the growing influence of the student body in campus affairs.

Perhaps more important, tough competition for student tuition dollars means that universities respond to student demands simply by appealing to their basic desires. Most obviously, universities offer better dormitories, dining halls, sports facilities, and extracurricular programs to attract students. Student demands have also had some impact on curricular decisions, with many colleges responding to demands for online courses and other cost-saving measures. Taken together, this growing emphasis on student input makes their views on higher education all the more relevant to university governance.

In short, we argue that divisions within the university are important and that shifts in power within the university require that we consider how professors, students, and administrators interact with one another to shape institutional culture. These interactions are shaped by the values, perspectives, and assumptions that each group brings to the dialogue. While there are many areas of agreement among these constituencies, they often hold opposing views that result in competing demands on the university. This disagreement may, in fact, be useful for higher education. A variety of perspectives on social and political issues, for example, is essential to the university's mission of promoting dialogue and the search for truth. However, at times, the various groups within the university appear to be talking past one another. With different priorities and expectations of the university, students, professors, and administrators may not be able to find common ground or even agree on what is worthy of debate. External pressures on the university have also changed considerably since earlier inquiries into the politics of academics. Ideological gaps between the public and the academy remain, yet charges against the academy have changed considerably. While leftist members of the faculty found themselves under assault from both external critics and their own administrations during the height of the McCarthy investigations, liberal academics appear to be relatively safe on the contemporary campus. In fact, even the most controversial of left-wing academics have enjoyed some protection under the umbrella of academic freedom. Ward Churchill, the University of Colorado professor who referred to the victims of the September 11, 2001, terrorist attacks as "little Eichmanns," enjoyed support from colleagues, the American Civil Liberties Union, and the American Association of University Professors. While he was eventually dismissed from his position, the university did not cite his remarks as cause for his dismissal. Rather, administrators argued that serious allegations of research misconduct were sufficient to justify his removal. Of course, Churchill's supporters will charge that his dismissal was encouraged by conservative talk show hosts and television news shows. Indeed, the controversial statements made by Professor Churchill and other fringe academics incited renewed interest in the politics of professors, with specific attention to those who espoused antiwar views. David Horowitz's (2007a) book, *The Professors: The 101 Most Dangerous Academics in America,* may be seen by many liberal academics—and especially by those unfortunate souls who grace its pages—as an echo of McCarthyism. In fact, prompted by Horowitz's charges, some state legislatures did sponsor investigations into the politics of university campuses, though they were careful to explain that they were not investigating individual people but rather university policies.

Despite the title of Horowitz's book, recent investigations into the politics of the academy are not prompted by concern that leftist professors are undermining our national security, at least for the most part. Rather, the more common accusations are that liberal professors are indoctrinating students and discriminating against conservatives in the academy. We explore these charges in some detail throughout the book, looking at the political values of professors, students, and administrators as well as their experiences within the university. We also contrast political perspectives within the academy with those of the general public, as measured by a number of public opinion polls.

Yet external political pressures in the modern era are not based solely on the ideological differences between elected officials and university employees. Rather, public policymakers and a number of advocacy groups have taken aim at issues of accountability, accessibility, and affordability. Public confidence in higher education has also declined in recent years. Colleges and universities are under considerable pressure from accreditation agencies and other external reviewers to define what it is they do and demonstrate that they are doing it both competently and efficiently. As a result, contemporary studies of conflict within the university must move beyond ideological division among the faculty and issues related to academic freedom. Political pressures on the university now force those within the academy to explain and justify distributions of power, use of resources, educational initiatives, and admissions policies. On these issues, there is also considerable disagreement within the academy. This makes it difficult for the higher-education community to provide a unified vision of its purpose. The academy's inability to articulate a coherent message leads to some public confusion about the nature of university education. We demonstrate that on some of these issues, differences in perspective also make productive dialogue difficult within the university. Some understanding of these differences, however, may allow students, professors, and administrators to seek some common ground and address one another's concerns in a more productive manner. At the very least, an understanding of the different values and expectations of those within the academy may provide some insight into the obstacles to reform.

THE NORTH AMERICAN ACADEMIC SURVEY STUDY

The data used for the original analysis in this book is derived from the 1999 North American Academic Survey Study (NAASS), which was designed by Stanley Rothman, Everett Carl Ladd, and Seymour Martin Lipset. The interviews were conducted by telephone between March 4, 1999, and May 3, 1999, by The Angus Reid Group (now Ipsos-Reid). Although this study originally included a sample of academics from both the United States and Canada, our analysis focuses solely on the American sample, which includes faculty, administrators, and students at 140 universities and colleges. Institutions were chosen using a random sampling procedure. Respondents from each university were randomly selected from lists of each population provided by the institution and were sampled in proportion to the size of the institution. All full-time faculty members who were teaching at the time were included in the sampling procedure, as well as both full-time and part-time undergraduate students, as long as they were pursuing a degree and taking at least two courses at the time of the survey. Administrators chosen for the survey included college presidents, provosts, academic vice presidents, senior academic officers, and a variety of academic deans. The response rates varied slightly for each group of respondents, with 53 percent of students, 72 percent of faculty, and 70 percent of administrators completing the survey. The resulting sample is comprised of 1,607 students, 1,645 faculty, and 807 administrators, although sample sizes are smaller in some specific analyses because of question nonresponse.[2]

Some of our specific analyses examine differences between types of institutions. For this purpose, we stratify these institutions by type according to their Carnegie classifications in 2000. Community colleges and two-year technical schools were not included in the survey. Our results must be interpreted accordingly. We aim to capture opinions and dynamics in four-year colleges and universities, with the appreciation for the fact that values and perspectives are likely to be different at the institutions excluded from this analysis. Even within this selective sample of institutions, we acknowledge that there is a good deal of variance. Some may question whether one can speak of a universal mission of higher education. Yet, despite differences in size, location, religious affiliation, and public or private status, we argue that the institutions involved in our analysis articulate many of the same basic objectives for their students. This is evidenced by the fact that a large and diverse number of institutions, ranging from the largest public universities to the smallest private colleges, are voluntarily members of the American Association of Colleges and Universities (AAC&U). In fact, almost all the institutions in our sample are members of the AAC&U. Thus, the AAC&U, along with other higher-education associations and accreditation agencies, helps to articulate a collective vision for higher education.

The timing of the NAASS presents both some benefits and some challenges to the study of the contemporary American university. Taking place just before the terrorist attacks on September 11, 2001, the survey provides a snapshot of values and opinions before America's involvement in Afghanistan and Iraq would exacerbate tensions between conservative organizations and the predominantly left-leaning academics. Consequently, the views of faculty, students, and administrators were codified before the onslaught of conservative criticism placed much of the academy in a defensive posture. Seen in a positive light, the pre–September 11 survey provides a glimpse behind the academic veil in a typical moment of relatively low social tension. In a more negative light, the timing of the survey does not provide researchers with an opportunity to examine the views of the academy's principle constituencies in a time of national crisis. In any case, given the dramatic swings of political fortune that have occurred since 2001, it is unclear whether a survey conducted just after September 11 would have been better at capturing the typical views of faculty, students, and administrators on issues of importance.

The most important challenges in interpreting the results of the NAASS center not on its timing relative to September 11 but rather on the delay in publication of the results. The unfortunate delay, prompted in large measure by the deaths of two members of the original researcher team (Seymour Lipset and Everett Ladd), means that some findings may not precisely reflect the current state of opinion among faculty, students, and administrators. In an effort to offset the uncertainties created by the passage of time, we draw on a number of other surveys to demonstrate that, although the American university may have changed somewhat since the time of the NAASS survey, the basic opinions and divisions within the university have remained fairly stable since the survey was completed. The results, while imperfect, closely approximate the views of faculty, students, and administrators in the present. Nevertheless, there have been changes in higher education in recent years, yet we believe that the analysis contained in the following chapters reveals long-term divisions within the academy that are applicable in the decade following the original survey. With that said, we are sensitive to the fact that opinions on some issues have shifted. On these more time-sensitive questions, we make a greater effort to present the NAASS findings alongside more recent studies.

This is especially important in the chapter on campus diversity, in which we discuss research findings from other scholars at considerable length. Additionally, although opinions may change over time, the forces that bear on these opinions have similar effects across each of the groups in our analysis, such that divisions and differences between groups would remain fairly stable. We support this assertion with data from recent surveys in higher education that reveal similar trends. Yet we cannot rely completely on these newer studies for our analysis, as they do not offer comparisons between students, administrators, and professors on many of these important issues.

Throughout our analysis, we consider how opinions within the academy differ from those of the general public. Since the NAASS survey does not include subjects outside of higher education, we also present findings from a number of reputable public opinion surveys in order to assess public sentiment. As a result, these measures sometimes differ in question wording and response options, resulting in minor differences in frequencies of response. We are careful to discuss these issues, when they arise, and are cautious about the interpretation of relatively minor differences.

LAYOUT OF THE BOOK

We begin our analysis in chapter 2 by examining various perspectives on the role and mission of the university. We also demonstrate that there is considerable disagreement within the university on the major problems facing higher education and on the performance of our colleges and universities. Here, we first reveal a finding that echoes throughout the book: administrators are far more positive about higher education than either professors or students. This positive perspective means that administrators may be unresponsive to the concerns of other groups. Where administrators do express concerns about the future of higher education, these concerns differ in meaningful ways from those expressed by students and professors. In short, we conclude that students, professors, and administrators identify different sets of problems, presenting challenges for shared governance and for educational reform.

In chapter 3, we explore perceptions of power and control within the university. The vast majority of colleges and universities operate under a system of "shared governance," with authority divided between the faculty and the administration. Our analysis reveals that faculty and administrators differ in perceptions of their own influence. We also find that students desire greater input, favoring more direct control over their graduation requirements. Again, these differences present challenges that, while not insurmountable, must be identified in order for educational reform to be successful.

In chapter 4, we delve more deeply into campus politics, exploring general partisan affiliations as well as specific issue positions on a range of issues. We demonstrate that there is some disagreement on issues within the university, as well as between the university and the public. We also find evidence that professors are further to the political left than their partisan identifications would suggest. The political orientations of college professors and administrators place them at odds with both their students and the general public on a number of issues. This disconnect has potential consequences for higher education and may contribute to the declining public trust in colleges and universities. Additionally, these political values have direct implications for campus governance, admissions policies, hiring procedures, and other institutional decisions. The political values of academics are especially important in that they affect perceptions of the university's mission. However, our analysis also reveals that academics' politics are more complicated than commonly portrayed, with a notable difference of position between social and economic issues.

In chapter 5, we explore these divisions as they relate specifically to the issue of campus diversity. Our analysis of campus diversity relies on our own findings from the NAASS survey, yet we supplement this research with a number of more recent studies in an effort to present the reader with a broad overview of the issue. We explore the campus climate for underrepresented groups and attitudes toward diversity. Again, we find important differences in opinion and priorities. While academics express general support for the concept of diversity, many are unwilling to sacrifice meritocracy in order to achieve it. Students are far less supportive of affirmative action policies and other diversity measures, which violate their sense of fairness. These differences present challenges for higher education, as most campus initiatives to increase diversity rely on methods that challenge established norms of meritocracy. We also consider the evidence for the effect of diversity on students' educational experience. Despite the common perception that diversity enhances students' experiences, we find no evidence that students' self-reported satisfaction with their college experience is enhanced by the diversity of the campus.

In chapter 6, we examine perceptions of academic freedom on campus and people's willingness to discuss viewpoints with others. While the university is heralded as a forum for debate, inquiry, and new ideas, we find some evidence that people self-censor their viewpoints if they believe they represent a minority on campus. Somewhat surprisingly, our evidence reveals that students feel relatively unconstrained in expression of their viewpoints, despite the fact that professors and administrators may hold political views that differ from their own. Professors report that they are more likely to self-censor if they believe that they are in the political minority. Surprisingly, administrators are most likely to avoid expressing their views out of concern for faculty reactions. However, this self-censorship appears to be unrelated to political orientation and is rooted in general disagreement with the faculty. Additionally, self-censoring on the part of administrators does not appear to diminish administrators' perception of their own influence. Rather, administrators may simply exclude faculty from discussions and decision making in order to avoid conflict.

The concluding chapter reflects on the consequences of our findings for educational reform. We consider the implications of our findings for campus debates on assessment, accessibility, and other contemporary issues. We argue that contradictory opinions and values within the academy come into conflict as the academy attempts to grapple with these new challenges and demands. Students, professors, and administrators differ in their concerns and priorities. At times, the goals and values of these groups are contradictory, making it difficult for institutions of higher education to address problems and adapt to new realities. On some issues, students, professors, and administrators articulate a shared vision of the university, grounded in a broad, general education. Yet the public's expectations of higher education are more vocational in nature, forcing academics to justify and defend the value of a traditional liberal education. The assessment movement is, in many ways, such an attempt to justify the value of higher education. Yet it remains to be seen whether this value can be defined and measured in terms that are acceptable to both the academy and the public it serves.

Much like *The Academic Mind* and *The Divided Academy*, our book offers a portrait of the American university in a moment of transition. Yet, unlike prior studies, the NAASS data set gives us the opportunity to explore some of the heretofore little-known differences between the university's primary constituencies. While faculty play an important role in shaping the objectives and direction of academia, our multidimensional survey provides important indications that, on issues like curriculum, affirmative action, and institutional reform, campus constituencies tend to see the world quite differently. Particularly in light of growing student and administrative influence, one must take into account all these views in order to understand the dynamics of the contemporary university and its response to external pressures.

Chapter Two

Visions of the University

As we begin our analysis of conflict and consensus within the American university, one of the most fundamental questions is whether the various groups charged with running the academy can actually agree on the basic goals of higher education. Disagreement and debate among intellectuals is, for the most part, useful. Ideally, the process of challenging and defending ideas contributes to our understanding of a problem and drives the search for objective truth. In this way, disagreement is essential to education insofar as education seeks to advance knowledge rather than merely transfer it from one generation to the next. However, there are a limited number of circumstances in which disagreement within the academy can undermine educational objectives. College professors, administrators, and students all share some responsibility for the governance of the university. If these internal constituencies cannot agree on the most fundamental goals of higher education, decision making will be mired by gridlock and inaction.

Any discussion on the purpose of higher education has the potential to degenerate into whatever clichés and buzzwords are currently fashionable in academic circles. In their book on the American college presidency, Cohen and March (1986) identify ambiguity of purpose as one of the greatest challenges facing a senior administrator, yet they rightly question whether this ambiguity can be resolved or even discussed in a meaningful way:

> Almost any educated person can deliver a lecture entitled "The Goals of the University." Almost no one will listen voluntarily. For the most part, such lectures and their companion essays are well-intentioned exercises in social rhetoric, with little operational content. Efforts to generate normative statements of the goals of a university tend to produce goals that are either meaningless or dubious. (195)

With Cohen and March's warning in mind and cognizant of the fact that people may also not willingly read a book chapter titled "The Goals of the University," we attempt to avoid hollow pronouncements about what higher education is or ought to be. Instead, we set our goals on a more modest but attainable target. Using a variety of sources, we demonstrate that there is wide support among administrators, professors, and students for the basic idea of "liberal education." However, we also demonstrate that there are significant differences of opinion about both the quality of education students receive and the major problems facing higher education. We argue that, in these areas, differences in perspective make cooperative efforts and dialogue difficult. While disagreement is often useful, it is most productive when people debate alternative solutions to a mutually recognized problem. When actors fail to agree about the presence or nature of a problem, it is difficult to have a meaningful exchange of ideas about solutions.

GOALS OF EDUCATION

Americans place a great deal of importance on higher education. Surveys of the American public demonstrate that the large majority of Americans agree that high school graduates should go to college and that doing so provides them with better job prospects (Immerwahr 1998). Not only do Americans believe that college is important for career success, but the majority of Americans regard higher education as a fundamental right that should be made available and affordable to all those who qualify (Immerwahr and Johnson 2007). As higher education becomes both more prized and more expensive, policymakers demand greater accountability. As a result, leaders in higher education spend a good deal of time explaining what it is the university strives to achieve and why it costs so much to achieve it. Some critics argue that our traditional system of educating students is both costly and ineffective. In an editorial in the *Wall Street Journal*, Charles Murray argues that a bachelor of arts degree is overvalued and that college degrees should be replaced by professional certification exams for specific professions, much like those currently required for certified public accountants (Murray 2008). Needless to say, his critique was not widely embraced by those in the academy.

Recently, the American Association of Colleges and Universities (AAC&U) launched the Liberal Education and America's Promise (LEAP) campaign to renew America's commitment to liberal education, defined as a broad, general education in science, culture, and society, as opposed to vocational training for a specific occupation.[1] While the AAC&U correctly asserts that this is not necessarily an either/or proposition, there is considerable debate about the appropriate balance between these two options. It is not a new debate. In fact, Richard Hofstadter wrote throughout the 1950s and 1960s about the democratization of American higher education and the resulting vocational nature of the college curriculum. Hofstadter argued that the American zeal for egalitarianism resulted in a rejection of classical learning, scholarly expertise, and anything related to class privilege. Instead, Americans favor a more practical education for the masses that is directly applicable to specific vocations (Hofstadter 1962; Hofstadter and Hardy 1952; see also Brown 2006, especially chapter 4).

Expanding enrollments and changing demographics prompt questions about the role of America's colleges and universities in preparing the workforce for a knowledge-based economy. In addition, other changes to the external sociopolitical environment may force a reexamination of postsecondary education. Since the 1980s, changes in U.S. education policy have placed increased focus on accountability in higher education (McClellan 2009). The resulting assessment movement has forced most colleges and universities to reconsider or at least defend their educational missions. Critics of the assessment movement argue that the broad intellectual gains often attributed to a liberal education are difficult to measure. For example, there is no universally accepted measure of students' growth in critical thinking and analytical skills. Since it is easier to measure students' factual knowledge and technical expertise, these critics charge that the assessment movement encourages colleges and universities to focus on developing narrow skills and areas of knowledge rather than broad intellectual growth (Jaschik 2005).

Using the NAASS data, we examine support for several basic goals of university education among students, professors, and administrators (see table 2.1). When asked to choose between two competing visions of higher educa-

Table 2.1. There Are at Least Two Visions about What the Role of Universities Should Be These Days. Which of These Two Broad Visions Comes Closest to Your Own?

	Faculty	*Student*	*Administration*
To encourage exploration of new ideas	70%	72%	67%
To respond to the changing needs of the economy	13%	22%	14%
Both/neither/depends	16%	6%	19%
Don't know	0%	0%	0%
Total	100%	100%	100%
n	1,645	1,607	807

tion, the vast majority of professors and administrators report that the primary role of the university is to encourage new ideas, as opposed to responding to the needs of the economy. Students, who are often accused of being overly career driven, also support the notion that the university exists to encourage new ideas. As we would expect, professors and students in professional studies programs are more likely than their social science and humanities counterparts to support the notion that higher education should respond to the needs of the economy. However, even among the professional studies, this viewpoint is expressed by a small number of respondents (see table 2.2).

We also find differences in faculty members' responses based on their political affiliation. Republican professors are three times as likely as Democrats to state that the university should respond to changes in the economy. Several researchers have demonstrated that political ideology is more than a measure of policy preferences. Rather, it reflects some underlying differences in disposition. For example, in previous work, researchers find that Republicans and Democrats cite different priorities in life, with Democrats being

Table 2.2. There Are at Least Two Visions about What the Role of Universities Should Be These Days. Which of These Two Broad Visions Comes Closest to Your Own?

	Professional	*Social Science*	*Humanities*	*Science*	*Total*
Faculty					
To encourage exploration of new ideas	62%	79%	76%	68%	72%
To respond to the changing needs of the economy	19%	7%	7%	14%	12%
Both/neither/depends	18%	14%	17%	17%	16%
Don't know	0%	0%	0%	0%	0%
Total	100%	100%	100%	100%	100%
n	464	539	275	275	1,553
Students					
To encourage exploration of new ideas	68%	78%	74%	71%	72%
To respond to the changing needs of the economy	28%	17%	19%	21%	22%
Both/neither/depends	5%	6%	6%	8%	6%
Don't know	0%	0%	0%	0%	0%
Total	100%	100%	100%	100%	100%
n	632	472	141	299	1,609

more likely to express a desire to create original works (Woessner and Kelly-Woessner 2009b). Similarly, Carney et al. (2008) find that political ideology correlates with personality traits such that "liberals are more open-minded, creative, curious, and novelty seeking, whereas conservatives are more orderly, conventional, and better organized." While using different measures, the results of the NAASS are consistent with the claim that Democrats are more interested in novelty and new ideas. However, it is still important to note that the majority of professors in both parties support the notion that colleges exist to explore new ideas (see table 2.3).

In a related survey question, professors and administrators who participated in the NAASS were asked to assign a score to a number of objectives, rating them on a seven-point scale from "not important at all" to "essential." On each of the four objectives, we find little difference between professors and administrators. For example, 50 percent of professors and 54 percent of administrators rate the goal of providing a broad, general education as "essential" to the mission of the university (see table 2.4). Among those who did not rate the goal as "essential," most still believe that it is very important,

Table 2.3. There Are at Least Two Visions about the Role of Universities. Which of These Two Broad Visions Comes Closest to Your Own?

Faculty Response	*Democrat*	*Independent*	*Republican*	*Total*
To encourage exploration of new ideas	74%	69%	54%	70%
To respond to the changing needs of the economy	10%	13%	30%	13%
Both/neither/depends	16%	18%	16%	16%
Don't know	0%	0%	1%	0%
Total	100%	100%	100%	100%
n	822	548	179	1,549

Table 2.4. Faculty/Administrators Who Rate the Following Goals as "Essential"

Educational Goal	*Faculty*	*Administrators*
Provide a broad, general education	50%	54%
Prepare students for employment after graduation	19%	21%
Learn about the classic works of Western civilization	15%	13%
Learn about the importance of non-Western cultures	18%	18%
n≈	1,645	808

assigning it a score of 6 on the seven-point scale. This support for a "broad, general education" may be interpreted as shared support for the goals of liberal education. While this measure may not capture all of the goals of liberal education, it is consistent with the AAC&U position that liberal education "provides students with broad knowledge of the wider world (e.g. science, culture, and society)" and "usually includes a general education curriculum that provides broad learning in multiple disciplines and ways of knowing."[2]

Both professors and administrators assign a much lower level of importance to preparing students for employment. It is important to note that this question does not ask respondents to prioritize between career preparation and general education. Respondents are able to conclude that both are essential to the mission of the university. However, only 19 percent of professors and 21 percent of administrators believe that preparing students for employment is "essential." Most of them do think that this goal is somewhat important, with over 75 percent of faculty and 84 percent of administrators rating this goal at a 5 or better on a seven-point scale. Still, this goal pales in comparison to providing the broad general knowledge associated with a liberal education. According to the NAASS, this pattern holds across all institution types in the sample, as defined by the 2000 Carnegie classifications. While professors and administrators at baccalaureate colleges are most likely to rate general education as essential, we see only small differences between them and their colleagues at master's universities and doctorate-granting institutions (see table 2.5).

In contrast, students are much more likely to identify career goals as their reason for attending college. While students are not asked the same question given to professors and administrators, the NAASS does ask them to provide their reasons for going to the university. Approximately half the student respondents make some mention of career prospects as their first reason. However, this is not to say that students are opposed to a broad, general education. Rather, they may echo the public's view that a college education, in general, is required for a successful career.

Table 2.5. Faculty Who Rate the Following Goals as "Essential"

Educational Goal	*Baccalaureate*	*Master's*	*Doctoral*
Provide a broad, general education	57%	52%	48%
Prepare students for employment after graduation	21%	26%	17%
Learn about the classic works of Western civilization	14%	13%	17%
Learn about the importance of non-Western cultures	18%	17%	18%
n≈	98	512	854

While professors and administrators agree on the importance of a broad education and show less concern for students' employment potential, it is important to ask whether this places them in opposition with the general public. According to one national survey, 58 percent of the American public believes that students should seek general skills that they can apply to multiple careers, while 41 percent believe that students should pursue a major that provides them with skills for a specific career (Immerwahr and Johnson 2007).

While it may initially appear that the public is in support of the broad, liberal education articulated by leaders in higher education, it is important to note that the public's focus is on broad skills rather than broad knowledge. In an earlier study, conducted around the time of the NAASS survey, Immerwahr and Foleno (2000) argue that there is some common ground between the public and higher education leaders in terms of the skills that both believe are necessary for success. However, the public is less likely to view a traditional liberal arts curriculum as the mechanism by which to achieve these skills. The authors explain,

> For supporters of the liberal arts curricula, the findings present good and bad news. Of the items on the list of expectations, the public places the least importance on "exposure to great writers and thinkers in subjects like literature and history." The value of the "great books"—or the humanities field itself—seems to be relegated to a lower level of interest. On the other hand, the public emphasizes skills also valued by advocates of the liberal arts, such as analytical thinking and top-notch writing and speaking skills. (12)

We conclude that professors, students, and administrators share a basic commitment to the idea that colleges and universities should provide students with a broad set of skills that may apply to a range of careers and that the majority of Americans support this goal. However, the end goal for students and for the public appears to be on improving people's potential for employment, something that professors and administrators are less likely to see as an essential function of the university. These differences in end goals present a challenge in that they demand quite different measures of institutional success. As the assessment movement gains steam, some institutions will undoubtedly measure success in terms of employment, which may undermine those programs and courses that do not speak as directly toward this goal. At the very least, institutions that desire to maintain a traditional liberal arts curriculum may need to better justify their approach and explain how a knowledge of history and literature translates into critical thinking and analytical skills.

It is important to note that support for the idea of liberal education may be significantly weaker at those institutions of higher education not included in our sample. Community colleges and vocational schools tailor programs more specifically to particular careers. We would expect, therefore, to find that professors, administrators, and students who choose these institutions are less supportive of liberal education.

Additionally, there is some evidence that faculty opinions on educational goals have changed somewhat. For example, surveys conducted by the Higher Education Research Institute (HERI) show a general increase in faculty commitment to preparing students for employment after graduation since the time the NAASS was completed.[3] However, this does not mean that faculty members are less committed to the goals of liberal education. In fact, HERI surveys also reveal that professors are increasingly committed to the goal of instilling a "basic appreciation of the liberal arts" (DeAngelo et al. 2009). Despite these changes, we believe that the observed differences between groups still persist, and there is some recent evidence to support this assumption. For example, one recent study finds a significant difference between faculty and students at one institution in the importance members of each group attach to career preparation (Myers 2008).

ENCOURAGING CULTURAL UNDERSTANDING AND MINORITY PERSPECTIVES

While we may find general agreement among professors and administrators on the principle of a broad, general education, this does not necessarily mean that campus constituencies agree on the essential components of a general education. In fact, there is considerable debate about appropriate course requirements in a common curriculum. In *The Closing of the American Mind*, Allan Bloom (1987) argued that America's colleges and universities have stopped asking the important philosophical questions about life and that, in an effort to impose moral and cultural relativism, they fail to teach the classics of Western civilization. More recently, the National Association of Scholars, the American Council of Trustees and Alumni (ACTA), and other organizations devoted to educational reform have furthered Bloom's argument that colleges and universities are neglecting to teach students about their own cultural heritage. According to a report by the ACTA, America's college graduates lack a basic understanding of their national history, a reflection of the fact that colleges no longer require students to take history courses:

> Instead of broad courses on the full sweep of American history, many universities require courses with a narrow focus on racism and inequality. At the University of Michigan, for example, students are required to fulfill a "Race & Ethnicity Requirement" from a list of approved courses that cover "issues relat-

> ing to race & ethnicity, racial and ethnic intolerance, and inequality." Wellesley's "Multicultural Requirement" requires one unit of coursework that focuses on "African, Asian, Caribbean, Latin American, Native American, or Pacific Island peoples, cultures or societies; and/or a minority American culture, such as those defined by race, religion, ethnicity, sexual orientation, or physical disability; and/or the processes of racism, social or ethnic discrimination, or cross-cultural interaction." Again, qualifying courses need not be grounded in history and can, in fact, be offered by a range of academic departments and programs. And while some view gains in knowledge of these topics as an essential component of undergraduate education, others contend that this is a poor substitute for an understanding of American history, which most students fail to gain in the pre-college years. (Neal and Martin 2002, 3)

The ACTA further identifies several areas of the curriculum as threats to the classic study of Western civilization and American history. First, the authors argue that colleges are increasingly requiring students to complete courses in non-Western cultures. According to the AAC&U, these multicultural courses are actually a positive development in the college curriculum and are encouraged as part of the AAC&U's "Shared Futures" program:

> Shared Futures is a multi-project, national initiative of The Association of American Colleges and Universities. It is based upon the assumption that we live in an interdependent but unequal world and that higher education can help prepare students not only to thrive in such a world, but to remedy its inequities. AAC&U seeks to support the academy in its vital role of expanding knowledge about the world's peoples and problems and developing individuals who will advance equity and justice both at home and abroad.

As Neal and Martin (2002) explain, the ACTA is not opposed to the advancement of knowledge in these areas. Rather, critics of the new curriculum appear to be concerned that these courses have replaced traditional courses on the history and philosophy of Western culture. Perhaps more important, opponents of the multicultural movement express concern that these specialized, global courses embrace the sort of absolute relativism that Bloom so vehemently opposed.

Groups on both sides of this debate use the term "liberal education" to define their educational objectives, defining a broad background according to their own perspective on what sort of knowledge will best prepare students for life after college. Thus, our earlier finding that college professors and administrators agree on the goal of providing a general education does little to explain what that education should entail. Using the NAASS survey, we examine opinions on required course content more closely (see table 2.6).

Table 2.6. Overall, Does Respondent Think That All Undergraduates Should Be Required to Take a "Common Core" of Courses in Literature, Humanities, Social Sciences, and Natural Sciences?

	Faculty	*Administrators*	*Students*
Yes, should require "common courses"	87%	84%	77%
No, should not require "common courses"	12%	15%	23%
Don't know	1%	0%	0%
Total	100%	100%	100%
n	1,645	806	1,608

Professors, students, and administrators are all highly supportive of the idea of a core curriculum, with required courses in literature, the humanities, social sciences, and natural sciences. Students are the least supportive of a core curriculum, with 23 percent opposing common, required courses (compared to 15 percent of administrators and 12 percent of professors). This again supports the conclusion that, within the academy, there is a general acceptance of broad educational goals and required exposure to different academic disciplines.

Professors and administrators also responded to a number of questions about the importance of specific educational goals, such as learning about the classic works of Western civilization and learning about non-Western cultures. Both questions were measured on a seven-point scale, ranging from "not important at all" to "essential." We find that professors and administrators provide nearly identical responses to these questions. A minority of members in both groups report that these are essential objectives. With that said, respondents assign slightly greater importance to learning about non-Western civilization than they do to learning about non-Western cultures. The difference is greatest among administrators, with a five-percentage-point gap between the two measures. We have reason to believe that these findings are relevant today, at least in part, with little change in importance assigned to the classic works of Western civilization.[4] Although it is possible that support for non-Western education has increased, it appears that, if this is the case, the change has little negative effect on support for Western cultural education.

In fact, although support for multicultural education is often cited as a contributing factor in the decline of the Western classics, we find that responses to these two questions are strongly correlated in a positive direction.[5] That is, those who believe that learning about non-Western civilization is important are also likely to support learning about Western classics (see table 2.7). This is an important finding, as it demonstrates that the two objec-

Table 2.7. Comparison of Importance Placed on Western Classics and Non-Western Cultures by Faculty

The Importance of Learning about the Classic Works of Western Civilization	The Importance of Learning about Non-Western Cultures				
	1–4	5	6	7 (essential)	Total
1–4	60%	23%	20%	14%	31%
5	21%	52%	27%	21%	33%
6	12%	18%	39%	21%	22%
7 (essential)	6%	7%	14%	44%	15%
Total	100%	100%	100%	100%	100%
n	442	539	372	289	1,642

tives are not mutually exclusive or incompatible, at least from the perspective of professors and administrators.

Although students, professors, and administrators are all highly supportive of requiring core courses in science, literature, the humanities, and social sciences, we see little broad support for the type of race and ethnicity requirement that Neal and Martin (2002) identify at some institutions. Approximately 17 percent of respondents in each group state that courses on the experiences of racial minorities should be required (see table 2.8). It is important to note, however, that although respondents may not support required courses focused specifically on racial understanding, a large percentage of faculty now rate the goal of "enhancing students' knowledge of and appreciation for other racial/ethnic groups" as an important goal for undergraduate education. In fact, support for this goal appears to be on the rise and the majority of faculty now agree that "racial and ethnic diversity should be more strongly reflected in the curriculum" (DeAngelo et al. 2009, 35).

All three groups of respondents are even less supportive of requiring courses on the experiences of women or gays/lesbians. Although they do not believe that such courses should be required, a fair number of professors, students, and administrators believe that students should be encouraged to take these courses. However, all three groups are considerably less supportive of courses that address the experiences of gays and lesbians. In fact, 12 percent of students believe that these courses should not be offered at all. This difference is a reflection of the nature of the questions. Few individuals would question equal rights for women or racial minorities. However, the issue of gay rights is a much more controversial issue, as we will demonstrate in chapter 4.

Table 2.8. For Undergraduates, Should These Be Required Courses?

	Faculty	*Students*	*Administrators*
Experiences of Racial Minorities			
Required	17%	16%	17%
Encouraged	42%	38%	46%
Made available	39%	45%	35%
Not offered at all	1%	1%	1%
Don't know	0%	0%	1%
Total	100%	100%	100%
n	1,646	1,608	807
Experiences of Women			
Required	12%	9%	11%
Encouraged	42%	37%	42%
Made available	43%	53%	46%
Not offered at all	2%	1%	1%
Don't know	1%	0%	1%
Total	100%	100%	100%
n	1,645	1,607	807
Experiences of Gays and Lesbians			
Required	4%	4%	3%
Encouraged	29%	19%	23%
Made available	57%	65%	66%
Not offered at all	9%	12%	7%
Don't know	0%	0%	1%
Total	100%	100%	100%
n	1,644	1,607	807

In general, higher educations' internal constituents appear to be in general agreement about the types of experiences students should have in college. With a few exceptions, these groups each support the ideal of liberal education and believe that college students should take a set of core courses in the humanities, social sciences, literature, and natural sciences. However, they also do not think that teaching Western classics is essential, nor do they believe that understanding of non-Western cultures is an essential goal of a college education. Likewise, students, professors, and administrators believe that courses should be offered on the experiences of racial minorities, women, and gays/lesbians but do not believe that these courses should be a part of the required curriculum.

PERCEPTIONS OF EDUCATIONAL QUALITY

The American system of higher education operates in a complex international marketplace. Colleges and universities from around the globe compete to attract the best and brightest students, both from within their own borders and from the growing pool of international students. College graduates also face the challenges of globalization as they encounter increased competition for jobs, both domestically and abroad. While the American system of higher education has been heralded as the best in the world, politicians, educators, and students express understandable concern about our relative position in the growing international marketplace. There is some debate about whether U.S. institutions continue to set the bar for educational quality. In fact, assessments of America's relative standing in the world depend a great deal on the measures used to judge greatness.

In reputation rankings of individual universities, select American institutions rank well among a large poll of international competitors. According to the Academic Ranking of World Universities, which ranks institutions according to research productivity and article citations, Harvard, Stanford, and the University of California, Berkley, top the list of the world's premiere universities (Institute of Higher Education 2007). According to the QS World University Rankings (2009), which are based largely on peer evaluation and reputation, Harvard and Yale rank best, followed by Cambridge and Oxford. While America's best universities may continue to hold the most prestigious reputations and produce the most cited scholarship, a small portion of college graduates matriculate from these highly prized institutions. As such, it is problematic to base an assessment of American higher education on the reputation of Harvard or the publications of a few distinguished scholars.

When measures are employed to assess our colleges and universities more broadly, there is some question about America's position of leadership. Again, rankings vary a great deal depending on the measures used to judge international standing. For example, if higher education is evaluated in terms of accessibility and affordability, the American system may fall behind some international competitors. According to a report from the National Center for Public Policy and Higher Education (Wagner 2006), a number of other nations have gained on or surpassed the United States in measures of degree completion. The report also finds that on specific assessment tests, America's college graduates rank below those of Sweden, Norway, Belgium, and the Czech Republic. The author concludes that the leadership position of the United States has eroded.

Despite some reports about America's educational decline, it has not yet been determined whether concerns about educational quality actually permeate academic culture. Critics of higher education frequently charge that those within the ivory tower are oblivious to criticism and unwilling to implement the types of reforms that would keep American institutions competitive. As such, we might expect college professors and administrators to be confident in the education they provide. Using the NAASS, we examine respondents' assessments of both their own institutions and the American system as a whole. The survey demonstrates that there are significant differences of opinion within the university.

When asked to evaluate American higher education, college administrators are overwhelmingly positive. The majority of college administrators, 58 percent, report that we have "one of the very best" systems in the world (see table 2.9). Administrators are significantly more positive about the state of American higher education than either professors or students. Among college professors, 38 percent rank the American higher-education system as one of the very best. Students are even less convinced of America's educational superiority, with only 20 percent of respondents characterizing the United States in such positive terms.

Divisions within the academy are not confined to occupational roles. As we demonstrated in the last chapter, differences in opinion are often rooted in core philosophical beliefs. As such, we also consider whether perceptions of American colleges and universities vary according to political orientation. We have some theoretical reason to believe this would be the case. As a general rule, Republicans tend to be less critical of U.S. institutions than Democrats. In fact, one of the explanations for the disproportionate number of liberals in academia is that liberals are prone to challenge existing orthodoxies. In theory, this questioning leads to original scholarship and the creation of new knowledge (see Ladd and Lipset 1975). A number of empirical studies pro-

Table 2.9. Compared to Other Industrialized Democracies, Would You Say the American Higher-Education System Is . . .

	Administrators	*Faculty*	*Students*
One of the very best	58%	38%	20%
Better than most	35%	42%	50%
More or less average	5%	14%	25%
Worse than most	0%	1%	2%
One of the very worst	0%	0%	0%
Don't know	2%	4%	2%
Total	100%	100%	100%
n	808	1,645	1,606

vide further evidence for this relationship between political orientation and criticism of the United States. For example, Schatz, Staub, and Lavine (1999) argue that Republicans are more likely to adopt an uncritical, pro-America perspective. Other researchers have argued that American conservatives are increasingly critical of European culture, suggesting that they would rank Europe's universities less favorably (Chamoral 2006). Surprisingly, we find that when the institution in question is higher education, those on the political left are not more critical of our national performance. In fact, based on the responses to the NAASS, there is no difference between Democrats and Republicans in their evaluation of America's colleges and universities (see figure 2.1). This is true for administrators, professors, and students. If liberal social criticism leads to positive social change in other areas, this force for change appears to be lacking in higher education. This also raises some questions as to whether liberals are, by nature, actually more questioning than their conservative counterparts or whether their critical nature is limited to specific social institutions and policies.

We find that most of our survey respondents are fairly positive about American higher education, reporting that it ranks above average compared to that of other nations. However, educational quality undoubtedly varies among the nation's colleges and universities, with some providing better educational experiences than others. It is possible that assessments of the nation's education system are based on the reputations of the top universities. Indeed, Harvard and Yale consistently rank at the top of international rankings, no matter which measures of excellence are employed. Objectively speaking, one could argue that these institutions are among the very best in the world. However, the vast majority of college professors, administrators, and students

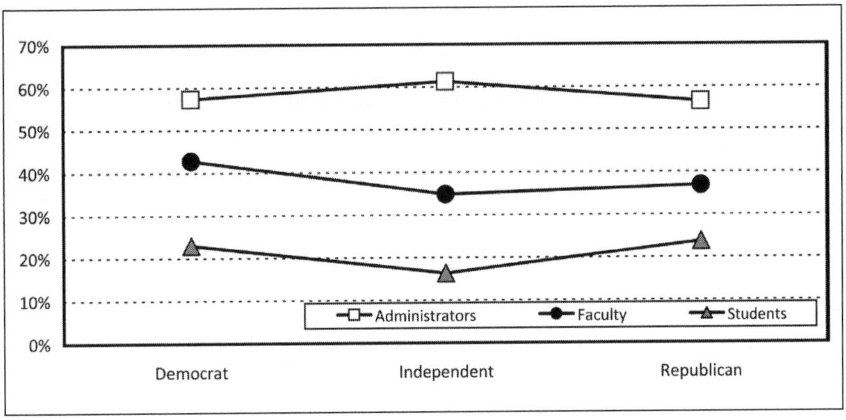

Figure 2.1. Respondents Who Feel American Universities Are "One of the Very Best"

have no personal experience with these elite institutions. As such, perceptions of one's own college or university may prove more useful in understanding the overall state of the nation's educational system.

When examining people's perceptions of their own institutions, the NAASS reveals what we find to be a familiar trend. Administrators are far more positive in their assessment of their own institutions than are professors and students. In fact, administrators are twice as likely as faculty to report that their institution does an "excellent" job of educating students. While the majority of both groups report that their college or university does either an excellent or a good job, a nontrivial number of professors, 16 percent, report otherwise, ranking their institution as merely fair or poor. Only 3 percent of college administrators report such a negative view of their own university. Compared to administrators and professors, students' assessments of their institutions lie somewhere in between but are more similar to the faculty than to the administration.

There are several possible explanations for these differences in assessment. First, faculty members and students have direct firsthand knowledge of the educational program and can more easily evaluate student learning than can campus administrators. Second, what information administrators do have about the educational program is likely to be relayed to them from faculty members. Since instructors are dependent on administrators for various resources and recognition, they have a real incentive to highlight the strengths and accomplishments of their educational programs. Third, members of the faculty tend to be more deeply affiliated with their professional associations and academic disciplines than with their places of employment. Ehrenberg (2000) describes academics as campers who set up tent at an institution but easily relocate if the weather or environment is not to their liking. This lack of institutional loyalty may permit or encourage a more critical evaluation of

Table 2.10. Overall, How Do Respondents Rate Their Institution's Job of Educating Students?

	Administrators	*Students*	*Faculty*
Excellent	52%	34%	26%
Good	45%	54%	58%
Fair	3%	11%	15%
Poor	0%	1%	1%
Don't know	0%	0%	0%
Total	100%	100%	100%
n	807	1,606	1,645

the institution. Finally, professors and administrators are driven by different motivations and goals because of the positions they occupy. Faculty members identify as members of an individual department or school within a university. Since they are in competition with other departments for students and resources, they have some incentive to be critical of other educational programs. This negative assessment of others may impact overall evaluation of the institution. Administrators, on the other hand, are increasingly involved in fund-raising efforts, alumni relations, community outreach, and accreditation. It is their responsibility to identify institutional strengths and convey these strengths to others. In short, administrators are institutional cheerleaders and are motivated to find evidence of quality, while professors are often motivated to point to areas of institutional weakness. This is not to say that either group is insincere in their assessment of their institutions. There is considerable evidence from research in social psychology that motivations to reach particular conclusions have a powerful influence on how people evaluate the evidence before them (see, for example, Kunda 1990).

Whatever the cause of this disparity, these differences in assessment are likely to have consequences. While administrative optimism may be useful in some regards, the fact that so many administrators view their institutions as "excellent" presents a challenge, especially since members of the faculty perceive there to be far more room for improvement. This division in perspective has the potential to negatively impact relations between the groups. As faculty members voice concerns about current practices, administrators may appear to be unresponsive or even defensive. Administrators, who view the institution more positively, may deem critical faculty members to be disgruntled, pessimistic, or disloyal. In the end, dialogue is frustrating for members of both groups as they struggle to find common ground.

Even among the faculty, there is a good deal of variance in assessments of educational quality. For example, compared to faculty at master's universities and doctorate-granting institutions, those at four-year baccalaureate colleges are more likely to report that their institution does an excellent job of educating students. As a general rule, the schools with more narrow educational objectives receive higher praise from faculty. Even among four-year colleges, we see differences in assessments based on the range of programs offered, with professors at traditional liberal arts colleges rating their educational success better than their colleagues at institutions that combine the liberal arts with professional programs.[6] Additionally, other institutional differences may contribute to the perception that educational quality is better at four-year undergraduate colleges. For example, baccalaureate colleges tend to have smaller class sizes and lower student-to-faculty ratios. These figures are often used by external ranking systems, such as *U.S. News & World Report*, as a measure of institutional quality. Additionally, there are financial differences between categories of colleges. At the time our survey was completed, the general expenditure for a baccalaureate college was $15,000 per student. However, per-student expenditures at "baccalaureate-liberal arts" colleges were nearly double those of schools defined as "baccalaureate-general," which award fewer than half of their degrees in liberal arts fields.

PROBLEMS FACING HIGHER EDUCATION

The NAASS also shows that students, professors, and administrators disagree about the main problems facing higher education. When asked to identify the most pressing problems confronting American colleges and universities, students rated the cost of tuition as their most common concern (see table 2.11). This is not a surprising discovery, especially given the rising cost of tuition and the expansion of enrollment to a broader sociodemographic constituency. In the year prior to the survey, college tuition had increased by 5.24 percent, while the national rate of inflation stood at 1.56 percent (Kantrowitz 2009). A wide range of surveys demonstrate that this concern about the rising cost of college tuition is widespread among the general public. According to a series of reports conducted for the National Center for Public Policy and Higher Education, the American public thinks that higher education costs are

Table 2.11. What Would You Describe as the Most Pressing Problem Confronting American Colleges and Universities?

	Faculty		*Administrators*		*Students*	
	First Response	*All Responses*	*First Response*	*All Responses*	*First Response*	*All Responses*
Funding/need more	28%	44%	36%	62%	12%	15%
Quality—students' skills	24%	38%	10%	16%	3%	4%
Tuition fees	4%	6%	8%	13%	17%	21%
Other	4%	7%	7%	12%	9%	12%
Courses/curriculum	5%	9%	6%	11%	7%	9%
Bureaucracy/ administration	6%	9%	4%	7%	3%	4%
Quality—teachers	3%	5%	3%	6%	7%	9%
Quality—general declining	5%	8%	5%	8%	2%	3%
Don't know	3%	4%	3%	5%	6%	7%
Nothing	1%	2%	1%	1%	5%	6%

rising quickly, that access to education is becoming more restricted, and that students have to borrow too much to pay for college (Immerwahr 2002, 2004; Immerwahr and Johnson 2007, 2009). Among parents of high school students, the majority report that they are concerned about their ability to pay for their child's college education. However, most of them believe that they will find a way to cover the costs. Perhaps most important, the public believes that higher-education costs can be better contained. The public is of the view that colleges can spend a lot less and still deliver high-quality education (Immerwahr and Johnson 2007).

Despite public sentiment, administrators and professors are considerably less concerned about the cost of college, at least compared to other issues. According to the NAASS, both groups believe that a shortage of funding or lack of financial resources is the most pressing problem facing higher education. This is a clear disconnect from the public and the students. While the public believes that colleges can operate with less money, professors and administrators believe that their ability to deliver quality educational programs is directly related to financial resources. As one former administrator explains, the difference in perspective is due to the nature of higher education (Ehrenberg 2000). Success is not measured in terms of profits; rather, schools are evaluated on the basis of the quality of students they attract, the productivity and reputations of the faculty, and their place in reputational rankings. As such, college administrators have little incentive to cut costs and improve efficiency. Rather, they are engaged in an "arms race of spending" (266), trying to outpace the competition by offering smaller classes, better research facilities, more student services, and higher faculty salaries:

> As nonprofit organizations, their institutions show no profits on their accounting books. Rather, maximizing value to these administrators means making their institutions the very best that they can be in almost every area of their activities. These administrators are like cookie monsters searching for cookies. They seek out all the resources that they can get their hands on and devour them. (Ehrenberg 2000, 11)

Other researchers have reported on this apparent disconnect between the public's demand for affordable education and the higher-education community's demand for more resources. Like the general public, legislative bodies are demanding greater accountability and more cost-effectiveness from colleges and universities. Yet, according a recent survey of college and university presidents, higher-education leaders believe that students continue to get good value for the money spent. Presidents express the view that efforts to control the cost of higher education will inevitably undermine quality or access to students. They also contend that students and families will need to pay even more for education because of reductions in state funding (Immerwahr, Johnson, and Gasbarra 2008). College professors appear to agree on the value of higher education. According to the 1999 American Faculty Poll, nearly 60 percent of college faculty believe that tuition and fees at their own institutions are appropriate. While approximately 24 percent believe that their college's tuition is too high, another 16 percent report that tuition and fees are actually too low (Pena and Mitchell 2000).

Our own analysis of the NAASS data confirms that there is a relationship between a college's expenditures per student and professors' assessments of educational quality (see figure 2.2). This relationship holds even when we control for the Carnegie institution type. In other words, even among doctorate-granting institutions, the more a school spends per student, the higher its internal constituents (students, faculty, and administrators) tend to rate the educational quality of the institution. While this finding might not be totally unexpected, it is somewhat surprising that, among all our available variables, per-student expenditures are the best predictor of perceived educational quality (see appendix 2).

It is important to recognize that this relationship does not necessarily mean that educational quality is directly dependent on financial resources. It is possible that the relationship is actually reversed in that the most prestigious institutions are simply in a better position to solicit funding and demand high tuitions. It is also important to recognize that perceptions of educational quality are just that and are not objective measures of what students actually learn.

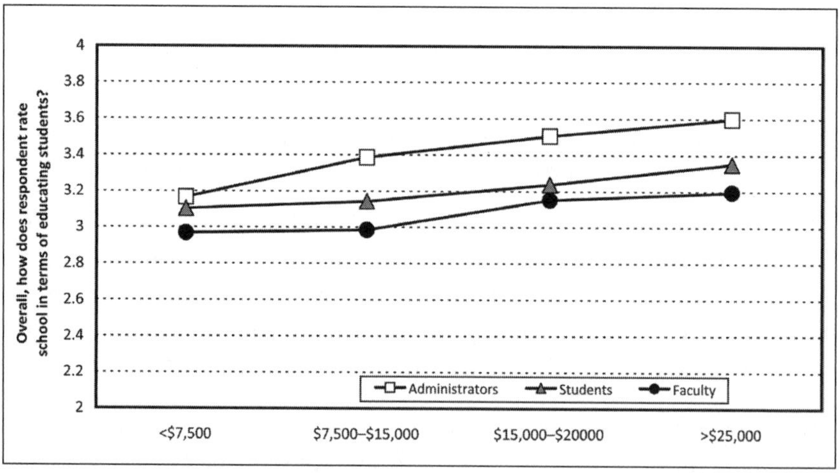

Figure 2.2. Relationship between Per-Student Expenditures and the Respondent's Rating of His or Her Own School (2 = Fair, 3 = Good, 4 = Excellent)

While professors and administrators largely agree that more funding is needed to deliver quality experiences for students, they disagree on the extent to which other challenges impact their educational objectives. Professors commonly cite the lack of student preparedness as a major problem facing American colleges and universities. In fact, they cite this problem almost as often as they cite funding issues, with 24 percent of professors mentioning it as the most pressing problem and 38 percent mentioning it as one of the most important problems. By contrast, only 4 percent of students and 16 percent of administrators make any mention of student quality when asked to identify the challenges to higher education. On the one hand, this is not surprising given that faculty members are most directly affected by students' level of preparation for college work. College professors spend a great deal of time with students and are most satisfied with their work when students are capable of meeting their expectations. A recent survey of faculty by the HERI demonstrates that the majority report some stress from working with underprepared students. Additionally, most professors believe that faculty members are not rewarded for their efforts to help these students (Lindholm, Szelényi, Hurtado, and Korn 2005). Still, administrators should also have reason to be concerned if student quality declines, both because student quality factors into the reputational rating of the college and because the need to provide remedial education is often cited as a factor that contributes to rising tuition costs.

Although many professors cite lack of student preparation as a problem, it is unclear whether lack of preparation is widespread or whether it is the case that a handful of unprepared students constitute a threat to higher education. According to the NAASS, most professors have some experience with underprepared students. Only 27 percent of the professors in our sample report that "almost all" of their students are academically prepared to be in their classes. While the majority of professors, 72 percent, report that at least most of their students are prepared,[7] this leaves more than a quarter who believe that most of their students are not prepared. These findings are consistent with more recent studies on the topic. For example, researchers at the HERI report that nearly a third of the professors in their survey believe that most of their students lack the necessary preparation for college work (DeAngelo et al. 2009; Lindholm et al. 2005).[8]

Administrators are much less likely to cite student preparedness as a major problem for higher education. This lack of concern is due, at least in part, to their different assessment of their students' skills. According to the NAASS, administrators are much more likely to believe that students at their institutions are academically prepared for college-level work, with approximately half of administrators reporting that nearly all their students are prepared.

Table 2.12. Assessments of Student Preparedness

What Proportion of the Students in Your Classes Is Academically Prepared to Be in Your Class?	*Faculty*	*Administrators*	*How Well Were You [Student Respondent] Prepared?*	*Students*
Almost all students prepared	27%	49%	Very well prepared	36%
Most students prepared	45%	41%	Fairly prepared	41%
Only some prepared	26%	9%	Not very	15%
Almost none students prepared	1%	0%	Not well	8%
Don't know	0%	1%	Don't know	0%
Total	100%	100%	Total	100%
n	1,645	808	*n*	1,608

Since administrators spend much less time in the classroom, if any time at all, it is possible that they are simply unable to assess students' skills. Administrators may also believe that faculty expectations for students are too high and that students are prepared if courses are taught at a level appropriate for the student body. However, our finding that administrators are more positive about their students' preparation is also consistent with our earlier observation that administrators are simply less critical of their institutions than are professors. In this case, students appear to agree more readily with campus administrators than with their professors. The majority of students in the NAASS sample report that they were academically prepared to enter college, with 36 percent reporting that they were "very prepared" and 41 percent reporting that they were "fairly prepared." One can look at this in several ways, however, as "fairly prepared" may be an admission that one was not fully prepared (table 2.12). Additionally, 23 percent of students admit that they did not feel prepared to enter college. This is a fairly high number, especially considering that the figure does not include students at community colleges, where preparation tends to be the lowest.

Other problems mentioned by survey respondents include issues related to quality of courses or the curriculum, problems with the administration or institutional bureaucracy, or concerns about teacher quality. However, the number of faculty, administrators, and students citing these concerns pales in comparison to the three top issues. It is also important to note that some of the problems commonly associated with higher education were simply not mentioned by the survey respondents. For example, despite a great deal of public commentary on the issue of "grade inflation," less than 1 percent of our survey respondents cited grading issues as an area of major concern. Similarly, survey respondents did not express concern over racial discrimination or diversity issues, nor did they find a lack of student services or facilities to be a major problem. Yet campus efforts to improve in these areas are commonly cited as the impetus for hefty tuition increases. According to a recent study by the Delta Cost Project (2009), the amount of money spent on classroom instruction has actually declined at most institutions, while spending on student services, administration, and facilities has increased.

We were also surprised to see that, despite concerns about college costs and lack of financial resources, few respondents identified a lack of accessibility to higher education as a major problem. While accessibility is sometimes used as a measure of a nation's progress (Usher and Cervenan 2005; Wagner 2006), we see little indication that it weighs heavily on the minds of those already at home within the academy. Other researchers have noted a similar trend among the public, with a disconnect between their concerns over costs and their views about accessibility. Although people express considerable concern about the rising price of college tuition, the vast majority believe that a student who really wants to go to college can do so if he or she is willing to make sacrifices (Immerwahr and Johnson 2007).

CONCLUSION

The results of our analysis demonstrate that students, professors, and administrators are in general agreement about the broad goals of a university education. We find widespread support for a general education, with required courses in literature, social science, humanities, and natural science. In this way, the universities' internal constituents appear to be rather traditional. While they believe that more contemporary courses on the experiences of minorities should be offered and even encouraged, the large majority are not yet willing to require these courses of all students. This is not to say that these types of courses are not offered within the contexts of the traditional requirements, and more recent survey evidence indicates that professors believe that these perspectives should be further integrated into the curriculum. The American Association of Trustees and Alumni has criticized the current core curriculum at most colleges and universities for the range of nontraditional courses that are allowed to fulfill various requirements (Latzer 2004). While students may not be required to take courses on minority experiences, it is possible that such courses would be among the range of options available to students to meet curriculum requirements. Thus, while professors, students, and administrators may support the traditional requirements of a liberal arts education, the courses offered within such a curriculum have become the source of some controversy, with critics charging that the academy has neglected to teach the great classics of Western civilization. There is some evidence that this is the case. Only a small number of survey respondents believe that learning about these classics is an "essential" part of the university experience. However, they are only slightly more likely to believe that the study of non-Western cultures is a necessity. Most important, we find that professors and administrators do not see these two goals as contradictory, as some of the critics of multiculturalism have charged. For the most part, those who believe students should learn about non-Western cultures also believe that they should learn the Western classics.

While students, faculty, and administrators largely agree about the general goals of higher education, they have different perspectives on the strength of American higher education and on the ability of their own institutions to educate students. In these areas, we find what will become a common theme throughout the book. Administrators are far more positive in their assessments of the university than professors and students. We attribute this difference to a number of factors but hypothesize that, in their role as institutional spokespeople, administrators are somewhat motivated to see and emphasize the positive. This certainly serves their institutions well in a number of ways. A positive administrator is more likely to secure funding, recruit faculty and students, and encourage others to serve the institution. However, these differences in assessment between administrators and professors have the potential to complicate the relationship between these two groups, which ultimately share responsibility for the governance of the university. Because administrators are more positive, faculty may regard them us oblivious to the problems facing the institution. When faculty raise concerns or are critical of the institution, administrators may appear to be unresponsive or defensive. Additionally, faculty members who are vocal about their concerns may compromise an administrator's ability to present the institution in a positive light. In this way, the two groups are often working at cross-purposes and may find productive dialogue to be difficult. For this reason, some administrators prefer to work with faculty through unofficial channels, bypassing faculty governance in exchange for ad hoc special committees comprised of agreeable appointees (Gumport 2001; Scott 1996). This has the potential to backfire, as committee actions may face opposition when they are brought before a more representative faculty forum.

Finally, we find that there are some important differences of opinion within the university about the most pressing problems for higher education. All three groups of survey respondents express some concern about finances, with notable differences. Students echo concerns expressed by those outside the academy. Most notably, they are concerned about the rising price of tuition. We find that professors and administrators show little concern about tuition costs. In fact, both groups appear to believe that students get good value for their money. Professors and administrators, however, believe that higher education is underfunded. Members of these groups appear to see money and quality as undeniably linked, a concept that is not shared by the majority of Americans, who believe that colleges can still cut excess costs without jeopardizing educational quality. This difference in opinion is likely to come to a head as states continue to reduce funding for higher education and college tuition continues to climb.

Among professors and administrators, few identify any problems within higher education itself. Rather, they tend to focus on the difficulties imposed on America's colleges and universities by outside forces. They believe that state governments do not provide enough funding and that the lack of financial resources compromises educational objectives. Professors cite a lack of student preparation as a problem, pointing to the failings of the country's primary education system. Yet external critics of higher education are quick to point to a variety of problems within the university system. Again, these differences in perspective make productive dialogue difficult. As Immerwahr et al. (2008) conclude, a lack of shared understanding between the different internal and external stakeholders means that cooperative efforts to improve higher education are unlikely.

Chapter Three

Perceptions of Power and Control in the American University

In the previous chapter, we argue that professors, administrators, and students have different perceptions of the problems facing higher education. We also provide some evidence that members of these groups disagree about the quality of education that their own institutions provide to students. These differences in perception are important, as views on the current status of higher education will undoubtedly influence people's willingness to consider major reforms. If professors, administrators, and students disagree about major issues facing their institutions, it is worth asking how much of a voice each group has in institutional decision making. While we cannot directly measure influence on university policy, we can measure people's perceptions of power and their willingness to engage in dialogue. Theoretically, power is shared within the institution, at least between the faculty and the administration. More than 90 percent of four-year colleges and universities have a faculty senate designed to participate in institutional decision making (Tierney and Minor 2003). However, the principle of shared governance may or may not translate into cooperative decision making.

For the past four decades, American colleges and universities have generally accepted the principles of shared university governance as articulated by the "Statement on Government of Colleges and Universities" of the American Association of University Professors (AAUP). The 1966 statement, which was developed in consultation with the American Council on Education (ACE) and the Association of Governing Boards of Universities and Colleges (ABG), calls for a joint effort between the faculty and the administration.[1] The faculty is given specific oversight of "such fundamental areas as curriculum, subject matter and methods of instruction, research, faculty status, and those aspects of student life which relate to the educational process." The statement also argues that, because of their academic expertise, faculty members are most qualified to evaluate, hire, and promote their colleagues. In addition to these specific responsibilities, the AAUP outlines a broad role for the faculty in the governance of the institution, requiring faculty input on practically all matters related to the general purpose of the university. At the same time, the organization recognizes the role of the university president as the "chief planning officer" of the institution, with "ultimate managerial responsibility for a large area of nonacademic activities."

The AAUP statement on shared governance was adopted near the end of what some historians have referred to as the "golden age" of American higher education, which occurred from the end of World War II through the 1960s. The postwar years were marked by a substantial increase in college admissions, due in part to the success of the 1944 GI Bill. During this period, the proportion of young people attending college grew from 15 to 45 percent (Geiger 2005). The federal government expanded financial support for higher education, recognizing a need to sponsor research programs to help build the peacetime economy. Colleges and universities struggled to keep up with the growth by hiring new faculty and expanding program offerings. In the 1960s, newly minted PhDs found easy employment. Institutions competed for the best and brightest new scholars by offering reduced teaching loads, competitive salaries, and other benefits, including influence in institutional planning (Baldridge, Curtis, Ecker, and Riley 1973; Honan and Teffera 2001):

> At most colleges and universities, the biggest gains in income, power, prestige and protections between 1945 and 1970 were those accumulated by the faculty. The prospect of a shortage of qualified college teachers, combined with the deference to expertise in some fields, gave a generation of professors unprecedented opportunities. The robust academic marketplace also had some spin-off in that faculty were sometimes able to negotiate gains in shared governance with presidents and boards. (Thelin 2004, 310)

It is not surprising that the AAUP statement on shared governance was written during this time period. Yet the academic job market, which was largely responsible for the growth in faculty authority, has change remarkably since the 1960s. By the 1970s, the academic boom had come to an end, and newly minted PhDs experienced much harsher competition for jobs within the academy. According to Thelin, administrators began to enjoy a "buyer's market." The sharp competition for academic work allowed administrators to negotiate conditions of employment that would have been unacceptable to the previous generation, leading to an increase in nontenured appointments and adjunct work. Even tenured faculty members suffered a loss in status, as reduced mobility left them with little leverage to negotiate salaries or other benefits.

At the same time, public confidence in the nation's academic institutions began to erode. The student protests of the 1960s had created a backlash against the academy, leading to greater governmental controls and reduced financing (Baldridge 1971). The academy faced further external pressure, as America moved from an industrial economy to a service and knowledge based economy. This redefined the role of higher education as a public utility, rather than an autonomous, elite institution (Lyons and Lyons 1973). Expected to provide a public service and contribute to the new global economy, higher education fell under even greater scrutiny (Schuster and Finkelstein 2006).

Now, as colleges and universities adjust to these external demands for accountability and cost cutting, the role of the faculty in institutional decision making continues to evolve. The political clout once held by the professoriate appears to be somewhat diminished, at least in the minds of the faculty. According to a 1997 survey, nearly three-quarters of American college professors believe that respect for the academic profession has declined. The same study demonstrates that faculty members' perceptions of professorial authority have been declining since the 1960s, with less than 20 percent now reporting a high level of influence in campus affairs (Schuster and Finkelstein 2006).

A decline in faculty influence may be attributed to several factors beyond the tightening of the academic job market. Pressures to reduce costs have led to what Schuster and Finkelstein (2006) call a "silent faculty revolution." The majority of college teachers hired in the past decade has filled part-time or non-tenure-track positions. The reliance on part-time, adjunct faculty strains campus governance systems, as fewer full-time professors are expected to carry the bulk of the committee assignments and other service duties (DeNardis 2001; Honan and Teferra 2001; Kezar and Eckel 2004). Faculty workloads have also shifted. Increased demands on teaching and research leave less time for institutional service, even among full-time faculty, who believe there are greater incentives and rewards for research than for service (Williams, Gore, Broches, and Lostoski 1987). The director of the Stanford Institute for Higher Education Research, Patricia Gumport (2001), suggests that new demands on academic administrators encourage them to bypass the traditional faculty governance system in favor of ad hoc committees filled with more agreeable, manageable appointees who can make timely decisions.

Concerned about the apparent decline in faculty governance, the AAUP issued another statement in 1994, reiterating the importance of shared governance by arguing that it is inextricably linked to academic freedom, a concept that is arguably held in high regard by the academic community. Yet while there appears to be a general consensus about the importance of the faculty's governance role, campus administrators express concerns about the limitations placed on their own offices (Bornstein 2003; Gumport 2001). As a former president of Harvard writes, "While leaders have considerable leverage and influence on their own, they are often reluctant to employ these assets for fear of arousing opposition from the faculty that could attract unfavorable publicity, worry potential donors, and even threaten their jobs" (Bok 2006). In 1996, the Association of Governing Boards of Colleges and Universities released a report (*Renewing the Academic Presidency 1996*) calling for efforts to strengthen the academic presidency. The report portrays the office of the presidency as weak, ineffective, and unnecessarily confined by "excessive consultation, a burdensome requirement for consensus, and a fear of change" created by the system of shared governance. It would appear, at least based on anecdotal accounts, that faculty and administrators have very different assessments of how power is and ought to be distributed within the system of "shared" governance. More important, there appears to be some disagreement about the usefulness of dialogue and discussion.

THE FACULTY–ADMINISTRATIVE DIVIDE

Analysis of the North American Academic Study (NAASS) survey data confirms the anecdotal evidence that professors have doubts about their own influence on university policy (table 3.1). When asked how much say professors have in how their institution is run, only 17 percent of the faculty believes that professors have a "great deal" of say, with an additional 46 percent indicating that they have "some" say. Thus, while the majority of professors believe that they have some influence, more than a third believe that they have little or no voice. Our findings here are consistent with other large-scale surveys of college professors (Schuster and Finkelstein 2006), although it is important to note that this is a general measure of perception of influence. Professors clearly have more influence in some areas than others. For example, according to one survey (Tierney and Minor 2003), the majority of faculty members do report having a great deal of influence on the undergraduate curriculum, tenure and promotion standards, and the evaluation of both teaching and academic programs. At the same time, relatively few faculty report having substantial influence on strategic priorities, budget priorities, personnel policies, and evaluation or selection of senior administrators. In all areas, senior administrators maintain that professors have more influence than the faculty perceive themselves to have. According to the authors of the report, "There is a certain irony that senior academic administrators believe faculty have influence, and faculty think they do not. Such perceptions carried to extremes are recipes for stalled decision-making" (Tierney and Minor 2003, 8).

While it may be the case that administrators perceive the faculty to have a fair amount of influence, this does not appear to take away from their perceptions of their own influence. In fact, the NAASS findings reveal that administrators are overwhelmingly confident in their own ability to influence the direction of the institution. Nearly two-thirds of administrators believe that, compared to faculty, they have "a great deal" of say in how the institution is run. In fact, there is comparatively little variance among the administrators, with 94 percent stating that administrators have "some" or "a great deal" of influence.

Perhaps it is not shocking to discover that administrators are more confident in their own institutional influence than the faculty given that they are, in fact, charged with running the day-to-day operations of the university. However, given traditions of shared governance, the fact that so many professors characterize the influence of the professoriate as weak may demonstrate an institutional failure. Either members of the faculty are correct in asserting that they have relatively little influence in matters of governance, or, alternatively, professors are quite influential but operate under the mistaken assumption that, on important matters, their opinions are inconsequential. Whether or not these perceptions are accurate, they are likely to have some effect on faculty morale, institutional loyalty, and commitment to university service and governance.

Table 3.1. "In Your View, Compared to Administrators/Professors, How Much Say Do Professors/Administrators Have in How This Institution Is Run?" [Question 4.2]

	Faculty: Professors' "Say" in This Institution				*Administrators: Administrators' "Say" in This Institution*		
	Assistant Professor	*Associate Professor*	*Full Professor*	*Faculty Overall*	*Held Teaching or Research Position*	*Never Held Teaching or Research Position*	*Administrators Overall*
A great deal	16%	16%	19%	17%	68%	54%	65%
Some	52%	46%	44%	46%	28%	34%	29%
A little	20%	26%	24%	23%	3%	9%	4%
Hardly any	11%	13%	14%	13%	1%	3%	1%
Don't know	0%	0%	0%	0%	1%	0%	0%
	100%	100%	100%	100%	100%	100%	100%
n	402	494	668	1,564	653	151	804

VARIED PERCEPTIONS OF INFLUENCE

In an attempt to account for the variance among professors in perception of faculty influence, we divided responses according to faculty rank. Previous research demonstrates that senior faculty report they have higher personal influence on both departmental and campus affairs than their junior colleagues (Schuster and Finkelstein 2006). Yet we find little difference between academic ranks in regard to perceptions of the faculty's voice as a whole. This may suggest that professors are able to assess group influence independent of their own personal participation in the decision-making process.

We also examined differences between groups of administrators according to whether they had previously held a teaching or a research position. Administrators who once occupied academic positions may have very different perceptions, perhaps more realistic ones, of faculty influence. According to Blackburn and Lawrence's (2002) study on faculty work, academics are socialized into a set of norms and values about higher education during their experience in graduate school. Since administrators who once held teaching or research positions have been introduced to these values, we might expect them to have assessments of relative influence that are more similar to those of the faculty. Indeed, the NAASS reveals that administrators who once occupied a faculty position rate administrative influence higher than those who have not risen from faculty ranks. While the differences are not dramatic, they are statistically significant.

Faculty members also differ in the assessments of influence according to the type of institution at which they are employed (table 3.2). We classify institutions according to the 2000 Carnegie classifications and find that professors at baccalaureate institutions perceive themselves to have more influence than those at master's universities, while those at research/doctoral institutions perceive they have the least amount of influence. This is consistent with other research findings. Peterson and White (1992), for example, find that at liberal arts colleges, which are included in the Carnegie baccalaureate grouping, "there is strong agreement on the purpose, culture, and climate patterns" (196) between members of the faculty and administrators, which allow them to adopt more collegial working relationships. Similarly, Chubb and Moe (1988) find that faculty at smaller, private schools report greater influence and better relationships with supervisors at the K–12 level. From the faculty perspective, organizational structures matter and have effects on the clarity of the institution's mission. However, while it may be the case that more narrowly focused institutions offer a more collegial environment based on shared visions, this improvement does not carry over to administrators' views of their own influence. In fact, there is no evidence that administrators recognize any difference in the distribution of faculty/administrative power on the basis of their institution classification.

This discrepancy raises a difficult question. Are professors more astute in observing their relatively high influence at baccalaureate institutions, or are administrators correct in noting that the administration is very powerful regardless of the college's classification? There are several explanations for these apparent differences in perceptions, all of which have implications for academic governance. First, on the basis of the literature suggesting that faculty governance is more effective at liberal arts colleges, one might conclude that administrators fail to recognize their considerably stronger influence on governance at larger institutions. However, a careful reading of the question wording suggests that perceptions of both groups may be accurate. It may be the case that faculty have a stronger voice at baccalaureate institutions. At the same time, administrators at these institutions may still have a great deal of say in institutional policy. In fact, active faculty participation in governance does not require that administrators surrender their own influence. Rather,

Table 3.2. "How Much Say Do Professors/Administrators Have in How This Institution Is Run?" [Question 4.2]

Professors' Perception: Professors' "Say"

	Baccalaureate	*Master's*	*Doctoral/Research*	*Total*
A great deal	39%	19%	13%	17%
Some	41%	46%	48%	47%
A little	14%	24%	24%	23%
Hardly any	5%	10%	15%	12%
Don't know	1%	0%	0%	0%
Total	100%	100%	100%	100%
n	131	542	957	1,630

Administrators' Perception: Administrators' "Say"

	Baccalaureate	*Master's*	*Doctoral/Research*	*Total*
A great deal	62%	66%	66%	65%
Some	35%	26%	30%	29%
A little	4%	4%	4%	4%
Hardly any	0%	3%	0%	1%
Don't know	0%	1%	0%	0%
Total	100%	100%	100%	100%
n	112	212	477	801

faculty influence may never rise to such a level that it seriously impedes on the administration. At its best, cooperative decision making allows both parties to perceive that they have a great deal of influence. When this ideal is not achieved, it would appear that the faculty is more likely to experience a loss of power, while the administration's perspective remains unchanged. Finally, it is quite possible that real power between faculty and administrators does not vary by type of institution but rather that faculty perceptions of their own power vary because of differences in government structures. For example, at small, baccalaureate institutions, the faculty assembly is more likely to be comprised of all faculty members as opposed to a small body of elected representatives. Direct participation may increase a professor's estimate of faculty voice. In reality, representative government at larger institutions may be as effective in advancing faculty interests, yet the actions and successes of these bodies may go unnoticed by the average professor. Whatever the case, it appears that professors at baccalaureate colleges believe that they have more say in the governance of their institutions than do faculty at master's or doctoral institutions.

Table 3.3 shows the major factors that contribute to a respondent's perceptions of power, including demographic/ideological, institutional, and rank/experiential factors. The most striking feature of these models is their inherent unpredictability. Even when accounting for a dozen theoretically useful factors, the model only explains 5 percent of the variance in faculty perceptions of voice and 2 percent of the variance in administrators' perceptions (see R^2 provided in table 3.3). Institutional factors do play some role in shaping faculty perceptions. Consistent with the results in table 3.2, we find that professors who work at baccalaureate institutions are significantly more likely than those at master's institutions to perceive that faculty have a "say" in the institution. Those serving at research/doctoral universities tend to think the faculty is considerably weaker. Furthermore, an institution's average expenditure per student plays a relatively important part in shaping professors' perceptions of power, with respondents from wealthier institutions indicating that their faculty is more influential than those from poorer schools. The standardized beta coefficients show that each of the statistically significant institutional predictors has roughly the same influence on perceptions of power. While we hypothesized that smaller schools lend themselves to greater faculty influence, the model illustrates that institutional size has no effect on perceptions of influence once institutional type is factored into the model. Thus, while faculty at baccalaureate colleges may, in fact, benefit from more direct participation in governance, compared to colleagues at master's and doctoral institutions, differences in size between institutions of the same classification are not relevant.

Table 3.3. Regression Showing Perceptions of How Much "Say" Faculty/Administrators Have in Governance

Independent Variables		*Professors' Perceptions: Professors' "Say"* — *Beta Coefficients*	*Administrators' Perceptions: Administrators' "Say"* — *Beta Coefficients*
	Constant	3.029 ***	3.186 ***
		(0.205)	(0.220)
Demographics and Ideology	Sex	−.067	−.141 **
		(0.062)	(0.052)
	Age	−.005	.010 *
		(0.004)	(0.004)
	Party identification	−.027	−.007
		(0.040)	(0.034)
	Social Liberalism Index	−.017	.040
		(0.031)	(0.029)
	Religious attendance	−.008	−.013
		(0.016)	(0.015)
	Income	.028 ***	.009
		(0.007)	(0.006)
Institutional Factors	Institution size	.000	.000
		(0.000)	(0.000)
	Expenditures per student	4.5E-06 ***	−7.1E-07
		−(1.3E-06)	(0.000)
	Doctoral institution	−.249 ***	.074
		(0.070)	(0.066)
	Baccalaureate institution	.382 ***	.042
		(0.098)	(0.077)
Rank and Experience	Years in higher education	.007	−.018
		(0.024)	
	Is professor tenured?	−.046	—
		(0.075)	
	Professor's rank	−.042	—
		(0.049)	
	n	1,331	753
	Adjusted R^2	0.049	0.021

Note: Standard errors listed in parentheses are * $p < .05$, ** $p < .01$, *** $p < .001$.

Again mirroring the results of table 3.2, administrators' perceptions of power appear completely unrelated to any of the institutional factors listed in table 3.3. The general assertion that administrators have "a great deal" of say in institution affairs is roughly the same, notwithstanding their institution's size, funding, or Carnegie classification.

One of the more interesting findings in table 3.3 is the statistically significant variations in perceptions of power based on the demographic characteristics of the individual respondent. Among professors, those with a higher income tend to perceive that the faculty is more influential than those with a lower income. This may be an accurate reflection of actual power since the most valued professors are likely to command the highest salaries, perhaps as the result of securing an endowed chair or other recognition. By contrast, administrators' views of power are related to their age and sex. Older administrators tend to perceive the administration as being slightly more influential than younger administrators, while female administrators tend to see their administrations as less influential than male administrators.

While the relationships are interesting, we must be careful about proclaiming the direction of causation. For example, perhaps male administrators do, in fact, command more authority, while female administrators are more likely to build institutional consensus. Thus, by engaging in more extensive consultation with the professoriate, female administrators would be less apt to characterize their own administrations as powerful relative to the faculty. It is also possible that women objectively yield the same authority as men but merely lack the confidence of their male counterparts. However, we are cautious about making definitive claims given that the models predict so little variance. Even among similar institutions, perceptions of power vary greatly, indicating that institutional culture and individual leadership styles are, in all likelihood, an important component of perceived influence.

CONFLICT AS A PREDICTOR OF INFLUENCE

According to Bacharach and Lawler (1980), the presence of conflict contributes to people's assessments of power (see also Bacharach and Lawler 1976). In the absence of conflict, it is difficult to evaluate the power of various groups since all parties can operate under the illusion that they have dictated the terms of agreement. However, when people or groups disagree about how resources should be distributed, the outcomes of the negotiations provide some evidence as to who controls those resources.

Based on our findings in the previous chapter, we hypothesize that professors and administrators differ in their goals and objectives often enough that there is potential for conflict between the groups. An analysis of the NAASS supports this theory, with an important exception. There does appear to be some faculty disapproval of administrative action, although there is a good deal of variance among professors (see table 3.4). When asked if they support the views of the administration about the direction the institution is going, a minority of professors, 42 percent, reports that they "usually" or "always" agree. A plurality of professors, 46 percent, says that they "sometimes agree," while only 11 percent "usually" or "always" disagree. As expected, faculty members at baccalaureate institutions report the most agreement with their administrations. Again, faculty attitudes appear to be relatively consistent over time. For example, according to the 2007–2008 Higher Education Research Institute survey of college faculty, a minority of 19 percent report that "faculty are typically at odds with campus administration" (DeAngelo et al. 2009). While this question varies somewhat from that used on the NAASS study, it demonstrates that few faculty members perceive the administration to be at war with faculty goals and objectives. However, the same survey also

Table 3.4. "When It Comes to the Direction Your Institution Is Going, Do You [Agree] with the Views of . . ." [Question 4.1]

Faculty, Do You [Agree] with the Views of Your Administration?

	Baccalaureate	*Master's*	*Doctoral/Research*	*Total*
Always/usually agree	54%	44%	38%	42%
Sometimes agree	38%	43%	49%	46%
Usually disagree	8%	12%	12%	11%
Always disagree	0%	0%	1%	0%
Don't know	1%	1%	0%	1%
Total	100%	100%	100%	100%
n	132	542	957	1,631

Administrators, Do You [Agree] with the Views of Your Faculty?

	Baccalaureate	*Master's*	*Doctoral/Research*	*Total*
Always/usually agree	69%	70%	71%	71%
Sometimes agree	31%	29%	27%	28%
Usually disagree	0%	0%	1%	1%
Always disagree	0%	0%	1%	1%
Don't know	0%	0%	0%	0%
Total	100%	100%	100%	100%
n	111	213	476	800

demonstrates that a small percentage of professors report that the administration is "open about its policies" (16.5 percent), and even fewer perceive that "administrators consider faculty concerns when making policy" (13 percent). Again, these are consistent with our findings from the NAASS survey (table 3.2), which is slightly more positive on faculty influence.

The important exception to our observation about conflict is that, among administrators, there is a greater perception of administrative–faculty agreement on the general direction of the university. The vast majority of administrators, 71 percent, report that they "always agree" or "usually agree" with their faculty. Only 2 percent of administrators state that they usually disagree with their faculty members. While there appears to be no difference among institution type, we find that those administrators who formerly held research or teaching positions report greater agreement with the faculty than other administrators. This is consistent with the theory that academics are socialized into academic norms and maintain these values as they move into other positions. The fact that other administrators report less agreement with faculty may be a concern for those committed to the concept of shared governance, given the current trend in higher education to employ administrators from outside the academy. According to a study by the ACE, 30 percent of college presidents in 2000 had never held a full-time faculty position (DeNardis 2001). Waugh (2003) warns that academic administrations are becoming increasingly professionalized and that the new academic presidents, recruited from the private sector, do not have the same commitment to academic values and shared governance.

Clearly, both professors and administrators cannot be correct about the degree to which they are in agreement about institutional agendas. The fact that perceptions of conflict are largely one sided raises some important questions about dialogue between professors and administrators. Either professors are not able to effectively communicate their dissent to administrators, or they are underestimating administrative support for their own positions. From the data in this chapter alone, it is difficult to determine the source of the miscommunication. However, in chapter 6 we explore communication between groups in more detail and are able to offer some clues as to how members of both groups could have such different perceptions of the institutional climate.

Since conflict may help to reveal power differentials, we would expect those professors who frequently disagree with the administration to have different assessments of faculty influence than those who most often agree with the views of the administration. Those who have little conflict with the administration would have fewer opportunities to evaluate their relative influence since the outcome of successful influence tactics would be identical to the outcome of unsuccessful tactics in that both would favor the shared agenda.

These more agreeable individuals may perceive that they have a strong voice in university matters since they are likely to be appointed to advisory committees. Those individuals who disagree with the administration may be less likely to be appointed to committees. When they do express opinions, it is less likely that their positions would guide university policy. Theoretically, these individuals would perceive the influence of the faculty to be relatively low.

The data from the NAASS supports this theory. There is a strong, positive relationship between a faculty member's agreement with the views of the administration and his or her perception of faculty influence. Those who usually or always agree with the administration have a strong sense of efficacy, with 83 percent of this group reporting that professors have "some" or "a great deal" of say in campus matters. Those who usually disagree with the administration tell a very different story, with nearly three-quarters reporting that the faculty has "a little" or "hardly any" influence (table 3.5). Many people will find these results discouraging. The fact that those with dissenting opinions believe they have little say in university matters may be a cause for concern. Even if these individuals' assessments are inaccurate and they grossly underestimate the power of their dissenting voices, the mere perception of inefficacy is likely to impact faculty morale and reduce participation in campus dialogue (Blackburn and Lawrence 2002; Brogan 1969). This disengagement is of some concern for institutional decision making since research on the role of divergent viewpoints in group deliberations demonstrates that disagreement improves decision outcomes (Schulz-Hardt, Frey, Lüthgens, and Moscovici 2000; Schulz-Hardt et al. 2006). More recent survey evidence provides additional cause for concern, as only 35 percent of faculty respondents report that the statement "There is respect for the expres-

Table 3.5. Faculty Agreement with the Administration versus "Say" in the Institution

		Question 4.1 "When it comes to the direction your Institution is going, do you [agree] with the views of your administration?"			
		Always/ Usually Agree	*Sometimes Agree*	*Usually/Always Disagree*	*Total*
Question 4.2: "How much say do professors have in how this institution is run?"	A great deal	28%	11%	4%	17%
	Some of the time	55%	46%	22%	47%
	A little	14%	30%	32%	24%
	Hardly any	3%	13%	42%	12%
	Don't know	0%	0%	1%	0%
	Total	100%	100%	100%	100%
	n	680	756	200	1,636

sion of diverse values and beliefs" is "very descriptive" of their institutions (DeAngelo et al. 2009).

COLLECTIVE BARGAINING

Faculty members who feel that they have little influence on campus policies may support actions designed to strengthen their position. Collective bargaining is often used as a last resort once cooperation between professors and administrators is no longer thought possible and the faculty has grown tired of "administrative encroachments" (Burgan 2006). Faculty movement toward unionization faces heavy administrative resistance and may result in the further breakdown of collegial relationships. Research demonstrates that campuses with unionized faculty groups have more adversarial relationships between professors and administrators (Putten, McLendon, and Peterson 1997). However, some could argue that the presence of a union is a reflection of poor faculty–administrative relationships rather than the underlying cause of conflict (table 3.6).

Overall, 62 percent of professors surveyed in the NAASS agree with the statement that "collective bargaining is important to protect the interests of the faculty." Support for collective bargaining is significantly higher among junior faculty, with 73 percent of assistant professors agreeing with the statement, compared to 52 percent of full professors (table 3.5). Support for collective bargaining is also highest among faculty at master's universities, with 72 percent of faculty offering support for collective bargaining, compared to 66 percent support among faculty at baccalaureate colleges and 56 percent among faculty at doctoral/research institutions. This may be due to the nature of the master's institution. According to Peterson and White (1992), faculty and administrators at master's universities disagree on questions of academic purpose more than their colleagues at baccalaureate colleges or doctoral/research universities. Perhaps most important, faculty employed at baccalaureate colleges are less likely to support collective bargaining, report the highest levels of faculty influence, and perceive that they have the most agreement with their administrations.

As one might expect, faculty members who disagree with the views of the administration are more likely to believe that collective bargaining is necessary to protect the interests of the faculty (table 3.7). Similarly, those who believe that professors have a great deal of say in how the institution is run are less likely to support collective bargaining than faculty who believe they have little influence. This provides some support for the claim that unionization is the result rather than the cause of adversarial faculty–administrative

Table 3.6. "Collective Bargaining Is Important to Protect the Interests of the Faculty" [Question 9.1b]

	Faculty								*Administrators*		
	By Professor's Rank				*Institution Classification*				*Held Teaching or Research Position*		
	Assistant	*Associate*	*Full Professor*	*All*	*Baccalaureate*	*Master's*	*Doctoral/ Research*	*All*	*Yes*	*No*	*All*
Strongly agree	36%	28%	22%	28%	19%	35%	24%	27%	6%	5%	6%
Moderately agree	37%	38%	30%	34%	47%	36%	32%	34%	18%	28%	20%
Moderately disagree	19%	25%	29%	25%	24%	21%	28%	25%	33%	32%	33%
Strongly disagree	9%	8%	19%	13%	10%	9%	16%	13%	42%	34%	41%
Total	100%	100%	100%	100%	100%	100%	100%	100%	100%	100%	100%
n	389	476	657	1,522	128	524	932	1,584	631	148	779

Table 3.7. Perceptions of Power and Importance of Collective Bargaining

		Faculty Question: "In your view, compared to administrators, how much say do *professors* have in how this institution is run?" [4.2]				
		Faculty				
		A Great Deal	*Some*	*A Little*	*Hardly Any*	*Total*
Question 9.1b: "Collective bargaining is important to protect the interests of the faculty."	Strongly agree	24%	25%	28%	37%	27%
	Moderately agree	32%	34%	37%	33%	34%
	Moderately disagree	28%	27%	23%	18%	25%
	Strongly disagree	15%	14%	12%	11%	13%
		100%	100%	100%	100%	100%
	n	274	744	383	195	1,599

		Administrative Question: "In your view, compared to professors, how much say do *administrators* have in how this institution is run?" [4.2]				
		Administrators				
		A Great Deal	*Some*	*A Little*	*Hardly Any*	*Total*
Question 9.1b: "Collective bargaining is important to protect the interests of the faculty."	Strongly agree	6%	6%	9%	29%	6%
	Moderately agree	19%	21%	16%	29%	20%
	Moderately disagree	32%	38%	31%	0%	33%
	Strongly disagree	42%	36%	44%	43%	41%
		100%	100%	100%	100%	100%
	n	508	228	32	7	779

relationships. Opinions on the usefulness of unionization are themselves divisive, with only one-quarter of the administrators in our study agreeing that collective bargaining is important to protect the interests of the faculty.

STUDENT DEMANDS AND INFLUENCE

Thus far, our analysis of power and influence in the university has been limited to the relationship between the faculty and the administration. However, students also place demands on the university. These demands have taken a variety of forms over the past several decades. The student protests of the 1960s moved beyond earlier calls for improved living conditions on campus and involved the university in the larger sociopolitical debates of the era. Students demanded that university administrators adopt policies that reflected their views on civil rights, war, and the university's relationship to the "military-industrial complex." Perhaps most important, the new student power movement demanded a formal voice for students in campus decision making (Lyons and Lyons 1973).

As the turbulence of the 1960s ended, students became less engaged in politics. However, the student power movement had a lasting effect on how students would view their relationship with the university. According to Thelin (2004), the "enduring legacy of the organized student movement was recognition by students of their rights as consumers and as members of the campus community . . . they had not forgotten the 1960s' lessons about the power of collective strength to influence the character of the campus" (327). Additionally, the declining enrollments of the mid-1970s created a competition for students and tuition dollars that forced administrators to increase campus services, improve dormitories, and provide a wide range of extracurricular activities.

As early as the 1970s, faculty bemoaned the new "consumerism" taking hold among students (Lyons and Lyons 1973). More recently, criticism has been focused on students' demands as related to the curriculum and includes claims that the American college student is interested in grades and degrees rather than knowledge. Professors also express concern that students prefer easy courses to challenging courses and that they evaluate professors on the basis of their ability to entertain and their willingness to hand out high marks. Some members of the academy claim that the consumer culture taking over higher education is counterproductive to higher education's goals of fostering inquiry and creating knowledge (Delucchi and Korgen 2002; Delucchi and Smith 1997).

Whatever power struggles exist between the faculty and the administration, there is some evidence that they are in agreement when it comes to limiting students' influence on academic policy and course requirements. Ladd and Lipset (1975) found that, although faculty members were politically liberal in the 1970s, they were fairly conservative on matters of university policy. They elected to maintain the status quo and safeguarded faculty control of the curriculum, admissions policies, and personnel decisions. Noel and Fontana (1974) reported similar results, finding that neither professors nor administrators showed much support for a student role in proposing new courses or evaluating faculty. Since both of these studies were conducted more than three decades ago, we must ask whether the recent wave of student consumerism reported by sociologists has had any effect on contemporary views of students' rights and responsibilities.

Using the NAASS data, we compare responses of professors, administrators, and students on two measures: students' ability to choose their own courses and deference to faculty in determining the educational needs of students. As expected, the overwhelming majority of professors believes that "faculty are the best judges of the educational needs of students" with 39 percent of respondents strongly agreeing with the statement (table 3.8). The majority of administrators also believe that faculty best determine educational needs. However, it is worth noting that they feel less strongly about the issue, with only 29 percent of administrators strongly agreeing with the statement. Students are divided on the question. Almost half the students surveyed disagree with the claim that faculty are best able to judge their educational needs. However, it is not clear from the question whether those students who disagree believe that they are better able to evaluate their own educational needs or whether they would grant this responsibility to some other authority, whether it be parents, administrators, or politicians.

The question on course selection more clearly demonstrates that students desire greater control over their own educational experience and that this desire places them at odds with the faculty and the administration (table 3.9). The majority of students, 59 percent, believe that "students should be able to choose

Table 3.8. "Faculty Are the Best Judges of the Educational Needs of Students" [Question 9.1ih]

	Faculty	*Student*	*Administrators*
Strongly agree	39%	13%	27%
Moderately agree	47%	40%	53%
Moderately disagree	12%	32%	18%
Strongly disagree	1%	14%	2%
Don't know	1%	0%	1%
Total	100%	100%	100%
n	1,644	1,607	807

Table 3.9. "Students Should Be Free to Choose Whatever Courses They Want for Their Degree Programs" [Question 9.1i]

	Faculty	*Student*	*Administrators*
Strongly agree	2%	27%	2%
Moderately agree	10%	32%	9%
Moderately disagree	33%	29%	29%
Strongly disagree	55%	11%	60%
Don't know	1%	0%	0%
	100%	100%	100%
n	1,646	1,607	807

whatever courses they want for their degree programs." Faculty and administrators overwhelmingly disagree with students but show remarkable agreement with one another. In fact, administrators are even slightly more opposed than faculty to granting students control over their own course selection. It appears that, at least in terms of academic course requirements, members of the faculty are opposed to giving into student consumer demands. More surprisingly, the administration does not appear to be torn between competing faculty and student constituencies as one might expect. Rather, administrators are even less inclined to allow students to dictate the terms of their academic experience.

Although professors and administrators are not inclined to let students dictate their own graduation requirements, both groups do recognize that students have a significant voice in university matters, especially in the area of faculty tenure and promotion. The vast majority of professors, administrators, and students agree that student evaluations of professors are important to faculty advancement (tables 3.10 and 3.11). Overall, administrators are most likely to rate student evaluations as "very important," a finding that may be unsettling to professors who had hoped the buzz about student evaluations was exaggerated. Among professors, perceptions differ according to faculty rank. Junior professors view student evaluations as most important, with 41 percent of assistant professors believing that they are "very important," compared to 36 percent of associate professors and 31 percent of full professors.

The biggest differences in perception of student evaluations occur somewhat predictably according to institutional classification. Professors, administrators, and students all consider student evaluations to be most important at baccalaureate institutions and least important at doctoral/research institutions. However, the difference in perception is most notable among the faculty. At doctoral/research institutions, only 29 percent of professors consider student evaluations to be "very important" for faculty advancement, compared to 58 percent of professors at baccalaureate colleges. This gap in perception may reflect the realities of the tenure and promotion systems, which place greater emphasis on teaching and less emphasis on research at undergraduate colleges. However, if this were the case, one would expect to see similar differences between administrators at these types of institutions. While administrators at doctoral/research universities do rate student evaluations as less important than their baccalaureate counterparts, the difference is not as substantial as that observed among the faculty. At research institutions, 37 percent of administrators rate student evaluations as "very important," compared to 49 percent of administrators at undergraduate institutions.

Although faculty, administrators, and students all agree that students do have a good deal of control over faculty careers, not all agree that this is appropriate or useful. The perception that career achievement depends on stu-

Table 3.10. "How Important Are Student Evaluations to Faculty Advancement at Your Institution?" [Question 4.3]

	Faculty by Institution Type				*Faculty by Rank*			
	Baccalaureate	*Master's*	*Doctoral/Research*	*Total*	*Assistant*	*Associate*	*Full Professor*	*Total*
Very important	58%	41%	29%	35%	41%	36%	33%	36%
Somewhat important	38%	47%	56%	52%	46%	50%	55%	51%
Not very important	3%	10%	14%	12%	11%	13%	10%	11%
Not at all important	1%	1%	1%	1%	1%	0%	2%	1%
Don't know	0%	0%	0%	0%	1%	0%	0%	0%
Total	100%	100%	100%	100%	100%	100%	100%	100%
n	130	542	957	1,629	401	494	670	1,565

Table 3.11. "How Important Are Student Evaluations to Faculty Advancement at Your Institution?" [Question 4.3]

	Administrators by Institution Type				*Students by Institution Type*			
	Baccalaureate	*Master's*	*Doctoral/Research*	*Total*	*Baccalaureate*	*Master's*	*Doctoral/Research*	*Total*
Very important	49%	46%	37%	41%	43%	39%	38%	39%
Somewhat important	46%	47%	52%	50%	44%	43%	45%	44%
Not very important	4%	4%	11%	8%	8%	12%	13%	12%
Not at all important	0%	2%	0%	1%	5%	5%	3%	4%
Don't know	1%	0%	0%	0%	0%	1%	0%	0%
Total	100%	100%	100%	100%	100%	100%	100%	100%
n	112	213	477	802	169	638	801	1,608

dent approval may make professors better educators if they perceive that students are objective, competent evaluators. However, if professors believe that students simply reward those who are less challenging, then they may simply adjust classroom demands accordingly. One survey of faculty found that 67 percent of professors agree that student evaluations promote lenient grading (Kolevzon 1981). Ryan, Anderson, and Birchler (1980) found that a third of professors admitted to lowering their own grading standards in order to improve evaluations.

CONCLUSION

Our analysis suggests that the university is a complex political environment with various internal constituencies competing for influence and power. Compared to professors and administrators, students are less confident in the faculty's ability to determine their educational needs and believe that they should have greater control over their own educational experiences. Professors and administrators are overwhelmingly opposed to granting students the type of control they desire. Thus, we find little support for claims that faculty and administrators are sympathetic to the "student as consumer" mentality. With that said, all three constituencies agree that student evaluations of teaching are important for faculty advancement, a realization that is likely to impact faculty behavior, whether it be for the better or for the worse.

While faculty members and administrators may agree on limiting the power of students to determine their own academic requirements, they disagree about the role that they themselves play in dictating the direction of the university. The vast majority of administrators believe that they have a substantial voice in institutional matters. Professors are less positive about their own influence, with a sizable number indicating that they have little or no influence. More important, faculty perception of influence appears to be related to agreement with the administration. Professors who disagree most with the direction of the administration rate faculty influence substantially lower than those who tend to agree with the administration. It is possible that these people do have less say in the institution, as administrators may be less likely to appoint them to advisory committees or other offices. It is also possible that these individuals merely perceive their influence to be lower than that of other members of the faculty since their policy preferences are implemented less often. However, we argue that professors cannot assess their capacity for influence without some conflict since outcomes would not reveal the distribution of power. Accordingly, the dissenting voices among the faculty may have the most accurate perspective of the division of power. Even if this is not the case, the perception of influence is itself a concern since it is likely to influence people's actions. Faculty who believe that their capacity to change university policy is low will be less likely to make demands or engage in campus dialogue. The fact that administrators report high levels of agreement with their faculty can be an indication that there is little conflict with the faculty. However, the results might also indicate that dissenting voices are present but not being heard.

Our results suggest that the system of shared governance is not operating to the satisfaction of the faculty and that the situation is likely to get worse before it gets better. The majority of professors surveyed believe that collective bargaining is necessary to protect the interests of the faculty. Those who disagree with the administration most often and those who perceive faculty influence to be low are more likely to support collective action than their agreeable, efficacious peers. The fact that junior faculty members are more likely to favor collective bargaining than their senior colleagues is something of an ominous sign for administrators, who tend to oppose unionization efforts. Unless this support for collective bargaining naturally fades as professors achieve greater professional success, one might expect a gradual increase in support for unions as this newer cohort of professors occupies an ever-greater proportion of the faculty ranks. Our results suggest that challenges to shared governance are also likely to increase as more administrators are hired from outside the academy. We find that administrators with no prior teaching or research experience have less collegial relationships with the faculty; they report greater disagreement with their faculty and perceive the faculty to have less say in campus matters.

The results of this chapter suggest some challenges for institutional growth and reform. A significant number of professors perceive that they are in disagreement with their administrations on the future and direction of their institutions. If this disagreement is real, professors and administrators may be working at cross-purposes. While faculty may perceive their influence to be low in some areas, they maintain considerable control over the curriculum and may fail to adopt curricular requirements that support the broader goals of the administration. Even if the disagreement is imagined, however, faculty who believe they are opposed to administrative objectives may adopt obstructionist positions. Perception of disagreement has consequences in and of itself.

It is also apparent that a sizable group of professors perceive themselves to have little voice in campus matters and that this is not an agreeable circumstance. In fact, those professors who rate the faculty as weak support measures to strengthen faculty influence, including collective bargaining agreements. External reformers may find themselves in the midst of a turf war and mired in the gridlock of shared governance.

Chapter Four

Politics and Culture Wars

Any analysis of conflict and values within higher education would be woefully incomplete without some discussion of political and social values. While it is true that political values are the source of some conflict within the academy, the larger division appears to be between the academy and the public. In times of political turmoil, these divisions in values and perspectives become more apparent, prompting the public and government officials to take notice of educational practices. Thus, during several periods in our nation's history, the academy has had to defend not only its educational practices but also the political practices of those it employs.

In the years following World War II, Senator Joseph McCarthy and the House Un-American Activities Committee accused several prominent academics of working with the Communist Party, a charge that, in the most severe cases, led to the firing of tenured professors. As John Thelin (2004) explains in *A History of American Higher Education*, this was a trying time for the academy:

> Although the highly publicized congressional hearings chaired by Senator McCarthy have received the most attention, these national episodes were only one part of the story of the postwar politics of higher education. The investigations conducted by state legislatures and campus administrations showed that local politics were especially important in shaping academic freedom . . . numerous state university presidents took the initiative to subject their faculties to loyalty oaths and codes of conduct exceeding anything that vigilant congressional or state officials might have required. Many campus presidents proved to be more interested in defusing external scrutiny than in defending their professors' traditional rights of academic freedom. (277)

While the McCarthy era was marked by an external assault on higher education, the Vietnam War presented another sort of challenge—an assault on the institution from within. Students organized campus demonstrations against U.S. involvement in the war and directly criticized universities for their support of the "military-industrial complex." The campus unrest attracted some media attention in the early years of the war. However, the violent confrontations between protesters and National Guard troops at Kent State University and Jackson State University "propelled the campus movement into the mainstream of American news and life with a force that was wrenching and riveting" (Thelin 2004, 310). These events further radicalized the student antiwar movement. Demonstrations became more aggressive, often interrupting classes and interfering with the basic function of the university. The inability or unwillingness of campus administrators to control the situation raised questions about the mission and integrity of higher education. Again, the academy faced intense scrutiny and was portrayed as a haven for radical leftism and anti-American sentiment.

While the academy routinely faces scrutiny, critics often claim that it is not responsive to external critiques. Because of a deep commitment to academic freedom and confidence in their own professional expertise, academics tend to resist government reforms and other intrusions into academic culture. Yet criticism of the academy often raises the very sort of questions that social scientists seek to answer. The McCarthy investigations raised questions about the values, politics, and loyalties of the professoriate. In response, sociologists Paul Lazarsfeld and Wagner Thielens (1958) published *The Academic Mind*, which included the first in-depth study into the attitudes and values of academics. Nearly two decades later, in the midst of campus unrest surrounding the Vietnam War, Carl Ladd and Seymour Martin Lipset (1975) expanded this line of research with their own study of professorial politics, *The Divided Academy*.

Following the September 11, 2001, attacks on the World Trade Center and the Pentagon, institutions of higher education once again found themselves in the midst of the culture wars. The threat of terrorism and the impending war in Iraq revealed a chasm between academic discourse and public sentiment. At a time when the majority of Americans favored U.S. military action against Iraq, college professors across the country opposed military action and organized to rally support for their position.[1] At the University of Pennsylvania, a group of faculty formed the "Penn Faculty & Staff Against War on Iraq," which issued a public statement condemning the war and held a teach-in to "protest the impending war."[2] Across the nation, similar faculty groups emerged at Stanford, the University of Colorado, and the University of Minnesota, to name but a few. At the University of California, Los Angeles (UCLA), the Academic Faculty Senate overwhelmingly approved, by a vote of 180 to 7, a resolution condemning the war in Iraq. Similar resolutions were passed by faculty governance organizations at the University of California, Santa Barbara (UCSB), and Oregon State University.[3] At some colleges and universities, activity was less structured, but the vast majority of institutions hosted some form of antiwar activity in the post-9/11 years, initiated by either faculty or students.

While much of the campus activity against the war went relatively unnoticed by those outside the academy, it was difficult for the public to ignore the controversy surrounding Ward Churchill, chair of the Department of Ethnic Studies at the University of Colorado. Churchill, who the university later charged with research misconduct and dismissed from his position, had written an essay claiming that the victims who died in the World Trade towers helped to provoke the attacks:

> They formed a technocratic corps at the very heart of America's global financial empire—the "mighty engine of profit" to which the military dimension of U.S. policy has always been enslaved—and they did so both willingly and knowingly. Recourse to "ignorance"—a derivative, after all, of the word "ignore"—counts as less than an excuse among this relatively well-educated elite. To the extent that any of them were unaware of the costs and consequences to others of what they were involved in—and in many cases excelling at—it was because of their absolute refusal to see. More likely, it was because they were too busy braying, incessantly and self-importantly, into their cell phones, arranging power lunches and stock transactions, each of which translated, conveniently out of sight, mind and smelling distance, into the starved and rotting flesh of infants. If there was a better, more effective, or in fact any other way of visiting some penalty befitting their participation upon the little Eichmanns inhabiting the sterile sanctuary of the twin towers, I'd really be interested in hearing about it.[4]

The conservative media discussed Churchill's statement at great length, with particular attention from Fox News's Bill O'Reilly, who expressed outrage and repeatedly called for Churchill's dismissal. Faculty initiatives to defend Churchill, in the name of academic freedom, furthered the perception that academia was again the bastion of radical, anti-American thought.[5]

Even before Ward Churchill became the poster boy for academic radicalism, David Howoritz began to mount an aggressive inquiry into the politics of higher education. In 2003, he founded Students for Academic Freedom, a group dedicated to promoting intellectual diversity on campus and securing the adoption of an "Academic Bill of Rights" aimed at protecting students from political and religious discrimination. In their mission statement, the group specifically notes that one-sided teach-ins, such as the one held at the University of Pennsylvania following 9/11, are violations of students' academic freedom rights. Prompted by the Academic Bill of Rights, several state legislatures held hearings on issues of academic freedom, faculty politics, and the politicization of the academy, with varying degrees of success. In response to these legislative inquiries, several state universities in Pennsylvania, Ohio, and elsewhere passed policies dictating the professional responsibility of professors to remain objective in the classroom and outlining grievance procedures for students who believe their professors have not acted accordingly.

According to Ladd and Lipset (1975), what made the Vietnam and McCarthy years especially problematic for academics is that these periods were marked by "deep tensions and conflicts in the polity." This is especially troublesome for those who discuss sensitive social issues as a matter of their profession—social scientists—and are hence vulnerable to criticism for the positions they take. The period following 9/11 is similar to these earlier eras in that political turmoil and disagreement served to reveal rather than to create a division between the intellectual elite and the mass public. The North American Academic Survey Study (NAASS), conducted two years before the 9/11 terrorist attacks, reveals that even in less tumultuous times, academics are consistently at odds with the rest of the nation on a wide range of policy issues.

POLITICAL VIEWS OF THE FACULTY

Surveys of academics reveal a long history of faculty support for left-wing political parties. After decades of studying the issue, Seymour Martin Lipset (1982) summarized the research findings as follows:

> A number of surveys of American professorial opinion, taken since World War II, have shown that, as a group, academics are more likely than any other occupational group, including manual workers, to identify their views as left or liberal, to support a wide variety of egalitarian social and economic policies, and to back small leftist third parties and/or vote Democratic. (144)

While Lipset based his conclusions on faculty surveys from the 1950s through the early 1980s, the propensity for academics to affiliate with the political left appears to extend beyond this time frame. According to the 1999 NAASS, the majority of faculty, 50 percent, report that they identify with the Democratic Party. A sizable group, 34 percent, identify as independents, while only 12 percent affiliate with the Republican Party. The University of Michigan's National Election Study reveals that the nation's politics are far more balanced, with 31 percent of the general public identifying with the Democratic Party and 29 percent identifying with the Republican Party.[6]

The NAASS also reveals that faculty members tend to take liberal positions on a range of policy issues, especially when compared to the rest of the population. This is true of all the social policy issues listed in table 4.1. For example, on the issue of abortion, professors are remarkably united, with 84 percent of those surveyed reporting that it is a woman's right to decide whether to have an abortion. According to the 2000 National Election Study, less than 40 percent of the general public supports a women's unconditional right to an abortion. Similarly, a 1998 General Social Survey (GSS) poll demonstrates that the issue of homosexuality divides the nation, with 58 percent of respondents signifying that the practice is "always wrong" and just under 30 percent indicating that it is "not wrong at all." By contrast, college professors are far more supportive of homosexual rights, with 67 percent of those surveyed reporting that homosexuality is as acceptable a lifestyle as heterosexuality.[7] Professors are also overwhelmingly supportive of cohabitation among unmarried couples, with 76 percent reporting that this is acceptable. Yet national survey results show that the rest of the population is less supportive of cohabitation, with only 44 percent of the public stating that it is alright for an unmarried couple to live together with no intention of marrying.[8]

Although attention to professorial politics tends to intensify during times of crisis, when the views of the academy most openly clash with public opinion, the results of the NAASS reveal that professors hold liberal views on a wide range of issues. Since professors are not normally compelled to form a faculty group on behalf of cohabitation or government regulation of business, the public is less aware of these divisions.

The fact that college professors tend to hold liberal policy positions and favor the Democratic Party is only part of the story. College professors are also not typical members of their own party. Strikingly, the NAASS shows that a majority of Republican professors "agreed" or "strongly agreed" with the assertion that "it is a woman's right to decide whether or not to have an abortion." By contrast, according to the 2000 National Election Study, only 26 percent of Republicans in the general population believe that "by law a woman should always be able to obtain an abortion as a matter of personal choice." Among Republican college professors, 45 percent indicated that they "agree" or "strongly agree" that "it is alright for a couple to live together without intending to get married." Among the general public, only 32 percent of Republicans "agree" or "strongly agree" with the same assertion.[9] In terms of their acceptance of homosexuality, 25 percent of Republican professors agree that "homosexuality is as acceptable a lifestyle as heterosexuality," while only 17 percent of Republican respondents in the general population believe that homosexuality is "not at all wrong." The differences are not just confined to social politics. Among Republican faculty, 39 percent agree that

Table 4.1. Political Views of the Faculty

	Party Identification				
	Democrat	*Independent*	*Republican*	*Don't Know/Other*	*Total*
Percent of faculty who "strongly agree" or "somewhat agree" with the following statement					
Social					
It is a woman's right to decide whether or not to have an abortion.	95%	80%	51%	78%	84% ***
It is alright for a couple to live together without intending to get married.	85%	72%	45%	77%	76% ***
Homosexuality is as acceptable a lifestyle as heterosexuality.	81%	60%	25%	67%	67% ***
Economic					
More environmental protection is needed, even if it raises prices or costs jobs.	96%	87%	63%	82%	89% ***
The government should work to reduce the income gap between rich and poor.	83%	66%	39%	72%	72% ***
The government should work to ensure that everyone has a job.	78%	56%	37%	70%	66% ***
The less government regulation of business the better.	19%	44%	80%	42%	35% ***
Competition is harmful. It brings out the worst in people.	19%	12%	7%	26%	16% ***
Race					
America is a racist society.	73%	58%	37%	70%	63% ***
No one should be given special preference in jobs or college admissions on the basis of their gender or race.	43%	64%	86%	61%	56% ***

Miscellaneous					
With hard work and perseverance, anyone can succeed in this country.	58%	74%	91%	51%	67% ***
Which do you think is more important: freedom or equality? (equality responses)	44%	24%	12%	38%	33% ***
How proud are you to be American? (proud responses)	84%	88%	94%	55%	85% ***
Party identification	50%	34%	11%	5%	100%
Approximate number of respondents (n)	822	548	179	79	1,627

Note: Statistical significance of a simple correlation between the respondents' views and their party identification excluding "don't know" and "other" (* $p < 0.05$, ** $p < 0.01$, *** $p < 0.001$).

"the government should work to reduce the income gap between rich and poor." According to the 1998 GSS, among the general population, only 20 percent of Republicans "agree" or "strongly agree" that "it is the responsibility of the government to reduce the differences in income between people with high incomes and those with low incomes."[10]

Like Republican professors, Democratic professors tend to hold far more liberal views than their counterparts outside of academia. Among self-identified Democrats in the professoriate, 95 percent "agree" or "strongly agree" that "it is a woman's right to decide whether or not to have an abortion." According to the 2000 National Election Study, only 48 percent of Democratic respondents believe that abortion should be made available without restrictions "as a matter of personal choice." Among professors, 85 percent of Democratic professors believe that it is alright for couples to live together without intending to get married. According to the 1998 GSS, only 46 percent of Democrats outside of academia agree. On the question of homosexuality, 81 percent of Democratic professors agree that "homosexuality is as acceptable a lifestyle as heterosexuality." According to the 1998 GSS, 34 percent of Democrats in the general population believe that homosexuality is "not at all wrong." When asked about the government's role in reducing the income gap, 83 percent of Democratic professors "agree" or "strongly agree" that the government should work to reduce the gap. Among Democratic respondents to the 1998 GSS, only 45 percent assign government this responsibility.

Researchers have noted that the political positions of elected officials are more extreme than those of the general public (Converse 1964; Jennings 1992). However, in these instances, the distinction is created largely by the public's failure to adhere to a strict ideological framework. In other words, the average person does not see a clear connection between issues like taxes, free trade, and same-sex marriage. They tend to hold a mix of policy positions that do not adhere to any clear ideological framework. As a consequence, Republican politicians tend to hold views that are consistently to the right of the average Republican, while Democratic politicians tend to hold views to the left of the average Democrat. In politics, elites simply hold extreme positions, compared to the party base. In academia, the ideological gap is unidirectional, with both Democrats and Republicans holding views that place them to the left of the average member of their own party. In this sense, recent concerns about the political imbalance within the academy may be understated. The small number of Republican faculty behave, on a number of issues, much like the average Democrat, while faculty Democrats are positioned at the left end of their party.

Our findings about the relative ideology of college professors are consistent with other studies on the politics of the academy. For example, Rothman and

Lichter (2009) find that self-identified moderates in academia tend toward the left in terms of their policy positions. Klein and Stern (2009) similarly argue that self-identification is a problematic measure of ideology in academia since it tends to be a relative concept. As such, policy positions in academia may be far more telling than either self-identified ideology or political party affiliation. While there is some evidence that professors are claiming more moderate political identifications in recent years (Gross and Simmons 2007), this appears to be a change in self-perception rather than a genuine change in political values. Even still, the evidence is that self-identified liberals continue to outnumber self-identified conservatives by a substantial margin.[11]

POLITICS OF THE ADMINISTRATION

College administrators are also academics, and we might expect their political views to be identical to those of the faculty. However, while most college administrators are former professors, the trend appears to be toward hiring external administrators with managerial experience in the corporate sector. According to the American Council on Education's report *The American College President*, 30 percent of college presidents in 2000 had never held a full-time faculty position. We demonstrated in the previous chapter that these individuals have different values and relationships with faculty. Even among administrators who move up through the faculty ranks, we might expect to see some difference in opinion with the faculty as a result of their unique goals and experiences.

If there is an ideological divide between professors and administrators, it is unclear how much this would actually influence the campus environment. On the one hand, professors have a great deal of autonomy in their classrooms and maintain the academic freedom to research and write without outside interference. On the other hand, administrative offices have grown in size over the past several decades and are becoming more influential in shaping the campus climate. As we demonstrate in chapter 3, faculty perceptions are that the administration exercises significant control over university policy.

Based on the results of the NAASS, we find little evidence that administrators serve to moderate the views of the faculty. In terms of party affiliation, our survey reveals no significant difference between faculty and administrators, with 50 percent of the administrators reporting a Democratic Party affiliation and 12 percent reporting a Republican Party affiliation (see table 4.2). On the social policy issues, administrators echo the views of the faculty, with similar majorities supporting homosexuality, cohabitation, and a woman's right to an abortion.

Table 4.2. Political Views of the Faculty, Students, and Administrators

	Survey Classification				
	Faculty	*Administrators*	*Students*	*Faculty–Administrator Gap*	*Faculty–Student Gap*
Party identification					
Democrat	50%	50%	32%	–1%	–19%
Independent	34%	36%	35%	3%	2%
Republican	11%	12%	26%	1%	15%
Don't know/other	5%	1%	7%	–3%	2%
Percent of respondents who "strongly agree" or "somewhat agree" with the following statement					
Social					
It is a woman's right to decide whether or not to have an abortion.	84%	86%	74%	2%	–11%***
It is alright for a couple to live together without intending to get married.	76%	74%	68%	–1%	–8%***
Homosexuality is as acceptable a lifestyle as heterosexuality.	67%	67%	55%	0%	–12%***
Economic					
More environmental protection is needed, even if it raises prices or costs jobs.	88%	89%	80%	1%	–9%***
The government should work to reduce the income gap between rich and poor.	72%	71%	75%	–1%	3%
The government should work to ensure that everyone has a job.	66%	63%	75%	–3% *	9%***
The less government regulation of business the better.	36%	41%	53%	5% ***	18%***

Competition is harmful. It brings out the worst in people.	16%	8%	21%	–7% ***	5% **
Race					
America is a racist society.	63%	58%	64%	–6% **	1%
No one should be given special preference in jobs or college admissions on the basis of their gender or race.	56%	47%	85%	–9% ***	30% ***
Miscellaneous					
With hard work and perseverance, anyone can succeed in this country.	67%	74%	85%	7% ***	19% ***
Which do you think is more important: freedom or equality? (equality responses)	33%	29%	36%	–4% *	2%
How proud are you to be American? (proud responses)	85%	94%	89%	9% ***	4% ***
Approximate number of respondents (n)	1,518	745	1,483		

Note: Statistical significance of a simple correlation between the respondents' views and their classification excluding "don't know" and "other" (faculty vs. administrator/faculty vs. student) (* $p < 0.05$, ** $p < 0.01$, *** $p < 0.001$).

On other issues, administrators show some modest differences from the faculty. Administrators are less supportive of government regulation of business and are half as likely as faculty to agree that competition is harmful. Perhaps because of their own career success, administrators are more likely to believe that anyone can succeed through hard work and perseverance. They are also slightly less likely than faculty to agree that America is a racist society, although the majority of them still believes this to be true. Yet, despite the fact that administrators perceive less racism and greater opportunity to succeed, they are also more likely than faculty to support preferential hiring and admissions policies for women and minorities.

STUDENTS' POLITICAL VALUES

A review of professorial and administrative politics may lead some to conclude that there is little difference of opinion on a college campus. While faculty and administrators appear to be of the same voice and largely support the Democratic Party and liberal policy positions, the same is not true of the student population. Students' party affiliations are far more in line with those of the general population, with 32 percent identifying with the Democrats and 26 percent identifying with the Republicans. Perhaps not surprisingly, students are far more likely to confess that they have no party preference or that they have a preference for a third party.

On social issues, students tend to be fairly liberal, perhaps in part because of their relative youth. The majority of students supports a woman's right to an abortion and believes it is acceptable for an unmarried couple to live together. Students are more divided on the issue of homosexuality, with only a slight majority agreeing that it is an equally acceptable lifestyle. On all three issues, students demonstrate greater ideological diversity than their professors, with smaller numbers taking a liberal position.

On several other issues, students take a more liberal stance than professors and administrators. For example, students are more likely to believe that the government should work to ensure that everyone has a job. They are also more likely to believe that competition is harmful, although the overwhelming majority still disagrees with this statement.

Students show great concern for the environment, yet are not as likely as professors and administrators to risk job loss or higher prices in order to protect the environment. Students are also more likely than their educators to believe that less government regulation of business is better. The greatest gap in opinion between students and their educators is on the issue of preferential treatment of minorities. Despite the fact that students are equally as likely as professors to say that America is a racist society, they are overwhelmingly opposed to affirmative action in jobs or college admissions; 85 percent of them agree that no one should receive preferential treatment because of race or gender. This resistance to preferential treatment may be due to their relative idealism, as they are overwhelmingly of the opinion that anyone can get ahead through hard work and perseverance. We explore these attitudes in more detail in chapter 5.

Some critics of the academy express concerns that students are being "indoctrinated" by liberal professors. In order for large numbers of students to be vulnerable to influence, they need to hold viewpoints that differ from their educators. On some issues, students tend to be fairly liberal themselves, which raises the question of whether professors' liberalism can have any real impact other than to reinforce students' prior beliefs. On some issues, such as the government's responsibility for providing jobs or reducing income inequalities, students are even more liberal than their professors, making it unlikely that college professors would have a great "liberalizing" effect in these areas. While it may be the case that a few conservative students are being pulled to the left on these issues, it would be more likely that a student would be pulled to the right. Yet on other policy issues, as well as on general political orientation, the average professor does appear to be well to the left of the average student. On the issue of homosexuality, for example, 45 percent of students believe it is not an acceptable lifestyle. These students find that the vast majority of their professors hold views that are in conflict with their own.

While there is less difference between students and faculty on other issues, this may be even more problematic for students who find themselves to be in the minority. For example, one-quarter of all students not only find that their views on abortion are in conflict with the views of their professors and administrators but also find that their beliefs place them at odds with two-thirds of their classmates. The same is true of the 20 percent of students who are skeptical of the need for more environmental protections. For these students, the college environment may appear to be stacked against them.

Given that students differ from faculty and administrators on a number of policy issues, one might ask whether college has a net effect on students' politics over the course of four years. The NAASS allows us to compare first-year college students to those who are further in their educational experience (see table 4.3). We observe some differences in attitudes between first-year students and those in their senior year. It is important to note that while some data sets allow researchers to observe changes in individual students at two distinct points in time (see Woessner and Kelly-Woessner 2009a, 2009b), the NAASS survey permits us to compare the views of first-year students only with their fourth-year counterparts. Accordingly, any observed differences

Table 4.3. Political Views of the Students by Year

	Year in School				
	First	*Second*	*Third*	*Fourth*	*Total*
Party identification					
Democrat	32%	29%	34%	31%	32%
Independent	35%	36%	33%	36%	35%
Republican	26%	26%	28%	26%	26%
Don't know/other	7%	8%	5%	7%	7%
Percent of students who "strongly agree" or "somewhat agree" with the following statement					
Social					
It is a woman's right to decide whether or not to have an abortion.	74%	68%	78%	73%	73%
It is alright for a couple to live together without intending to get married.	67%	70%	68%	68%	68%
Homosexuality is as acceptable a lifestyle as heterosexuality.	50%	55%	56%	57%	55%*
Economic					
More environmental protection is needed, even if it raises prices or costs jobs.	80%	82%	76%	81%	80%
The government should work to reduce the income gap between rich and poor.	81%	78%	71%	72%	75%**
The government should work to ensure that everyone has a job.	79%	77%	73%	73%	75%**
The less government regulation of business the better.	54%	52%	51%	54%	53%
Competition is harmful. It brings out the worst in people.	22%	24%	20%	19%	21%
Race					
America is a racist society.	62%	62%	67%	64%	64%
No one should be given special preference in jobs or college admissions on the basis of their gender or race	87%	87%	84%	84%	85%
Miscellaneous					
With hard work and perseverance, anyone can succeed in this country.	86%	86%	83%	86%	85%
Which do you think is more important: freedom or equality? (equality responses)	38%	38%	31%	36%	36%
How proud are you to be American? (proud responses)	90%	89%	88%	90%	89%
Approximate number of respondents (n)	399	313	357	538	1,607

Note: Statistical significance of a simple correlation between the respondents' views and their year in school (* $p < 0.05$, ** $p < 0.01$, *** $p < 0.001$).

are not necessarily the result of changes in opinion, as we cannot know for certain what the fourth-year respondents believe when they too were in their first year. Nonetheless, if concerns over the political indoctrination of undergraduates are correct, we would expect to see some evidence of systematic shifts in students' beliefs by cohort. When students from different cohorts hold roughly the same views, it is reasonable to infer that their beliefs are not meaningfully shaped by their institution.

On the issue of homosexuality, students appear to be more liberal in their senior year than in their first year, with a gain of seven percentage points in acceptance of homosexuality.[12] In this case, students appear to be moving toward their professors and administrators. It seems less likely that this change would be due to peer influence since peers are divided on the issue and could exert influence in either direction. While it is possible that the mere exposure students have to different groups of people makes them more accepting of others, it is worth noting that administrators and faculty play a role in forming a campus culture that fosters acceptance of alternative lifestyles. Most colleges and universities have an "Office of Diversity" or similarly named entity whose primary function is to promote diversity and acceptance of people of a different race, ethnicity, and sexual orientation. Compared to these issues, the other policy issues on our survey have little institutionalized support. With perhaps a rare exception, there is not a large, campuswide coordination of efforts to promote abortion rights, environmental protection, or cohabitation.[13]

On several issues, college seniors are slightly to the right of their first-year counterparts. College seniors are more conservative on issues dealing with redistribution of wealth, with a nine-percentage-point difference between first-year students and fourth-year students. College seniors are also less likely to believe that the government should work to ensure that everyone has a job. It is interesting to note that, on these issues, professors are more conservative than students. In other words, if students' views are becoming more conservative, they are, nonetheless, moving in the direction of the faculty.[14] However, it is unclear whether this is due to faculty influence or, rather, to educational gains in the area of economics. In one study of college students, Whaples (1995) found that students were more likely to believe that the free market is "fair" after taking a general economics course and that this change occurred in courses taught by both liberal and conservative professors.

Students' partisan loyalties are consistent across the cohorts. Since party affiliation often involves deep loyalties that are passed down from parents or acquired through other forms of socialization, we would not expect to see dramatic changes in these attachments over the course of a four-year period.

However, people's policy positions are more malleable, and it is reasonable to expect some attitudinal change on these issues as young people examine and refine their values. However, even in most of the policy areas, students' aggregate attitudes do not appear to vary much between their first and final years. This raises some question about charges that campuses politically indoctrinate students. However, as Sidanius, Levin, van Laar, and Sears (2008) note, the steadfastness of college students' attitudes over four years' time also raises serious questions about the effectiveness of campus programs aimed at changing racial attitudes, an issue we address in chapter 5.

DIVISIONS WITHIN THE PROFESSORIATE

Thus far in this chapter, we have treated the faculty as one general body. However, it is important to recognize that there are notable differences among professors based on discipline, sex, and other characteristics. These divisions within the professoriate are important, as students may be exposed to more or less diversity of opinion depending on their area of study and/or the professors with whom they have contact.

Disciplinary Differences

There is some debate about whether there are enough conservative Republicans in higher education to provide students with the variety of viewpoints required in a "free marketplace of ideas." While it may be possible for 11 percent of the faculty to adequately challenge the general consensus, not all professors are equally skilled, equipped, or willing to discuss the contentious issues of the day. In some disciplines, there may be relatively little discussion of political events. Thus, the distribution of political views within areas of study is an important component of the campus culture.

In the fields where political, social, and moral issues are most likely to be discussed, the social sciences and the humanities, faculty are the most politically imbalanced. In the humanities, 61 percent of faculty members identify with the Democratic Party compared to 5 percent with the Republican Party (see table 4.4). The social sciences exhibit a similar tilt, with 59 percent Democrats and 9 percent Republicans. The most political diversity occurs among faculty in fields we have marked as "other," which are composed largely of agriculture and physical education. The sciences and professional studies lie somewhere in between. It is important to note, however, that although the social sciences and humanities faculty have the distinction of being the most Democratic and the most liberal on policy issues, faculty in the

Table 4.4. Political Views of the Faculty by Field

	Field					
	Humanities	*Social Science*	*Science*	*Professional*	*Other*	*Total*
Party identification						
Democrat	61%	59%	46%	42%	25%	50%
Independent	29%	28%	36%	39%	46%	34%
Republican	5%	9%	14%	13%	22%	11%
Don't know/other	5%	4%	4%	5%	8%	5%
Percent of faculty who "strongly agree" or "somewhat agree" with the following statement						
Social						
It is a woman's right to decide whether or not to have an abortion.	89%	88%	80%	81%	72%	84%***
It is alright for a couple to live together without intending to get married.	80%	83%	68%	70%	65%	76%***
Homosexuality is as acceptable a lifestyle as heterosexuality.	73%	77%	60%	60%	52%	67%***
Economic						
More environmental protection is needed, even if it raises prices or costs jobs.	95%	91%	87%	84%	83%	88%***
The government should work to reduce the income gap between rich and poor.	80%	77%	68%	64%	66%	72%***
The government should work to ensure that everyone has a job.	75%	74%	55%	59%	60%	66%***
The less government regulation of business the better.	23%	26%	38%	50%	52%	36%***
Competition is harmful. It brings out the worst in people.	20%	17%	9%	16%	13%	16%***

(continued)

Table 4.4. Political Views of the Faculty by Field (continued)

	Field					
	Humanities	*Social Science*	*Science*	*Professional*	*Other*	*Total*
Race						
America is a racist society.	67%	69%	54%	61%	57%	63%***
No one should be given special preference in jobs or college admissions on the basis of their gender or race	52%	46%	67%	59%	70%	56%***
Miscellaneous						
With hard work and perseverance, anyone can succeed in this country.	55%	59%	74%	76%	76%	67%***
Which do you think is more important: freedom or equality? (equality responses)	43%	38%	23%	29%	29%	33%***
How proud are you to be American? (proud responses)	81%	84%	87%	87%	88%	85%***
Approximate number of respondents (n)	275	539	275	464	92	1,645

Note: Statistical significance of a one-way analysis of variance on the respondents' views factoring in their field of study (* $p < 0.05$, ** $p < 0.01$, *** $p < 0.001$).

professional studies and natural sciences are also slanted heavily toward the Democratic Party. Likewise, the majority of the faculty in the physical sciences and professional studies hold liberal views on abortion, homosexuality, cohabitation, and a number of economic issues. Even among the professional studies faculty, the majority agree that the government should work to reduce income inequality and provide employment.

It appears that, although certain disciplines are more liberal than others, the underrepresentation of Republicans is generally a widespread phenomenon. More important, the fact that Republicans are more concentrated in the fields that are least likely to be engaged in political discussions may have the effect of exaggerating the political imbalance in campus discourse. This may also contribute to the appearance that the campus is even more politically homogeneous than the facts indicate.

Sex and Politics

As one might expect, there are notable differences between men and women in the professoriate, with women holding policy positions and party loyalties to the left of their male colleagues. The sex-based differences in academia are especially interesting since they occur among individuals of similar educational obtainment, economic level, and employment status (see table 4.5). Despite these similarities, women identify with the Democrats by a margin of fourteen percentage points over men, exceeding the gender gap of nine percentage points found in the population at large.[15]

On specific policy issues, we see further evidence of division between the sexes. Women are more liberal than men on all the social issues. For example, women are more accepting of homosexuality by fifteen percentage points. Women are more supportive of a woman's right to an abortion and are more likely to support cohabitation. Women are also slightly more likely to call for increases in environmental protection. On issues regarding the role of government in economic affairs, which include regulating business, providing jobs, and reducing income inequalities, there is relatively little difference between men and women. As a whole, women appear to be more concerned with issues of equality, with 42 percent of women rating equality as more important than freedom, compared to 30 percent of men. Women are much more likely to agree that competition is harmful, although the overwhelming majority does not believe this to be true.

The most notable difference between men and women is on the issue of racism in America. Female members of the faculty are far more likely than men, with a gap of twenty percentage points, to agree that America is a racist society. Perhaps as a result, women are less likely than men to believe

Table 4.5. Political Views of the Faculty by Sex

	Sex		
	Male	*Female*	*Total*
Party identification			
Democrat	47%	61%	50%
Independent	36%	27%	34%
Republican	12%	7%	11%
Don't know/other	5%	5%	5%
Percent of faculty who "strongly agree" or "somewhat agree" with the following statement			
Social			
It is a woman's right to decide whether or not to have an abortion.	82%	90%	84%***
It is alright for a couple to live together without intending to get married.	74%	81%	76%**
Homosexuality is as acceptable a lifestyle as heterosexuality.	63%	78%	67%***
Economic			
More environmental protection is needed, even if it raises prices or costs jobs.	87%	93%	89%**
The government should work to reduce the income gap between rich and poor.	72%	71%	72%
The government should work to ensure that everyone has a job.	64%	70%	66%*
The less government regulation of business the better.	36%	36%	36%
Competition is harmful. It brings out the worst in people.	13%	23%	16%***
Race			
America is a racist society.	58%	78%	63%***
No one should be given special preference in jobs or college admissions on the basis of their gender or race.	58%	49%	55%**
Miscellaneous			
With hard work and perseverance, anyone can succeed in this country.	69%	59%	67%***
Which do you think is more important: freedom or equality? (equality responses)	30%	42%	33%***
How proud are you to be American? (proud responses)	86%	81%	85%**
Approximate number of respondents (n)	1,224	421	1,645

Note: Statistical significance of a simple correlation between the respondents' views and their sex (* $p < 0.05$, ** $p < 0.01$, *** $p < 0.001$).

that anyone can succeed through hard work and perseverance and are more likely to favor preferential admissions and employment policies for women and minorities.

These differences are important given the demographic changes that have occurred in the professoriate. When Ladd and Lipset's faculty survey was distributed in 1969, women occupied one position in six. At the time the NAASS was conducted, the ratio of women to men had grown to one in three (Schuster and Finkelstein 2006). This would suggest that, as women continue to join the academic ranks and advance into senior positions, the campus may become even more dominated by the political left.

GENERATIONAL DIFFERENCES AMONG FACULTY

The July 3, 2008, edition of the *New York Times* featured a front-page article titled "The '60s Begin to Fade as Liberal Professors Retire." The author, Patricia Cohen, reported that younger professors are more ideologically moderate than their baby-boomer counterparts. She concludes that the university will undergo significant change as the radical baby boomers begin to retire. The article relied heavily on data from sociologists Neil Gross and Solon Simmons (2007), who surveyed over 1,400 faculty members and asked them to self-rate their political ideology. The researchers concluded in their report, *The Social and Political Views of American Professors*, that younger faculty members are less likely than their senior colleagues to identify as "liberal" and more likely to identify themselves as "moderate."

The research findings are sound and raise some interesting questions about generational changes in the professoriate. However, it is unclear from the Gross and Simmons report whether the difference in ideological rating is a real difference in political opinion or merely a difference in self-perception. Ideological self-rating is a limited measure of political orientation because it is relative. Former president of Harvard Larry Summers has quipped that when he worked for the Clinton administration in Washington, he viewed himself to be on "the right half of the left" but that in academia he found himself to be "on the right half of the right" (Jaschik 2007). The baby boomers may be more likely to identify as radicals because their views were extreme at one time, when their political self-identities were being formed. Faculty members of the younger generation may hold the same views or be even more liberal, and yet they may perceive these to be moderate positions within the academic community. For these reasons, we chose to focus our analysis on people's party identification and policy positions, since placement on these items is not measured in comparison to others; one is objectively pro-choice no matter how many colleagues share this position.

In fact, Gross and Simmons report some evidence that would suggest that younger professors are objectively more liberal on some measures. Although younger professors report that they are less ideological, they take more liberal positions on social issues involving sex and gender, including acceptance of homosexuality and abortion. The authors also find that younger faculty members are more inclined to allow personal politics to influence their careers. More so than their senior colleagues, younger respondents agree that it is acceptable for a professor's political and religious beliefs to influence their choice of research topics.

Our own data analysis, based on the NAASS, demonstrates that, when measured in terms of policy preferences, younger professors do not appear to be more moderate (see table 4.6). For example, they are a bit more likely to identify with the Democratic Party. Although self-perception may be moderating as the baby boomers retire, the overrepresentation of Democrats in academia appears to increase with the newer generation. We also find that younger professors are more liberal on some policy issues. For example, they are more likely than their older colleagues to say that America is a racist society. Additionally, 61 percent of the "pre-baby-boomer" generation agreed that homosexuality is "as acceptable a lifestyle as heterosexuality," while three-quarters of the faculty classified as "late and post-baby-boomer" felt that homosexuality was morally on par with heterosexuality.

It is worth noting that there are other potentially important differences between our study and the Gross and Simmons study that warrant additional consideration. First, the Gross and Simmons study was conducted seven years after the NAASS study. If, within those seven years, the youngest cohort suddenly embraced more moderate positions on ideological controversies, the abrupt shift in issue positions would not be reflected in the NAASS study. Second, whereas the NAASS study was designed to examine the opinions of those at four-year institutions, Gross and Simmons elected to include faculty respondents from community colleges, arguing that it better reflects the values of academia as a whole. If the shift they report toward professorial moderation is driven largely by the unique contribution of professors from America's community colleges, the ideological realignment would not show up in the NAASS study. Nonetheless, the drift toward social liberalism, observed in the NAASS data set, would still be readily applicable to professors at America's four-year institutions.

From our perspective, the most likely explanation for the difference between our findings comes down to the difference between self-identified ideology and policy positions. Whereas Gross and Simmons find that younger

Table 4.6. Political Views of the Faculty by Generation

	Generation			
	Pre Baby Boomers	*Early Baby Boomers*	*Late and Post Baby Boomers*	*Total*
Party identification				
Democrat	49%	50%	53%	50%
Independent	36%	35%	29%	34%
Republican	11%	12%	10%	11%
Don't know/other	3%	4%	8%	5%
Percent of faculty who "strongly agree" or "somewhat agree" with the following statement				
Social				
It is a woman's right to decide whether or not to have an abortion.	86%	83%	83%	84%
It is alright for a couple to live together without intending to get married.	72%	77%	80%	76%***
Homosexuality is as acceptable a lifestyle as heterosexuality.	61%	68%	75%	67%***
Economic				
More environmental protection is needed, even if it raises prices or costs jobs.	86%	90%	90%	88%**
The government should work to reduce the income gap between rich and poor.	70%	71%	75%	72%
The government should work to ensure that everyone has a job.	65%	68%	65%	66%
The less government regulation of business the better.	35%	34%	39%	36%
Competition is harmful. It brings out the worst in people.	15%	15%	17%	16%
Race				
America is a racist society.	55%	67%	70%	63%***
No one should be given special preference in jobs or college admissions on the basis of their gender or race.	60%	50%	56%	56%*
Miscellaneous				
With hard work and perseverance, anyone can succeed in this country.	68%	64%	68%	67%
Which do you think is more important: freedom or equality? (equality responses)	32%	34%	35%	33%
How proud are you to be American? (proud responses)	91%	84%	78%	85%***
Approximate number of respondents (n)	627	542	470	1,639

Note: Statistical significance of a simple correlation between the respondents' views and their age in years (* $p < 0.05$, ** $p < 0.01$, *** $p < 0.001$).

academics perceive themselves to be more mainstream than their older counterparts, there is no evidence that the positions of college faculty are becoming more moderate. In the final analysis, a professor's actual views may be of greater societal consequence than his or her perception of personal ideology. From this standpoint, the considerable gap between the views of the public and those of the professoriate are still quite large, and, on the basis of the NAASS survey, we see no evidence that this chasm will narrow anytime in the foreseeable future.

POLITICS AND SCHOLARLY ACHIEVEMENT

The research on faculty politics leaves little doubt as to the political leanings of the professoriate. The overall consensus is that academics tend to be well to the left of the general population. This is true whether we measure their politics in terms of party affiliation, ideological self-rating, or policy positions. With that said, there is still some question as to why this is the case. David Horowitz and other critics contend that conservative thinkers are intentionally shut out of the academy by liberal academics. Others argue that there is some degree of self-selection involved.

In earlier studies of faculty political values, both Lazarsfeld and Thielens (1958) and Ladd and Lipset (1975) found a relationship between liberalism and academic achievement. Ladd and Lipset (1975) concluded that academia rewards original thought. Thus, a successful scholar is one who challenges the social and political structure:

> The intellectual community, of which faculty are a part, is inherently questioning, critical, and socially disruptive. . . . Intellectuals, as distinct from professionals, are concerned with creation of knowledge, art, or literature. In awarding status within the occupation, the emphasis is on creation, innovation, avant-gardism. Professionals are the users of knowledge. And many writers such as Thorstein Veblen, Joseph Schumpeter, and C. P. Snow have pointed out that inherent in the obligation to create, to innovate, has been the tendency to reject the status quo, to oppose the existing or the old as philistine. Intellectuals, as Tocqueville noted, are also more likely than those in other occupations to be partisans of the ideal, of the theoretical, and thus to criticize reality from this standpoint. (11)

Ladd and Lipset (1975) found that, when ranked by the quality of their respective schools, professors at the most prestigious universities not only identified more readily as liberals but also held left-leaning positions more often than colleagues at less prestigious institutions. For example, professors at elite institutions were more likely to favor bussing for school integration, prefer an immediate withdrawal of U.S. forces from Vietnam, and support "radical student activism" on college campuses.

Conducted more than twenty-five years after the Ladd and Lipset (1975) study, the NAASS provides an important opportunity to reexamine this link between liberalism and scholarship. Rather than compare the accomplishments of liberal and conservative scholars purely on the basis of their institution's reputation, we also examine the publishing record of the survey respondents. The results, while not entirely inconsistent with Ladd and Lipset's earlier findings, do provide a more nuanced understanding of the link between a scholar's worldview and the propensity to succeed in the academy.

Much like the analysis conducted by Ladd and Lipset in 1975, table 4.7 breaks down faculty views based on the prestige of the institution. We divided colleges and universities into three tiers, based on a synthesis of *US News & World Report*'s reputational rankings and the Carnegie classifications (see appendix 3). Our analysis reveals that the difference in partisan affiliations between those employed at the top institutions and those employed at bottom-tier schools is relatively modest. Among top-tiered schools, 52 percent of respondents reported that they were Democrats, as compared to 48 percent of the lowest-ranked schools. Indeed, the higher-ranking schools have only half as many faculty aligned with the Republican Party. However, given the scarcity of Republicans in academia overall, this represents only a seven-point difference.

On specific issue positions, liberalism and institutional prestige are more closely linked. Nevertheless, the ideological gap between those at the most prestigious institutions and those at lower-ranked institutions appears to be confined to social issues rather than economic issues. For example, we find a twenty-percentage-point gap in opinion between academics at high- and low-ranking schools on the issue of homosexuality. On economic issues, we find that the differences among tiers of institutions are small, with those at top institutions showing slightly more support for environmental regulations and a government role in correcting income inequality. Among America's most elite institutions, there is also greater faculty support for affirmative action programs.

Measures of scholarly productivity reveal similar patterns, with more productive scholars taking more liberal positions on social issues. Interestingly, we find that the most productive scholars in the professoriate actually tend to hold more conservative views on a range of nonsocial issues.

The partisan gap in scholarly productivity looks much the same as the divide based on institutional prestige. Just over half of all academics identify as Democrats, regardless of their publishing history. Whereas Republicans constitute 13 percent of the least prolific publishers, they constitute only 8 percent

Table 4.7. Political Views of the Faculty by University Rankings

	University Ranking			
	Bottom	*Middle*	*Top*	*Total*
Party identification				
Democrat	48%	51%	52%	50%
Independent	34%	33%	34%	34%
Republican	15%	12%	8%	11%
Don't know/other	4%	4%	6%	5%
Percent of faculty who "strongly agree" or "somewhat agree" with the following statement				
Social				
It is a woman's right to decide whether or not to have an abortion.	79%	85%	87%	84%***
It is alright for a couple to live together without intending to get married.	66%	75%	83%	76%***
Homosexuality is as acceptable a lifestyle as heterosexuality.	56%	67%	76%	67%***
Economic				
More environmental protection is needed, even if it raises prices or costs jobs.	88%	87%	90%	88%*
The government should work to reduce the income gap between rich and poor.	70%	70%	74%	72%*
The government should work to ensure that everyone has a job.	67%	63%	67%	66%
The less government regulation of business the better.	40%	40%	29%	36%
Competition is harmful. It brings out the worst in people.	17%	19%	12%	16%
Race				
America is a racist society.	64%	64%	63%	63%
No one should be given special preference in jobs or college admissions on the basis of their gender or race.	62%	56%	50%	56%***
Miscellaneous				
With hard work and perseverance, anyone can succeed in this country.	69%	68%	64%	67%
Which do you think is more important: freedom or equality? (equality responses)	33%	32%	35%	33%
How proud are you to be American? (proud responses)	91%	85%	80%	85%***
Approximate number of respondents *(n)*	486	525	635	1,645

Note: Statistical significance of a simple correlation between the respondents' views and their college ranking (* $p < 0.05$, ** $p < 0.01$, *** $p < 0.001$).

of the most prolific publishers.[16] The pattern holds when political views are measured by issue positions. On social issues, the most productive scholars tend to take more liberal positions than their less productive counterparts. As shown in figure 4.1, the link between social liberalism and publishing success is statistically significant but substantively modest. The most important variations appear to occur between those who report between zero and four publications and those who published four or more articles in the last five years.

On economic questions, we find only one statistically significant relationship between policy positions and publishing success. Yet, in this case, faculty with the highest rates of publication tend to take the more conservative position. Those who report the most scholarly productivity are substantially less likely to agree that "competition is harmful."

On racial issues, the relationship between professional achievement and political attitudes is mixed. We find that publishing success is unrelated to support for affirmative action. However, the most accomplished scholars are less likely to characterize America as a "racist society." Among the least published scholars, 18 percent "strongly agree" that America is a racist society, compared to only 10 percent for the most published professors. Part of this difference is a function of gender and race. According to the data, women and minorities tend to publish less prolifically than white males. Consequently, they constitute a disproportionately large segment of professors with the least publications. Since women and minorities are more likely to view America as a "racist society," much of this difference can be explained on the

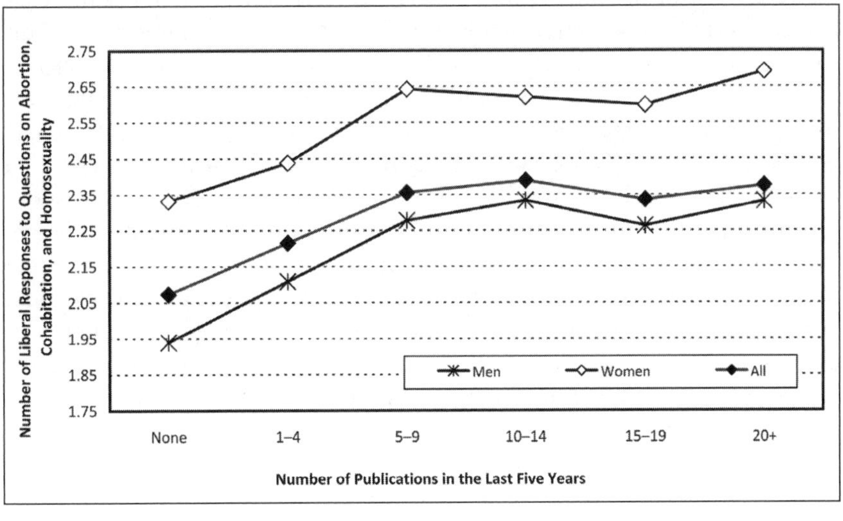

Figure 4.1. Publishing and Social Liberalism

basis of demographic differences between the groups. Yet, even controlling for race, sex, and sexual orientation, the least productive professors are still more likely to characterize America as a racist society.

The relationship between ideology and scholarship is complicated, with social issues and economic issues operating in competing directions. The complexity of these relationships was identified, to some degree, by the earlier work of Ladd and Lipset (1975). For example, Ladd and Lipset concluded that on the issue of affirmative action, professors were divided into a number of camps. While the researchers found that many liberals favored affirmative action, they also concluded that the most successful academics were more likely to oppose affirmative action, precisely because it violated norms of meritocracy. Our results from the NAASS echo this finding, with higher-publishing professors placing greater importance on meritocracy. For example, respondents are asked questions about the merits of hard work and the importance of equality. When asked to respond to the claim that "with hard work and perseverance, anyone can succeed in this country," the most published professors were slightly more likely to agree. When asked which value is more important, freedom or equality, those who had published the most were less likely to choose equality.

Taken together, tables 4.7 and 4.8 provide a more comprehensive view of the link between ideology and academic success. We find some support for Ladd and Lipset's claim that liberals are more productive scholars, but only when ideology is measured on social dimensions. On questions of competition, self-reliance, and equality, there are either no observable differences between high-achieving and low-achieving academics, or, by some estimates, the most productive scholars are actually more conservative. This finding does, however, reflect Ladd and Lipset's claims that productive scholars were liberal but that the highest-achieving academics also placed a priority on meritocracy. Hence, it would appear that high-achieving scholars are more apt to challenge the status quo on some social issues but do not exercise the same level of criticism for the competitive economic marketplace that rewards their efforts. One might conclude that successful academics, thus, have merely learned to adopt the norms of the profession in order to advance their own careers, embracing both liberal social policies and a commitment to meritocracy. Louis Menand (2010) argues that young academics are heavily socialized into the norms of the professoriate, through graduate school and their pretenure years, such that the academic profession is essentially "cloning" itself.

As we mentioned earlier, women are both more liberal and less likely to publish. As such, it is useful to examine the relationship between scholarship and ideology while accounting for differences in sex. Figure 4.1 demon-

Table 4.8. Political Views of the Faculty by Publishing

	Refereed Articles or Chapters in the Past Five Years			
	0–4	*5–14*	*>14*	*Total*
Party identification				
Democrat	51%	50%	51%	50%
Independent	31%	35%	37%	34%
Republican	13%	9%	8%	11%
Don't know/other	5%	5%	4%	5%
Percent of faculty who "strongly agree" or "somewhat agree" with the following statement				
Social				
It is a woman's right to decide whether or not to have an abortion.	81%	87%	86%	84%**
It is alright for a couple to live together without intending to get married.	72%	79%	78%	76%***
Homosexuality is as acceptable a lifestyle as heterosexuality.	63%	70%	72%	67%*
Economic				
More environmental protection is needed, even if it raises prices or costs jobs.	87%	89%	90%	88%
The government should work to reduce the income gap between rich and poor.	71%	73%	71%	72%
The government should work to ensure that everyone has a job.	65%	68%	66%	66%
The less government regulation of business the better.	37%	33%	35%	36%
Competition is harmful. It brings out the worst in people.	19%	17%	5%	16%***
Race				
America is a racist society.	66%	64%	55%	63%***
No one should be given special preference in jobs or college admissions on the basis of their gender or race.	58%	53%	55%	56%
Miscellaneous				
With hard work and perseverance, anyone can succeed in this country.	66%	64%	74%	67%**
Which do you think is more important: freedom or equality? (equality responses)	35%	35%	24%	33%**
How proud are you to be American? (proud responses)	88%	80%	86%	85%
Approximate number of respondents *(n)*	793	555	295	1643

Note: Statistical significance of a simple correlation between the respondents' views and number of refereed articles in press in the past five years (* $p < 0.05$, ** $p < 0.01$, *** $p < 0.001$).

strates that there is a similar relationship between social liberalism and publication success for both men and women. However, low-publishing women are still more liberal than high-publishing men. This supports our earlier claim that women will have a liberalizing effect on the academy, and it appears that this would happen across a range of institutions, regardless of their demands for scholarship.

If the relationship between scholarship and social liberalism were confined only to the social sciences, one could make a plausible argument that this provides some evidence for discrimination. In an ideologically charged discipline where political controversies are often an important component of scholarly research, conservatives might have a difficult time getting articles into refereed journals. However, looking to figure 4.2, the data suggest quite the opposite. While there is a modest statistical relationship between publishing and liberalism in every field (minus the category specified as "other"), the relationship is strongest among professors in the natural sciences. The most prolific publishers among professors of the natural sciences tend to hold the most liberal views on abortion, cohabitation, and homosexuality, issues that would, theoretically, have little to do with their publication records.

Ladd and Lipset did note that, while the creation of knowledge is something more suited for liberals, the transmission of existing knowledge suits

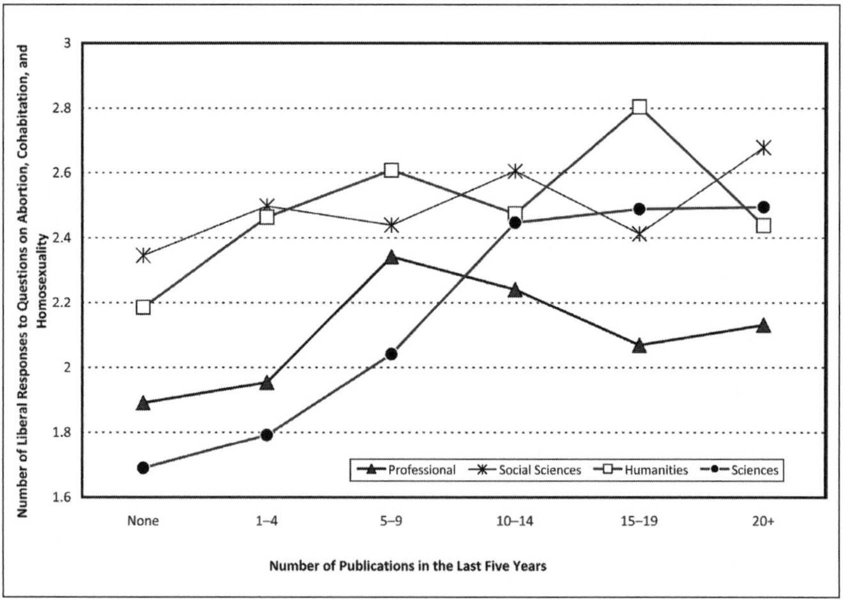

Figure 4.2. Publishing and Social Liberalism by Field

those with conservative ideologies. Thus, those on the political right may be more inclined toward teaching and, as a consequence, be less inclined toward scholarship. This commitment to teaching and transmitting knowledge could apply to those in the physical sciences as well. This may also help to explain why Republicans are found in greatest numbers at community colleges and in lowest numbers at top research institutions. Indeed, there is some relationship between political orientation and interest in teaching. Among Democratic professors who responded to the NAASS, 29 percent state that they would like to spend half their time or more on teaching, as opposed to research and administrative work. Among Republican professors, 44 percent would prefer to spend the majority of their time on teaching.

Woessner and Kelly-Woessner (2009b) provide additional evidence to support the argument that politics is related to interest in scholarship. For example, liberal college students are most likely to say that they desire to "create original works." This desire increases the likelihood that students will pursue a PhD. However, one should not confuse a *desire* to do academic work with the *ability* to do academic work. The authors further demonstrate that conservative college students earn similar grades compared to liberal students and have academic records that would allow them to pursue graduate education in equal numbers if they so chose. The relationship between faculty achievement and ideology is a bit more complicated.

Among our sample, liberals/Democrats tend to be employed at more prestigious institutions than their conservative/Republican counterparts. On an eight-point scale, where a value of 8 denotes a highly prestigious institution and a 1 denotes a minimally prestigious institution, Democratic professors averaged an institutional score of 5.3, while Republican professors averaged a 4.5. When measured in terms of the three-part social liberalism scale[17] (e.g., abortion, homosexuality, and cohabitation), those who provide liberal answers to all three questions were employed by institutions with an average prestige score of 5.5, while those who offered conservative responses averaged a 4.4.

The fact that left-leaning scholars tend to publish more often than their right-leaning counterparts suggests that some differences in their institutional placement might be perfectly logical. The question remains, to what extent does the difference in scholarly productivity account for the prestige gap? Replicating the basic statistical model first reported by Rothman, Lichter, and Nevitte (2005), we examined the extent to which a professor's social liberalism is related to the prestige of his or her academic appointment. The first model is designed to replicate the basic elements of the original Rothman et al. model, including controls for ideology, demographics, and scholarship. When Rothman and Lichter (2009) replicated the original model, they defined productivity as follows:

> To determine whether any political differences could be traced to different achievement levels by right- and left-leaning faculty, we constructed an academic achievement index from items measuring the number of refereed journal articles, chapters in academic books, books authored or co-authored, service on editorial boards of academic journals, attendance at international meetings of one's discipline, and proportion of time spent on research. (70–71)

Concerned that one element of the aforementioned achievement variables may itself be largely a product of a professor's institutional prestige,[18] we constructed a second model in which the "time devoted to research" is omitted from the equation. The results of both the original model and the revised model are reported in table 4.8.

According to our analysis, the most important predictors of a professor's institutional prestige are publishing success and time spent on research. This is precisely what one would expect to find, as universities naturally reward scholarly productivity. However, both model 1 and model 2 provide evidence that a number of other factors also predict a respondent's institutional prestige. All else being equal, noncitizens tend to have more prestigious posts than U.S. citizens. Men tend to have more prestigious appointments than women, and nonblacks tend to be at more prestigious schools than blacks.[19] Again, even controlling for publication achievement, social liberals tend to work at more prestigious institutions than do social conservatives.[20]

It is interesting that noncitizens enjoy a slightly higher institutional ranking than their American citizen counterparts. However, given the emphasis that higher education has placed on providing a "global" education, it is possible that universities perceive international scholars to provide a benefit that may offset their relative lack of publications. International professors may be useful in providing different perspectives, teaching courses in foreign cultures and languages and recruiting high-quality international students.

Accounting for variations in merit, it is more difficult to explain the difference in institutional prestige found on the basis of sex, race, and ideology. There are several possible explanations for the apparent discrepancy between merit and institutional prestige. Nonetheless, since the data cannot provide a definitive explanation of the prestige gap, each alternative is worthy of serious consideration.

First, it is possible that the apparent discrepancy in institutional prestige is the result of imperfections in the way the model measures merit. For example, a simple enumeration of refereed articles fails to capture the quality of those publications or their prominence in the academic literature. If, within any given discipline, women, blacks, and social conservatives are more apt to publish in specialized journals with a somewhat more narrow focus in the discipline, the model might overestimate their scholarly contribution. As such, their tendency to be employed at less prestigious institutions may be a result of their inability to publish in top journals.

Second, it is possible that women, blacks, and social conservatives select out of competitive placements because of a belief that academia discriminates against members of their group. While this is theoretically possible, we find little evidence to support this. As we demonstrate in chapter 5, the majority of conservatives do not believe that they are discriminated against on the basis of their political orientation. While many blacks do report that they believe they experience difficulty in the hiring process, whites actually report that they have the more difficult time. Similarly, women are actually less likely to believe they face hiring discrimination than men. Hence, we conclude that the lower placement of these three groups is probably not due to self-selection, based on the belief that they will be discriminated against in the hiring process.

Third, it is possible that the gap in institutional prestige is linked to conscious choices that women, blacks, and social conservatives make as they enter the job market. Women, blacks, and conservatives may simply place less importance on working at elite institutions. For blacks and women, these elite institutions may represent old systems of power and influence. Blacks and women may have more egalitarian perspectives that enable them to place greater value on less prestigious institutions. Likewise, conservatives may be more likely to value institutions that focus less on liberal education and offer more cost-effective career training. We do find some evidence that women and social conservatives prefer to spend a greater proportion of their time teaching when compared to males and social liberals. There is no statistically significant difference in teaching preferences based on race. Additionally, professors who are more concerned with balancing work and family may opt to teach at a less demanding institution. Indeed, other research concludes that, at least for women and conservatives, the desire to raise a family may influence career paths and workplace behavior (Drago et al. 2006; Mason and Goulden 2002; Woessner and Kelly-Woessner 2009b).

Among black faculty, the prestige gap could be a by-product of a conscious decision to teach at a historically black college or university. In her synthesis of the relevant literature, Johnson (2004) argues that, while the reasons black professors are drawn to historically black institutions are complex, many faculty have a special affinity for educating black students. Since historically black colleges are typically rated lower in terms of institutional prestige, such a decision would impact the group's rankings overall. In fact, if we remove historically black colleges and universities from our analysis, the relationship between race and institutional prestige vanishes.[21]

Taken together, if women, blacks, and social conservatives are even marginally less motivated to teach at prestigious institutions, it might well ex-

Table 4.9. Regression Predicting the Ranking of a Professor's Institution

	Independent Variables	*Model 1*	*Model 2*	*Model 2A: Minus Socio-Liberalism*	*Model 2B: Minus Merit*
	(Constant)	−9.416	−16.085	−18.336	−12.680
		(11.499)	(11.436)	(11.491)	(11.938)
Politics/ideology	Index of liberal responses to social-ideological questions	.267***	.293***		.391***
		(0.069)	(0.068)		(0.072)
	Index of liberal responses to economic-ideological questions	−.009	−.011	.029	−.043
		(0.049)	(0.048)	(0.048)	(0.052)
	Party identification	−.107	−.098	−.198*	−.137
		(0.095)	(0.094)	(0.091)	(0.100)
Demographics	Is respondent female?	−.395**	−.478***	−.412**	−.767***
		(0.132)	(0.130)	(0.129)	(0.137)
	Is respondent black?	−.530	−.614*	−.751**	−.686*
		(0.271)	(0.266)	(0.266)	(0.286)
	Is respondent Asian?	−.233	−.117	−.219	.142
		(0.279)	(0.272)	(0.273)	(0.291)
	Is respondent a U.S. citizen?	−.617*	−.669*	−.657*	−.948**
		(0.291)	(0.285)	(0.287)	(0.304)
	English native language	.044	.016	.039	−.145
		(0.182)	(0.182)	(0.183)	(0.194)
	Age	.007	.011	.013*	.010
		(0.006)	(0.006)	(0.006)	(0.006)
	Is respondent married?	.105	.111	.088	.391**
		(0.140)	(0.137)	(0.138)	(0.146)
	Is respondent a religious Christian?	−.229	−.214	−.483***	−.400**
		(0.147)	(0.145)	(0.132)	(0.155)
	Is respondent a homosexual?	.165	.295	.366	.196
		(0.278)	(0.276)	(0.278)	(0.296)

Scholarly productivity	Percent of time devoted to research	.284*** (0.039)			
	Articles, chapters published in past five years	.321*** (0.045)	.458*** (0.041)	.462*** (0.042)	
	Books published or in press	−.019 (0.051)	−.002 (0.049)	.002 (0.049)	
	Has respondent served on the editorial board of an academic journal?	−.229 (0.130)	−.218 (0.129)	−.234 (0.130)	
	Does respondent attend international meetings?	−.071 (0.059)	−.142* (0.058)	−.160** (0.058)	
	n	1,432	1,506	1,506	1,514
	Adjusted R^2	0.221	0.200	0.190	0.079

Note: Standard errors listed in parentheses were * $p < 0.05$, ** $p < 0.01$, *** $p < 0.001$.

plain the gap between their scholarly productivity and their placement, which we observe in table 4.9. It is important to reiterate that while the limited research suggests that blacks, women, and conservatives *may* have different priorities when seeking employment, the self-selection hypothesis is merely one alternative, and the results are not conclusive.

Finally, the prestige gap observed for women, blacks, and social conservatives may be the result of discriminatory practices. While measures of merit do account for the majority of difference in career placement, women, blacks, and conservatives end up at less prestigious institutions even after controlling for these factors. In the case of women and blacks, the academy often views this as a sign of a clear problem. Even if there is no evidence of blatant discrimination, the higher-education community argues that more effort is needed to recruit members of these groups into elite institutions. Yet the same claim could be made for social conservatives, who are also likely to end up at lower-ranked institutions than their publication records would warrant.

Perhaps ironically, minorities (particularly conservatives) considering entering the academy can take some solace in the results of table 4.9. In their totality, the models demonstrate that whatever bias *may* cloud the academic hiring process, it is truly small compared to objective measures of academic performance. To demonstrate the overriding importance of academic merit in securing a prestigious position, we constructed two additional variations on model 2, one that excludes the social-ideology variable (model 2A) followed and one that excludes various measures of merit (model 2B).

The key to understanding the relative importance of both merit and ideology can be found in the line indicating each model's R^2. To social scientists and statisticians, the R^2 (variance explained) value provides an important clue as to whether a group of independent variables (e.g., age, articles published, social-liberalism, and so on) can be used to accurately predict the value of a dependent variable (e.g., the professor's university prestige). An R^2 of 0.00 would reveal that the independent variables provide no useful information about the value of the dependent variable and thus explains 0 percent of the variation observed in the sample. If our statistical model had an R^2 close to 0, we would know that none of our predictors, like merit or ideology, were in any way related to the university prestige. On the opposite extreme, an R^2 of 1.00 means that the independent variables can perfectly predict the behavior of the dependent variable, explaining 100 percent of the differences observed in the sample. Because of the complexity of human behavior and the limitations on the data, in the social sciences, R^2s exceeding 0.40 (where the variable explains 40 percent of the variation observed in the sample) are exceedingly rare. Generally R^2 values ranging between 0.20 and 0.30 are considered strong models, explaining a fair portion of the otherwise mysterious variations in the observed behavior. By comparing the results of alternatively configured statistical models, it is possible to identify which variables have the greatest impact on the behavior in question.

Based on the changes in the explained variance (R^2), it is clear that success in publishing is the overriding factor in explaining a respondent's placement at a more prestigious institution. Model 2, with its complete battery of ideological, demographic, and scholarly predictors, explains 20 percent of the total variation in institutional prestige. By eliminating the social-ideological variable (model 2A), the explained variance drops to 19 percent. When we restore the social-ideological variable but eliminate the measures of professional merit,[22] the explained variance drops to just under 8 percent. By these estimates, merit constitutes a vast majority of the model's explained variance. If bias plays any systematic role in hiring and promotions, it would typically occur in borderline cases, where a person's professional accomplishments placed them at the edge of a job offer or promotion. In these instances, even a small, unconscious bias on the part of a faculty committee could make a critical difference. On balance, the results listed in table 4.9 suggest that for most professors, their position within academia is defined by their scholarship, not their beliefs, sex, or race.

Finally, as Rothman, Lichter, and Nevitte (2005) observed, the highest-publishing women, blacks, and social conservatives (with more than 14 publications each) hold placements that are equal in rank to the highest-publishing men, whites, and social liberals. Among moderate publishers (between five and fourteen publications), the prestige gap applies only to social ideology, with conservatives in this group being employed at less prestigious institutions. When the regression estimations used in model 2 are confined to professors with fewer than five articles/chapters published in the past five years ($n = 694$), we observe a statistically significant link between university prestige and race, sex, and social ideology. At the lower end of the publishing scale, women, blacks, and conservatives fair worse than their publication history, alone, would indicate.

To place the ideological gap in some perspective, we looked to the NAASS interviews to determine how often faculty believe that they had been treated unfairly on the basis of politics (we explore reports of unfair treatment against women and blacks in chapter 5). In the course of the NAASS interview, faculty, students, and administrators are asked, "Have you ever personally been treated unfairly because of [your] race, ethnicity, gender, sexual orientation, religious beliefs, or political views?" Those respondents who report problems are given up to three opportunities to characterize this unfair treatment with an open-ended response. Table 4.10 provides a summary of those responses, focusing specifically on respondents who believe that their mistreatment is re-

Table 4.10. Did Respondent Report Any Unfair Treatment Based on Politics?

	Faculty Party ID				*Administrators' Party ID*				*Students' Party ID*			
	Democrat	*Independent*	*Republican*	*Total*	*Democrat*	*Independent*	*Republican*	*Total*	*Democrat*	*Independent*	*Republican*	*Total*
No	98%	98%	98%	98%	98%	99%	99%	99%	99%	99%	98%	99%
Yes—NOT "ongoing"	1%	1%	1%	1%	1%	0%	1%	1%	0%	0%	1%	0%
Yes—some "ongoing"	1%	2%	1%	1%	1%	0%	0%	0%	1%	1%	1%	1%
Total	100%	100%	100%	100%	100%	100%	100%	100%	100%	100%	100%	100%
No	98%	98%	98%	98%	98%	99%	99%	99%	99%	99%	98%	99%
Yes—NOT "harassment"	1%	1%	2%	1%	1%	0%	1%	1%	1%	1%	2%	1%
Yes—some "harassment"	0%	1%	1%	1%	1%	0%	0%	0%	0%	0%	0%	0%
Total	100%	100%	100%	100%	100%	100%	100%	100%	100%	100%	100%	100%
n	822	548	179	1,549	399	293	99	791	495	555	415	1465

	Faculty Liberal Social Views				*Administrators' Liberal Social Views*				*Students' Liberal Social Views*			
	3	2	0–1	Total	3	2	0–1	Total	3	2	0–1	Total
No	98%	97%	99%	98%	98%	100%	98%	99%	99%	99%	99%	99%
Yes—NOT "ongoing"	0%	1%	1%	1%	1%	0%	1%	1%	0%	0%	0%	0%
Yes—some "ongoing"	1%	2%	0%	1%	0%	0%	1%	0%	1%	0%	0%	1%
Total	100%	100%	100%	100%	100%	100%	100%	100%	100%	100%	100%	100%
									0	0	0	0
No	98%	97%	99%	98%	99%	100%	98%	99%	99%	99%	99%	99%
Yes—NOT "harassment"	1%	3%	1%	1%	1%	0%	1%	1%	1%	1%	1%	1%
Yes—some "harassment"	1%	1%	0%	1%	0%	0%	1%	0%	0%	0%	0%	0%
Total	100%	100%	100%	100%	100%	100%	100%	100%	100%	100%	100%	100%
n	967	318	361	1,646	452	187	169	808	665	440	502	1607

lated to politics. Among faculty, just over 2 percent of respondents believe that they have been treated unfairly as a result of political beliefs. Overall, liberal/Democratic professors are as likely to cite politics as the root of their mistreatment as their conservative/Republican counterparts. Similarly, administrators and students report very few incidents of political mistreatment. While the statistical models in table 4.9 show that there may, in fact, be a prestige gap among social conservatives, based on the open-ended portion of the NAASS, it does not appear that conservative respondents would characterize it as overt or serious ideological discrimination.

Further evidence that conservative/Republican faculty are not necessarily the victims of widespread mistreatment can be found in a retrospective question posed to faculty that asks, "If you were to begin your career again, would you still want to be a college professor?" The results in table 4.11 show that, overall, 55 percent of Republicans and 58 percent of Democrats answer "definitely yes," with fewer than 5 percent of either group responding "definitely no." Overall, 58 percent of socially liberal faculty and 57 percent of social conservatives answer "definitely yes," with fewer than 5 percent of either group responding "definitely no." Similarly, examining levels of career satisfaction, we find no statistically significant difference by partisanship and social ideology.

It is important to note, however, that Republicans' satisfaction with their careers may not be due to their relative treatment within the academy. Rather, Pew Center surveys convey that Republicans are happier in general, with about 45 percent of Republicans reporting that they are "very happy," compared to 30 percent of Democrats. The difference in happiness is persistent and appears regardless of which party is in control of the government and even holds up after controlling for income (Taylor, Funk, and Craighill 2006). In fact, given that liberals are far more likely to perceive the campus environment as discriminatory, which we demonstrate in the following chapter, it is somewhat surprising that they are not less satisfied with their careers than Republicans.

CONCLUSION

During periods in our nation's history, political and social crises have served to unveil deep ideological divisions between the general public and the academic elite. We demonstrate that these divisions are present on a wide range of issues and exist in the absence of a national political crisis. The results of our analysis confirm some of what we already know, that college professors are located well to the left of the general public and that Democrats outnum-

Table 4.11. Measures of Faculty Career Satisfaction by Partisanship and Ideology

"If you were to begin your career again, would you still want to be a college professor?"

	Party Identification			
	Democrat	Independent	Republican	Total
Definitely yes	58%	58%	55%	58%
Probably yes	32%	31%	39%	33%
Probably no	6%	6%	5%	6%
Definitely no	3%	5%	2%	3%
Total	100%	100%	100%	100%
n	788	510	174	1,472
	Liberal Positions			
	3	2	0–1	Total
Definitely yes	58%	54%	57%	57%
Probably yes	33%	33%	33%	33%
Probably no	6%	8%	6%	6%
Definitely no	3%	5%	4%	3%
Total	100%	100%	100%	100%
n	921	306	338	1,565

"In general, how satisfied are you with your career?" (seven-point scale)

		Party Identification			
		Democrat	Independent	Republican	Total
Very satisfied	7	24%	26%	33%	26%
—	6	42%	41%	37%	41%
—	5	24%	22%	22%	23%
Less satisfied	<5	10%	10%	8%	10%
Total		100%	100%	100%	100%
n		819	546	180	1,545
		Liberal Positions			
		3	2	0–1	Total
Very satisfied	7	23%	25%	31%	23%
—	6	42%	38%	40%	42%
—	5	25%	26%	18%	25%
Less satisfied	<5	10%	10%	11%	10%
Total		100%	100%	100%	100%
n		963	318	361	1,642

ber Republicans in the professoriate by substantial margins. However, our analysis in this chapter also produces some new revelations about the politics of the academy. For example, we demonstrate that both Republican and Democratic professors hold policy positions that are to the left of their partisan brethren. This suggests that the political tilt among the professoriate may actually be more severe than mere party identification would indicate. Further analysis of professors' views on specific issues would serve to strengthen our understanding of academic politics.

In the first study to examine the political views of the administration, we demonstrate that administrators are quite similar to faculty, with equal proportions identifying with the Democratic Party. On most policy issues, administrators and professors hold similar positions. Yet there are some notable distinctions. Administrators are more supportive of affirmative action policies, despite the fact that they are less likely to believe that the country is racist and more likely to believe that people can succeed on their own. This combination of responses may appear peculiar if one views affirmative action as a means to provide opportunities for disadvantaged populations. However, if administrators assign value to diversity in and of itself, then their responses are completely consistent. Affirmative action may be used as a recruitment tool, much as scholarships are used to recruit other groups of students.

For the most part, professors and administrators are similar in terms of their politics. Students, however, show greater division, both in terms of party identification and on issues such as acceptance of homosexuality. However, on some issues, students are actually more liberal than their professors, raising some question about the ability of professors to "liberalize" their views. In comparing first-year students to fourth-year students, we find mixed evidence for the liberal indoctrination thesis. Students move very little in terms of party affiliation. We do find that students are more liberal on the issue of homosexuality after four years of college, but we also find that seniors tend to be more conservative than freshman on economic issues. The impact of college on students' social and political views tends to be fairly complicated. It is important to note that, when change does occur, students are still moving in the direction of their professors, as professors actually hold more conservative economic views than do students.

Our analysis of divisions within the professoriate both confirms and contradicts previous research. We find, much as others have noted, that women are more liberal than men on social issues. However, we find little gender difference on economic issues. We also find that professors in the social sciences and humanities are more liberal on a number of positions than are professors in other disciplines. Our analysis challenges recent claims that the academy is moderating. We find that younger faculty disproportionately identify with the Democratic Party and take political positions to the left of their senior colleagues. We conclude that self-perception may be moderating but that actual political positions will remain the same or move to the left as the baby boomers begin to retire.

We find some evidence that is consistent with Ladd and Lipset's finding that those on the political left are higher achievers than are those on the right. However, we find that this is true when liberalism is measured on a social dimension but not when it is measured on an economic dimension. When examined in terms of scholarly productivity, high achievers take a number of more conservative policy positions than faculty who publish infrequently. More important, the difference in publication rates between Democrats and Republicans appears to be partially explained by interest. Compared to Democrats, Republicans report that they would like to spend more time teaching and less time on scholarship and administrative work. Additionally, we find that the relationship between social liberalism and publication success holds for professors outside the social sciences and humanities. This raises some interesting questions about Ladd and Lipset's social criticism theory, as it is unclear how it would apply to chemistry, mathematics, and more technical fields.

Consistent with the findings of Rothman, Lichter, and Nevitte, we find evidence that controlling for a variety of other factors, social liberals (as well as whites and males) tend to work at more prestigious colleges and universities than their socially conservative counterparts. However, the politics of the professor are far less important than their publication record and their time spent conducting research. Combined with the survey results that show very few complaints of mistreatment related to politics and high job satisfaction rate among professors of all political persuasions, the prestige gap between liberal and conservative professors does not appear to be a function of widespread ideological discrimination. Nevertheless, when taken together, the dearth of conservatives in academia, combined with their unique underrepresentation at America's most prestigious colleges and universities, does raise interesting questions about the range of probable causes for the ideological imbalance.

Combined, these findings reveal a common theme: social liberalism and economic liberalism are distinct concepts and affect the university in different ways. Professors are to the left of students socially but not economically. Students appear to collectively move to the left on some social issues over four years, but they move to the right on economic issues. Faculty publication rates increase with social liberalism but do not increase with economic liberalism. These differences add to our concerns about the use of self-reported ideology in assessing faculty politics, as it is not clear which dimension most influences self-assessment and thus is likely to vary for each individual. Future studies of faculty politics should strive to capture these distinct dimensions.

The findings of the NAASS clearly illustrate that, while the views within the university are well to the left of the public at large, the political views of academics are complex. Far from espousing the leftist diatribes exemplified by radicals like Ward Churchill, academics represent a range of viewpoints that differ according to sex, age, field, and even success within the academy. Even as critics may have exaggerated the radicalism of the typical college professor, most of the data suggest that, far from moderating or becoming more ideologically heterogeneous, the university may continue to drift leftward. The influx of women, combined with the gradual retirement of older, socially conservative faculty, will gradually transform the politics of the faculty. Given the enormous public resources used to finance higher education, there is no indication that vocal criticisms of academia's left-leaning tradition will abate anytime soon.

The findings of this chapter have important implications for the future of higher education. The division in values between the academy and the public it serves is likely to remain a source of contention. While academics may not simply indoctrinate students into their own political camps, the political values of academics undoubtedly shape their priorities and bleed into institutional decision making. For example, liberalism in academia leads to greater support for racial and ethnic diversity, affirmative action programs, and environmental protections than we find among the public. This translates into support for campus initiatives to promote environmental sustainability and social justice, which may direct time and financial resources to programs that the public deems unnecessary or even objectionable. On these issues and others, political differences create fundamental disagreements about the role of the university in society. In the next chapter, we see how differences in core political values translate into disagreement about affirmative action and other diversity initiatives, with a notable divide between professors and students. At the very least, the perception that the academy is a haven for political radicalism appears to diminish public trust and confidence in higher education.

Chapter Five

Campus Diversity

The issue of campus diversity presents an opportunity to explore how conflicts in values and priorities between academics and the public result in heated battles over higher-education policy. For the most part, the higher-education community enjoys a great deal of autonomy. Colleges and universities are self-governing institutions, free to design their own educational missions and to determine the means for achieving them. Because they view this autonomy as essential to their mission, higher-education associations and professional organizations usually resist intrusion by government agencies or other external entities. Recently, the academy has identified campus diversity as a central component of its educational mission. Yet the means by which universities achieve diversity have produced a great deal of legal controversy, forcing the state and federal courts to issue rulings on the legality of race-based admissions policies. As a direct result, the higher-education community has been called on to justify and defend the relationship between its educational mission and its admission policies. A substantial amount of time, energy, and resources has already been devoted to this task. Yet we demonstrate that the conflict has not been resolved and argue that academics will be forced to make some difficult choices both as they encounter external opposition to institutional practices and as they are forced to confront tensions in their own values and traditions.

The need to justify diversity initiatives in terms of their educational value is a relatively recent phenomenon and a direct result of Supreme Court rulings on race-based admissions. The courts have not only required that universities defend their admissions policies but also have redefined the criteria by which such policies are to be evaluated. Prior to the 1978 *Bakke* decision, colleges and universities implemented affirmative action programs with the goal of providing opportunities to members of certain disadvantaged groups.

The main objective was both a social and a political one, based on the idea that some people deserved opportunities that would not otherwise be available to them and that higher education should contribute to positive social change. In this regard, increased representation of minorities was a goal in and of itself. Yet in the *Bakke* decision, Justice Powell outlined a new imperative for higher education. Russel Nieli (2004) explains,

> Only because of Lewis Powell's subsequent declaration that compensatory justice and "social needs" arguments are insufficiently important to override the Fourteenth Amendment's colorblind imperative—but that educational diversity and the educational benefits it allegedly brings about are concerns of sufficient constitutional seriousness to outweigh such an imperative—did the diversity-enhancement rationale assume its present dominance among supporters of race-based preferences in college and professional school admissions. Before Powell's decision, diversity-enhancement arguments were rare to nonexistent. (411)

The idea that diversity has educational value for all students now serves as the primary justification for race-based admissions policies.[1] Because of the recency of the argument, critics of the new diversity imperative contend that these educational benefits are merely a post hoc rationale for a system of racial preferences that is motivated by ideological agendas. However, the courts have not required that educational benefits be the only objective for race-based admission policies. Even if the educational benefits of diversity are an afterthought, they may still be real and sufficient to satisfy the Supreme Court's criteria. Nor has the educational community denied that "social justice" is at the heart of its diversity programs. Rather, the educational benefits of diversity are cited as one of many factors that shape higher education's commitment to diversity.

It is not difficult to find evidence of this commitment among institutions of higher education. Perhaps the most compelling example is the statement issued by thirty national education associations, including the Association of American Colleges and Universities, the American Association of University Professors, and the American Association for Higher Education, following the Supreme Court's ruling on the University of Michigan's admissions policies:

> In a nearly unprecedented expression of consensus, virtually the entire higher education community had urged the Court to recognize that racial diversity on campus is a compelling national interest. . . . Higher education has an important role to play in this unfinished work of racial inclusion and civic commitment, as the outpouring of national support for Michigan's policies attests. Success at expanding educational opportunity is the key to addressing the racial and economic inequities that are so harmful to our society. The civic benefits of campus

> diversity go far beyond admissions decisions, important as these are. Great gains come when students from different backgrounds achieve together the interracial understanding and mutual respect that are indispensable in a diverse democracy. We now know, from experience and from a growing body of research, that engaging diversity on campus deepens students' individual learning and reaps rich dividends—in both knowledge and values—for democracy. (Diversity and Democracy: The Unfinished Work, http://www.aacu.org/about/statements/diversity_democracy.cfm)

The statement is worthy of discussion for a number of reasons. First, it demonstrates the higher-education community's commitment to promoting social and political change. While some argue that this is a natural role for such a powerful American institution, this admission will undoubtedly give pause to those who are concerned about the predominance of liberals among college faculty and administrators. While defenders of the academy have argued that the political orientations of professors are irrelevant to what it is they do in the classroom, political values undeniably influence people's views on social change and the mechanisms for achieving it.

Second, the statement ties the goals of achieving racial equality and expanding opportunities to the far more controversial policy of giving preferences to minorities in college admission decisions, a policy that fails to garner widespread public support. In this way, the statement may demonstrate a growing divide between those within the academy and those on the outside. However, as we demonstrate in this chapter, opinion within the academy is more divided than the previous statement would seem to suggest, at least on matters related to preferential admissions and hiring policies. While students are the most likely to challenge race-based admissions policies, there are a fair number of professors and administrators who also disagree with preferential treatment for minorities.

Finally, the statement implies that the academy is united in its conclusion about the relationship between structural diversity and student learning. "We now know, from experience and from a growing body of research, that engaging diversity on campus deepens students' individual learning and reaps rich dividends." But social science evidence is rarely conclusive, and there is no clear consensus to either accept or reject. Rather, people on both sides of the debate tend to be suspicious of evidence that challenges their position and are far too quick to accept faulty evidence that supports their position. It is against this politically charged backdrop that we endeavor to shed light on the debate, clarify the positions of the competing camps, and highlight the values and opinions of the academy's most important constituencies. In this chapter, more than others, we often depart from the North American Academic Study Survey (NAASS) data. We do this for several reasons. First, it is important to provide some background on the issue and to place the NAASS findings in context, comparing and contrasting them with other research. Second, we recognize that the opinions on diversity change over time and that the age of the NAASS data presents some limitations. Thus, when possible, we compare our findings to those from more recent studies in order to demonstrate that our basic conclusions remain unchanged, even if there has been some shift in opinion strength.

While this chapter centers primarily on the issue of racial and ethnic diversity, we also consider the environment for other groups on campus, including women, gays and lesbians, and religious minorities. The research shows that, with few exceptions, the academy has created a welcoming environment for various groups to live and work together, even if people continue to disagree on the means by which colleges achieve a diverse community.

THE CAMPUS CLIMATE FOR DIVERSITY

American colleges and universities are undergoing significant changes in the demographic composition of the student body, the faculty, and the administration. In a ten-year period, between 1995 and 2005, minority student enrollment on college campuses increased by 50 percent (Ryu 2008), with students of color now making up 29 percent of all college students. In the southern states, black student enrollment in colleges and universities is now equal to or greater than the proportion of blacks living in the region (Marks and Diaz 2007). For a quarter of a century, women have outnumbered men among college students nationwide, and the gender gap is widening, leading the *New York Times* to conclude that "women are leaving men in the dust" (Lewin 2006).

These changes present the academy with several challenges as it adapts to the educational needs of an increasingly diverse constituency. Most colleges and universities now devote some nontrivial amount of campus resources to creating an inclusive environment. Administrative offices often include an Office of Diversity, whose central mission is to facilitate positive relationships between the various racial and ethnic groups on campus. Frequently, a separate office is assigned to handle the specific needs of international students. Faculty members and administrators sit on a wide variety of committees and task forces designed to address sexual harassment and other forms of discrimination. Theoretically, one might expect to find that the campus environment is an extremely tolerant one.

Yet because higher education attempts to identify discriminatory practices, in an effort to eliminate them, it is quite possible that the campus environment produces a heightened awareness or perception of sexism, racism, and other forms of discrimination. There is some evidence that such a connection occurs. Alexander Astin (1993) reports that the greater a university's emphasis on diversity, as measured by policies to increase minority representation and emphasis on multiculturalism, the more likely students are to conclude that America is still a racist society. Some may see this change in perspective as a positive growth in students' awareness, while others may view this as a symptom of political indoctrination and oversensitivity to identity politics. Whichever interpretation one accepts, the point is that campus efforts to identify and address discrimination may actually contribute to the perception of a hostile environment, simply by sensitizing students to these claims. Thus, college students may perceive there to be a great deal of discrimination on campus despite obvious efforts to eliminate it.

Measuring the campus climate for diversity presents some challenges. On the one hand, members of the campus community may be naively unaware of the conflict between different groups. On the other hand, some individuals may be oversensitive to group conflict. Even if people are capable of correctly assessing their own attitudes toward others, they may be reluctant to share those feelings with researchers. Because of these difficulties, researchers do not often agree on appropriate measures of prejudice and group relations. As a result, different studies provide widely varying conclusions about the campus environment, depending on the measure used. In some research, estimates of group conflict are notably flawed.

For example, one study of racism at a southern university concludes that instances of race discrimination are fairly common in the classroom, affecting between 17 and 32 percent of students (Marcus et al. 2003). While it may be the case that this specific campus is particularly prone to racial conflict, we believe that these high estimates are an artifact of the measure used. The authors consider all conflict with anyone of a different race as an indication of racism, failing to recognize that conflict also occurs between members of the same race. For example, the researchers ask students to report whether "an instructor (of a race other than my own) has been unfair to me in grading an exam" or if "an instructor (of a race other than my own) belittled my intellectual ability in class." If the student agreed that either of these things had occurred, the researchers concluded that this was racial discrimination, merely because the unfair instructor happened to be of a different race. Needless to say, many white students may also believe that their white professors grade exams unfairly or belittle their intellectual ability. Without a measure of conflict between members of the same race to establish a baseline, it is difficult to assess the extent to which such unfair treatment is actually a consequence of race.

Other measures of racism are more sound but still generate some controversy. Theorizing that "old-fashioned" expressions of blatant racism have been driven underground by social mores, some researchers have devised methods designed to root out these subtle, complex, "symbolic" forms of racism. But this is a difficult thing to measure, and the very fact that it is hidden means that we must search for abstract signs of it. As a result, it is not always clear whether these measures truly capture racist sentiments. For example, some early measures of "symbolic racism" included opposition to affirmative action and other race-based government programs as a measure of racism (Kinder and Sears 1981; Sears and Citrin 1982), a technique that others criticized for confusing conservative values and preference for small government with racism (Sniderman and Piazza 1995; Sniderman and Tetlock 1986a, 1986b; Tetlock 1994).

Recently, the measure of symbolic racism has been more consistent but still somewhat controversial. Researchers now define it as the belief that blacks are no longer disadvantaged in our society and therefore no longer need special programs to get ahead (Sidanius, Levin, van Laar, and Sears 2008). For example, if one believes that government policies adequately address the needs of blacks or that blacks can "get ahead without special favors," one would rate high on the symbolic racism scale. By defining racism as a lack of awareness or recognition of discrimination, researchers are in danger of confusing racism with idealism and naïveté, traits common among young college students. While ignorance of others' situations may not be desirable, it is also not racism. Under this definition, we suspect that we would find alarming levels of racism among America's kindergarten classes. Additionally, the researchers conflate racism with assessments of the government's responsiveness to racial issues. Those who believe that the government is doing enough for blacks score higher on the symbolic racism scale than those who believe the government should do more. Hence, if government policy toward minorities actually changes, such that people's evaluations are more positive, then it would appear that symbolic racism has increased. We expect this to create a problem under the Obama administration. In fact, many blacks may now have a more favorable opinion of the government's attempts to address minority needs and would, hence, also score higher on the symbolic racism scale.

We mention these studies not to present a comprehensive review of the literature on racial prejudice and discrimination. Rather, we merely hope to highlight some of the difficulties involved in assessing attitudes on these sensitive topics. Our approach to measuring the campus climate is less novel but perhaps also less problematic. We do not claim to measure racism, sexism, or other forms of discrimination. We simply cannot tap into people's hidden or latent prejudices. Rather, we examine attitudes toward diversity by simply asking respondents to describe their perceptions, their experiences, and their values. In so doing, we learn a great deal about the different perceptions of the campus climate. While this may not be an objective measure of prejudice, perceptions are important and may impact student and faculty retention, group relations on campus, faculty job satisfaction, and other educational outcomes.

Using the NAASS, we find that survey respondents are generally positive about their campus environment. With that said, there are notable differences between groups of respondents and some disconnect between people's general values and their specific policy preferences. While some critics on the political right and left often portray the university as an ideological monolith, on the issue of diversity politics we find that the university is a surprisingly complex entity.

One of the most noticeable changes to the college campus in the past several decades is the increase in women among students, professors, and administrators. Despite these large gains, most of the educational associations still have sections devoted to improving the status of women on campus. This leaves some questions as to how the campus community views the environment for women. According to our survey results, the majority of students, professors, and administrators agree that sexual harassment is not a serious problem on their campus (see table 5.1). However, there are some notable differences between the groups. Among students, 62 percent believe that sexual harassment is not a problem at all, and another 20 percent believe that it is not a serious problem. Notably, we find very little difference between male and female students. Among professors and administrators, responses are generally less positive. However, the majority of both groups still report that sexual harassment is either not a problem or not a serious problem. Yet women professors and administrators are more likely to perceive a problem, with female faculty being twice as likely as men to maintain that harassment is a fairly serious or very serious issue. In fact, nearly 30 percent of women professors believe that sexual harassment is a problem. This perception alone may have implications for faculty retention and work relationships. More recent survey evidence suggests that this continues to be a concern for some faculty. According to a 2008 survey of faculty, 10 percent of female professors reported that they had been "sexually harassed" at their institution, while 39 percent reported that subtle forms of discrimination (racism, sexism, and so on) were a "source of stress" (DeAngelo et al. 2009).

People appear to have similar perceptions of the environment for other groups on campus. When asked about racial discrimination, students are again the most positive in their evaluation of the campus. What is most remarkable is that students' responses are fairly consistent across racial/ethnic groups (see table 5.2). For example, 60 percent of white students and 56 percent of black

Table 5.1. To What Extent Does Respondent Believe That Sexual Harassment Is a Problem on His or Her Campus?

	Faculty			*Administrators*			*Students*		
	Males	*Females*	*Total*	*Males*	*Females*	*Total*	*Males*	*Females*	*Total*
Not a problem	47%	37%	44%	38%	36%	38%	64%	61%	62%
Not a serious problem	36%	32%	35%	45%	40%	43%	19%	20%	20%
Fairly serious problem	14%	24%	17%	14%	21%	16%	13%	15%	14%
Very serious problem	1%	5%	2%	2%	1%	2%	3%	3%	3%
Don't know	2%	3%	2%	1%	2%	1%	1%	1%	1%
Total	100%	100%	100%	100%	100%	100%	100%	100%	100%
n	1,223	421	1,644	562	245	807	704	904	1,608

students report that racial discrimination is not a problem at all on campus. Of those who think there might be some problem, the largest group of respondents believes that it does not constitute a serious problem. Taken together, 82 percent of white students and 79 percent of black students believe that racial discrimination is not a serious problem on campus.[2] Faculty members and administrators are slightly less positive in their assessments of the environment for minorities on campus, yet the majority still believes that racism is not a serious problem. With that said, there are significant differences among professors based on race. Black professors are the most likely to perceive there to be a problem, with over 40 percent maintaining that racial discrimination is a fairly serious or very serious problem. While white professors report less of a problem, it is interesting to note that white professors are more likely to think racism a problem than are black students. This highlights the significant difference in perception between students and their educators.

These numbers are somewhat optimistic, however, in that they include professors at historically black colleges and universities (HBCUs). When these individuals are removed from the analysis, we find that perceptions of racial discrimination among blacks increase. For professors outside the HBCU system, a majority, 58 percent, of black professors reports that racial discrimination is a problem (combination of "fairly" and "very" serious; n = 43). Among black administrators at non-HBCUs, 45 percent report that discrimination is a problem (n = 29). Predictably, not one of the sixteen black administrators at HBCUs believes racial discrimination to be a problem on their own campuses. Among students, the results are also less positive when HBCUs are removed from the analysis, though the difference is not as dra-

Table 5.2. To What Extent Does Respondent Believe That Racial Discrimination Is a Problem on His or Her Campus?

	Faculty						*Administrators*						*Students*					
	White	*Black*	*Hisp.*	*Asian*	*Other*	*Total*	*White*	*Black*	*Hisp.*	*Asian*	*Other*	*Total*	*White*	*Black*	*Hisp.*	*Asian*	*Other*	*Total*
Not a problem	46%	30%	12%	49%	48%	45%	37%	24%	33%	33%	36%	36%	60%	56%	58%	58%	49%	59%
Not a serious problem	27%	26%	18%	29%	16%	27%	36%	44%	33%	50%	43%	36%	22%	23%	23%	24%	16%	22%
Fairly serious problem	22%	30%	65%	12%	24%	22%	23%	24%	33%	17%	21%	23%	14%	14%	15%	13%	19%	14%
Very serious problem	4%	11%	6%	4%	12%	4%	4%	4%	0%	0%	0%	4%	3%	7%	3%	4%	13%	4%
Don't know	1%	3%	0%	7%	0%	2%	1%	2%	0%	0%	0%	1%	0%	0%	0%	1%	1%	0%
Total	100%	100%	100%	100%	100%	100%	100%	100%	100%	100%	100%	100%	100%	100%	100%	100%	100%	100%
n	1,421	76	17	76	50	1,640	733	45	3	12	14	807	1,228	149	60	92	67	1,596

matic. Twenty-nine percent of black students at non-HBCUs report that discrimination is a "fairly" or "very" serious problem ($n = 105$). Thus, our conclusions about relative perceptions among these groups are true whether we include HBCUs in the analysis or not.

In general, people also perceive the climate for gays and lesbians on campus to be fairly positive. The majority of students, professors, and administrators believe that discrimination is either not a problem at all or not a serious problem. Predictably, perceptions of discrimination on the basis of sexual orientation vary tremendously by the sexual orientation of the respondent (see table 5.3). Among the faculty, 74 percent of heterosexual respondents agree that discrimination against homosexuals was either "not a problem" or "not a serious problem," as compared with 54 percent of gay and lesbian respondents. While the majority of self-identified gays and lesbians think discrimination is not a serious problem, this group is the most likely to report discrimination, more so than either women or any of the racial groups in our survey. While at first glance it looks as though homosexual administrators and students are less concerned about discrimination than faculty, we are cautious about drawing conclusions about these groups because of the small sample sizes. Recognizing the difficulty of conducting any survey where the respondents are asked to discuss something as personal as sexual orientation, the results seem to suggest that the vast majority of the campus community does not see discrimination against homosexuals as a serious problem, even though a somewhat larger proportion of homosexuals expresses some concern.

Our findings regarding the general perceptions of the faculty appear to hold up over time, with similar responses to more recent surveys. For example, 81 percent of faculty now report that "gay and lesbian faculty are treated fairly" on their campus, 86 percent believe that women are treated fairly, and 89 percent believe that "faculty of color" are treated fairly. Only 10 percent of the faculty perceive there to be "a lot of campus racial conflict" (DeAngelo et al. 2009).

Conscious that American campuses might be perceived as hostile toward religious groups, particularly those closely tied to conservative political causes, the NAASS also asked respondents to evaluate whether they considered discrimination against "religious groups" to be a problem on their campus (see table 5.4). Much like racial and sexual discrimination, virtually all students, faculty, and administrators perceive there to be little mistreatment of religious groups on campus, with just under 80 percent of all respondents indicating that it is "not a problem." Beyond the aggregate figures, it is noteworthy that perceptions of religious discrimination hardly vary as a function of either the respondent's religion or the importance that people attach to religion in their everyday life. At best, there is a five-point difference between

Table 5.3. To What Extent Does Respondent Believe Discrimination against Gays and Lesbians Is a Problem on His or Her Campus?

	Faculty			*Administrators*			*Students*		
	Heterosexual	*Homosexual*	*Total*	*Heterosexual*	*Homosexual*	*Total*	*Heterosexual*	*Homosexual*	*Total*
Not a problem	50%	26%	49%	46%	33%	46%	57%	39%	57%
Not a serious problem	24%	28%	25%	31%	33%	32%	19%	29%	20%
Fairly serious problem	18%	28%	18%	18%	33%	18%	17%	23%	18%
Very serious problem	5%	18%	5%	3%	0%	3%	5%	6%	5%
Don't know	3%	0%	3%	1%	0%	1%	1%	3%	1%
Total	100%	100%	100%	100%	100%	100%	100%	100%	100%
n	1,566	72	1,638	788	12	800	1,574	31	1,605

Table 5.4. To What Extent Does Respondent Believe That Discrimination against Religious Groups Is a Problem on His or Her Campus?

What is respondent's religious preference?

	Faculty					*Administrators*					*Students*				
	Protestant	*Catholic*	*Jewish*	*Other*	*Total*	*Protestant*	*Catholic*	*Jewish*	*Other*	*Total*	*Protestant*	*Catholic*	*Jewish*	*Other*	*Total*
Not a problem	78%	80%	83%	75%	79%	76%	83%	81%	80%	78%	78%	79%	83%	81%	79%
Not a serious problem	17%	13%	11%	17%	15%	20%	13%	13%	20%	18%	14%	14%	10%	13%	14%
Fairly serious problem	3%	6%	4%	5%	4%	3%	3%	3%	0%	3%	8%	7%	7%	5%	7%
Very serious problem	1%	0%	1%	0%	1%	0%	1%	3%	0%	0%	1%	0%	0%	1%	1%
Don't know	1%	2%	2%	3%	1%	0%	1%	0%	0%	0%	0%	0%	0%	1%	0%
Total	100%	100%	100%	100%	100%	100%	100%	100%	100%	100%	100%	100%	100%	100%	100%
n	910	342	138	253	1,643	514	191	62	41	808	761	448	41	357	1,607

How important is religion in respondent's life?

	Faculty				*Administrators*				*Students*			
	Very Important	*Somewhat Important*	*Not at All Important*	*Total*	*Very Important*	*Somewhat Important*	*Not at All Important*	*Total*	*Very Important*	*Somewhat Important*	*Not at All Important*	*Total*
Not a problem	78%	77%	81%	79%	77%	75%	85%	78%	79%	78%	80%	79%
Not a serious problem	16%	18%	12%	15%	19%	20%	13%	18%	13%	14%	14%	14%
Fairly serious problem	4%	3%	5%	4%	3%	4%	2%	3%	7%	8%	4%	7%
Very serious problem	1%	1%	0%	1%	0%	1%	0%	0%	1%	1%	0%	1%
Don't know	1%	2%	1%	1%	1%	0%	0%	0%	0%	0%	1%	0%
Total	100%	100%	100%	100%	100%	100%	100%	100%	100%	100%	100%	100%
n	544	568	526	1,638	296	328	179	803	783	523	299	1,605

Protestant, Catholic, and Jewish respondents, with similar disparities observed depending on the self-reported importance of religion. As with reports of sexual and racial discrimination, there is comparatively little variation among students based on either religion or religiosity.

One of the most notable features of perceived discrimination on campus is the surprisingly gloomy outlook of college administrators. Within the NAASS, one of the defining characteristics of an administrator is the tendency to see virtually everything related to the university in the best possible light. In regard to perceptions of campus discrimination, they consistently state that the problem is more serious than either students or professors believe it to be. This finding holds true for perceived offenses against women, minorities, and religious groups. By contrast, students are consistently most positive in their assessment of the campus climate.

There are several possible explanations for why students view discrimination as less serious than either faculty or administrators. One possibility is that students' favorable impressions of their campus are a result of campus programs designed to foster a tolerant environment. However, the evidence on the effect of these programs is mixed. While multicultural programs might prompt students to behave more appropriately toward other students, these diversity initiatives can actually sensitize people to claims of discrimination, thereby reducing misbehavior on the one hand and heightening perceptions of misbehavior on the other.

Another possible explanation for students' positive assessment of the campus climate centers on the distinct demographic makeup of the student population when compared to either faculty or administrators. For example, since women now make up more than half of college students, it would be difficult for students to imagine that there is gender discrimination in the enrollment process. However, among faculty and administrators, women are still largely underrepresented when compared to the general population, especially among the higher ranks. Since minority hiring and promotions tend to lag behind changes in admissions, students are surrounded by a more diverse group of peers than any other group within the university.

The differences in perspective between students and other campus constituencies may also be due to generational differences. For example, younger generations of women are less likely to exhibit the sort of "feminist consciousness" found among older women. While they are highly supportive of the goals of the women's movement, these "postfeminists" tend to believe that the war has already been won, and they are relatively satisfied with the status of women (Aronson 2003). Similarly, on race, traditional college-aged students have no living memory of separate washrooms, lynching, Martin Luther King Jr.'s assassination, or race riots. Left with only a historical perspective on what seems to be a distant civil rights struggle, young people may simply be less inclined to view the world through a racial lens.

Finally, administrators' relative pessimism regarding discrimination on campus may be due to the procedures for handling charges of discrimination and harassment. Colleges routinely handle such complaints at an administrative level and do so confidentially in order to protect both the accuser and the accused. As a result, administrators are simply more likely to be aware of complaints and incidents involving discriminatory behaviors. On the one hand, this may give them a more accurate portrayal of the campus climate. On the other hand, administrators may assume that the problem is bigger than it is, based on their involvement with a few problematic cases.

To understanding respondents' views of campus climate, it is also important to consider the role of ideology in shaping perceptions of discrimination. At least among professors and administrators, there are profound differences in the perceived seriousness of campus discrimination based on the respondent's partisan affiliation. This may provide some indication that views of discrimination on campus are shaped by assumptions about the distribution of power outside the university (see table 5.5). For example, nearly two-thirds of Republican professors characterize sexual harassment, racial discrimination, and discrimination against homosexuals as "not a problem," compared to about 40 percent of Democratic faculty. These divisions hold, although not as dramatically, for administrators, while among students the differences are practically nonexistent.

Recognizing that correlation is not the same as causation, the differences among the perceptions of the partisan camps might suggest that experience with discrimination shapes partisan affiliation. A person who has experienced sexual harassment may be more likely to side with the Democrats than with the Republicans. However, with the exception of religion, Democrats' perceptions of discrimination do not vary significantly based on their sex, race, or sexual preference. Whereas just over half of the Democratic respondents are female and thus more likely to be the victims of sexual harassment, very few of the faculty reported that they considered themselves members of the gay or lesbian community. Yet faculty respondents (the vast majority of whom were self-identified heterosexuals) showed similar concerns for both the treatment of women and homosexuals. Thus, it seems unlikely that a professor's partisan affiliation is being driven by personal experiences with discrimination. To the extent that there are differences in the perceptions of campus climate between Republican and Democrats, it would appear that ideology tends to shape perception rather than the other way around. In general, Democrats are more likely than Republicans to see their campus environment as discriminatory.

Table 5.5. Reports That Various Forms of Discrimination Are "Not a Problem" on Respondent's Campus by Partisan Identification

	Faculty				*Administrators*				*Students*			
	Democrat	*Ind.*	*Republican*	*Total*	*Democrat*	*Ind.*	*Republican*	*Total*	*Democrat*	*Ind.*	*Republican*	*Total*
Sexual harassment	38%	46%	64%	44%	33%	40%	47%	38%	63%	61%	64%	62%
Racial discrimination	39%	48%	67%	45%	30%	42%	40%	36%	55%	59%	62%	59%
Discrimination against homosexuals	41%	56%	64%	49%	41%	52%	45%	46%	58%	57%	53%	56%
Discrimination against religious groups	78%	78%	84%	79%	80%	78%	74%	78%	79%	81%	77%	79%
n ≈	821	547	179	1,547	400	292	99	791	495	555	414	1,464

PERSONAL EXPERIENCES WITH ONGOING DISCRIMINATION OR HARASSMENT

It is important to recognize that people may simply be unable to accurately estimate the occurrence of discrimination and harassment on campus. One or two high-profile instances may give the impression that discrimination occurs more frequently than it does. Likewise, if cases of discrimination or harassment go unreported or are kept confidential, the campus community may underestimate the extent of the problem. Accordingly, while both measures are still subjective, individuals' reports of their own experiences, *in the aggregate*, may be more telling than their estimates of the larger campus climate.

In order to measure individuals' personal experiences with discrimination, the NAASS asks respondents if they have ever "personally been treated unfairly because of your race, ethnicity, gender, sexual orientation, religious beliefs, or political views."[3] Using an open-ended question, those who respond in the affirmative are given three opportunities to describe incidents in which they have been treated unfairly. Furthermore, respondents are asked if the mistreatment is ongoing and whether the respondent considers the incident to constitute "harassment." It is from this mixture of open- and closed-ended questions that we derive concrete estimations of perceived mistreatment that may prove more telling than general, overarching estimations of the campus climate.

Reports of mistreatment vary quite considerably among students, faculty, and administrators, with most reporting that they have not personally been the victims of discrimination. Still, a sizable proportion of some groups report unfair treatment over the course of their academic career. Reports of mistreatment are least common among students, perhaps as a result of their relatively short careers within the university.

As shown in table 5.6, fewer than 10 percent of respondents report any unfair treatment on the basis of gender, but this tells only half the story. Looking at female respondents, nearly a quarter of faculty and administrators report some unfair treatment on the basis of gender, with almost a fifth of women reporting that the problems are ongoing. Of those who report unfair treatment, only 5 percent of professors and 2 percent of administrators consider the incident to constitute actual "harassment." While men have not historically been the target of sexual discrimination, some recent literature suggests that the educational environment has become more hostile toward men because of feminist agendas, which may promote women at the expense of men (Sommers 2000). Yet we find that men rarely state that they have suffered unfair treatment as a result of their gender.

Table 5.6. Did Respondent Report Any Unfair Treatment Based on Gender?

	Faculty			*Administrators*			*Students*		
	Males	*Females*	*Total*	*Males*	*Females*	*Total*	*Males*	*Females*	*Total*
No	98%	76%	92%	99%	73%	91%	98%	94%	96%
Yes—NOT "ongoing"	1%	5%	2%	1%	9%	3%	1%	3%	2%
Yes—some "ongoing"	2%	19%	6%	1%	19%	6%	1%	3%	2%
Total	100%	100%	100%	100%	100%	100%	100%	100%	100%
No	98%	76%	92%	98%	73%	91%	98%	94%	96%
Yes—NOT "harassment"	1%	19%	6%	1%	25%	9%	1%	5%	3%
Yes—some "harassment"	1%	5%	2%	0%	2%	1%	0%	1%	1%
Total	100%	100%	100%	100%	100%	100%	100%	100%	100%
n	1,224	421	1,645	561	246	807	703	904	1,607

Among students, very few respondents report unfair treatment on the basis of gender, with virtually none of the respondents characterizing the treatment as outright "harassment." This finding holds even among students who major in male-dominated fields, such as the natural and physical sciences. Unlike faculty and administrators, there is virtually no difference between male and female students as it pertains to experience with unfair treatment on the basis of sex.

On questions of race, we see many of the same patterns, with a vast majority of whites reporting no unfair treatment and a small but significant proportion of minorities expressing concerns that they attribute to their race (see table 5.7). Again, students are far less likely to report unfair treatment on the basis of race. As with gender discrimination, a fair proportion of the complaints are labeled as ongoing, while very few respondents characterize their mistreatment as outright harassment. Interestingly, minorities' perceptions largely mirror those of their white counterparts. It is impossible to say whether this reflects objectively positive conditions for minority students or merely a failure on the part of undergraduates to recognize when they are the target of racially motivated mistreatment. In any case, the results suggest that students have relatively high levels of satisfaction with their treatment, regardless of their racial or ethnic background.

Table 5.8 breaks down reports of unfair treatment on the basis of sexual orientation. Perhaps not surprisingly, virtually no heterosexual respondents identify their sexual orientation as the basis for unfair treatment.[4] However, among the relatively limited number of respondents who self-identified as homosexuals, a surprisingly small percentage report that they have been

Table 5.7. Did Respondent Report Any Unfair Treatment Based on Race/Ethnicity/Nationality?

	Faculty						*Administrators*						*Students*					
	White	*Black*	*Hisp.*	*Asian*	*Other*	*Total*	*White*	*Black*	*Hisp.*	*Asian*	*Other*	*Total*	*White*	*Black*	*Hisp.*	*Asian*	*Other*	*Total*
No	98%	78%	71%	68%	82%	95%	99%	65%	100%	91%	92%	97%	98%	90%	90%	88%	91%	96%
Yes—NOT "ongoing"	1%	9%	6%	12%	4%	2%	1%	15%	0%	0%	8%	2%	1%	5%	5%	3%	1%	2%
Yes—some "ongoing"	1%	13%	24%	20%	14%	3%	1%	20%	0%	9%	0%	2%	1%	5%	5%	9%	7%	2%
Total	100%	100%	100%	100%	100%	100%	100%	100%	100%	100%	100%	100%	100%	100%	100%	100%	100%	100%
No	98%	78%	71%	68%	84%	95%	99%	65%	100%	91%	92%	97%	98%	89%	90%	88%	91%	96%
Yes—NOT "harassment"	1%	20%	24%	31%	14%	4%	1%	33%	0%	9%	8%	3%	2%	5%	7%	10%	9%	3%
Yes—some "harassment"	1%	3%	6%	1%	2%	1%	0%	2%	0%	0%	0%	0%	0%	6%	3%	2%	0%	1%
Total	100%	100%	100%	100%	100%	100%	100%	100%	100%	100%	100%	100%	100%	100%	100%	100%	100%	100%
n	1,420	76	17	76	51	1,640	733	46	3	11	13	806	1,227	149	60	93	68	1,597

treated unfairly as a result of their sexual orientation. Again, the sample size of self-identified homosexuals is predictably small. The fact that personal reports of unfair treatment among homosexuals are uncommon provides additional evidence that, for gays and lesbians, the academy is a relatively safe environment. Yet, when asked about discrimination on campus as a whole, a large number of homosexuals perceived there to be a serious problem. It appears that this perception is not rooted in personal experience with unfair treatment. This may be due to the fact that gay and lesbian students are not open about their sexual identity, thus making it unlikely that they would personally suffer from discriminatory behavior, even in a hostile environment.

The results presented in table 5.9 appear to contradict some claims about the environment for religious groups on campus. To an even larger extent than gender, race, and sexual orientation, personal reports of unfair treatment on the basis of religion are considerably rare among professors, administrators, and students. In each group, no more than 1 percent of respondents reported mistreatment due to religious beliefs. The propensity for unfair treatment does not meaningfully vary based on the respondent's religious preferences. Axiomatically, very few respondents reported unfair treatment as ongoing or serious enough to be called harassment.

Overall, the results of the survey reveal that the university is somewhat balkanized into factions who view discrimination in different terms. For the most part, the campus community does not consider discrimination to be a serious problem. Nevertheless, a fair number of professors and administrators, especially women and minorities, do perceive there to be serious problems with the campus climate. These differences in perception will undoubtedly contribute to disagreements about the use of campus resources to combat various forms of discrimination.

The NAASS also allows us to measure professors' views of discrimination in the hiring process. Respondents were asked to judge which group faces the toughest time getting hired for a faculty position at the average American university: minority females, white females, minority males, or white males (see table 5.10). The survey results show tremendous variance in the responses, depending on the respondent's own gender and race. Whites and nonwhites are sharply divided as to which group suffers the most disadvantage. While nearly half of white faculty identified white males as the most disadvantaged group, the majority of blacks and Hispanics identified minority males as the most disadvantaged. Nonwhite faculty appear to believe there are still effects from historical disadvantages created by race, while white faculty perceive the tables to have turned because of affirmative action programs and efforts to diversify the campus. Perhaps most strikingly, comparatively few faculty identify women as the most disadvantaged class, with re-

Table 5.8. Did Respondent Report Any Unfair Treatment Based on Sexual Orientation?

	Faculty			*Administrators*			*Students*		
	Heterosexual	*Homosexual*	*Total*	*Heterosexual*	*Homosexual*	*Total*	*Heterosexual*	*Homosexual*	*Total*
No	100%	89%	99%	100%	100%	100%	100%	87%	100%
Yes—NOT "ongoing"	0%	3%	0%	0%	0%	0%	0%	13%	0%
Yes—some "ongoing"	0%	8%	1%	0%	0%	0%	0%	0%	0%
Total	100%	100%	100%	100%	100%	100%	100%	100%	100%
No	100%	89%	99%	100%	100%	100%	100%	87%	100%
Yes—NOT "harassment"	0%	7%	1%	0%	0%	0%	0%	10%	0%
Yes—some "harassment"	0%	4%	0%	0%	0%	0%	0%	3%	0%
Total	100%	100%	100%	100%	100%	100%	100%	100%	100%
n	1,565	72	1,637	789	12	801	1,574	31	1,605

Table 5.9. Did Respondent Report Any Unfair Treatment Based on Religion?

	Faculty					*Administrators*					*Students*				
	Protestant	*Catholic*	*Jewish*	*Other*	*Total*	*Protestant*	*Catholic*	*Jewish*	*Other*	*Total*	*Protestant*	*Catholic*	*Jewish*	*Other*	*Total*
No	99%	99%	97%	100%	99%	100%	98%	97%	98%	99%	98%	99%	100%	99%	99%
Yes—NOT "ongoing"	1%	0%	3%	0%	1%	0%	1%	0%	0%	0%	1%	1%	0%	1%	1%
Yes—some "ongoing"	1%	1%	0%	0%	1%	0%	1%	3%	2%	1%	1%	0%	0%	0%	0%
Total	100%	100%	100%	100%	100%	100%	100%	100%	100%	100%	100%	100%	100%	100%	100%
No	99%	99%	97%	100%	99%	100%	98%	97%	98%	99%	98%	99%	100%	99%	99%
Yes—NOT "harassment"	1%	1%	3%	0%	1%	0%	1%	3%	2%	1%	2%	1%	0%	1%	1%
Yes—some "harassment"	0%	0%	0%	0%	0%	0%	1%	0%	0%	0%	0%	0%	0%	0%	0%
Total	100%	100%	100%	100%	100%	100%	100%	100%	100%	100%	100%	100%	100%	100%	100%
n	909	344	139	253	1,645	514	190	62	42	808	761	448	41	356	1,606

spondents identifying minority women as the most disadvantaged only 19 percent of the time and white women a mere 9 percent of the time. At least in the realm of hiring, men are, from the perspective of the faculty, the most disadvantaged group in the academy.

This division in perspective is important. First, it helps to demonstrate the difficulty involved in assessing disadvantage. While whites believe that efforts to diversify the campus have created a disadvantage for white job applicants, blacks and other minorities believe that they continue to be judged unfairly and are the least likely to find employment. In fact, according to the NAASS, 64 percent of black and Hispanic professors agree that "traditional standards of merit for jobs and school admissions are basically affirmative action for white males," compared to just 28 percent of their white counterparts. It is difficult, if not impossible, to sort out which group is correct since hiring decisions hinge on a multitude of factors, some of which are not clearly articulated. Unsuccessful applicants must draw their own conclusions about the basis of the decision. Second, the division helps to explain why affirmative action policies have become so divisive. Whites continue to challenge such policies, contending that racial preferences place them at a considerable disadvantage. Minorities see affirmative action policies as a means to correct a disadvantage. The higher-education community has attempted to bridge the gap between these two perspectives by demonstrating that affirmative action policies benefit whites by enriching the campus climate for everyone.

CAMPUS SUPPORT FOR DIVERSITY

Colleges and universities across the country have, for the most part, devoted a great deal of institutional resources to encouraging an environment that is accepting of people from diverse backgrounds and cultures. But colleges' commitments to diversity appear to go well beyond ridding the campus of discrimination and prejudice. Rather, most colleges and universities also devote some effort toward increasing the physical representation of minority groups on campus, both through their admissions policies and through hiring procedures.

Despite the proclamations from leaders in higher education about the importance of exposing students to those unlike themselves, the NAASS survey demonstrates that opinions on efforts to increase diversity are a bit more nuanced (see table 5.11). While there is general support for greater diversity, the methods by which greater diversity is obtained are more controversial. The vast majority of college students, 85 percent, agree with the statement that "no one should be given special preference in jobs or college admissions on

Table 5.10. Who Does Faculty Respondent Think Faces the Toughest Time Getting Hired for a Faculty Position at the Average American University?

	All Faculty by Race						*Males*			*Females*		
	White	*Black*	*Hispanic*	*Asian*	*Other*	*Total*	*White*	*Nonwhite*	*Total*	*White*	*Nonwhite*	*Total*
Minority females	18%	34%	24%	22%	15%	19%	15%	20%	16%	25%	37%	27%
White females	10%	0%	6%	6%	6%	9%	7%	4%	7%	18%	3%	16%
Minority males	13%	57%	53%	31%	27%	16%	13%	41%	17%	11%	42%	16%
White males	46%	5%	12%	18%	37%	42%	50%	19%	46%	33%	15%	31%
No difference	6%	3%	0%	6%	13%	6%	7%	8%	7%	4%	0%	3%
Don't know	8%	1%	6%	16%	2%	7%	7%	8%	7%	8%	3%	8%
Total	100%	100%	100%	100%	100%	100%	100%	100%	100%	100%	100%	100%
Females	28%	34%	29%	29%	21%	28%	23%	24%	23%	43%	40%	43%
Males	59%	62%	65%	49%	63%	59%	64%	59%	63%	44%	56%	46%
n	1,419	76	17	77	52	1,641	1,061	158	1,219	358	62	420

Note: Shading depicts modal response.

the basis of their gender or race." Professors are a bit more divided, with 56 percent agreeing with the statement that "no one should be given special preferences" and 44 percent generally opposing it. Our findings in this regard are consistent with a more recent study of faculty attitudes that also finds broad support among faculty for the general concept of diversity yet less enthusiasm for affirmative action as a means to achieve it (Flores and Rodriguez 2006). As we mentioned in the introduction to this chapter, we are sensitive to the fact that attitudes about campus diversity may have changed over the past decade, rendering the results from the NAASS inaccurate by today's standards. Yet we have reason to believe that these tensions are persistent, and we find evidence for them in the 2007–2008 Higher Education Research Institute (HERI) faculty survey. For example, the vast majority of faculty, nearly 94 percent, agree that "a racially/ethnically diverse student body enhances the educational experience of all students." Yet nearly a quarter believe that "promoting diversity leads to the admission of too many underprepared students," and the faculty is evenly divided on the importance of recruiting minority students, with 50 percent believing that recruitment of more minority students should be a high priority. Even fewer believe it is a high priority to increase the representation of minorities in the faculty and administration.[5] In fact, these questions may produce a more generous measure of faculty support for diversity initiatives than the NAASS since it does not ask respondents to agree to "preferences" or advantages but merely to the efforts to "recruit" a more diverse student body. Similarly, only about half of faculty respondents believe it is a high priority to "create a diverse multicultural campus environment." According to the HERI study, the issues that faculty are most likely to rate as a high priority are promoting the intellectual development of students, increasing prestige, and enhancing the institutions' image. Since prestige and rankings are related to selectivity and retention, commitments to diversity may come into conflict with these higher priorities, an issue we discuss further in the following pages.

The NAASS also reveals that administrators, who are most often associated with promoting and implementing affirmative action programs, are also divided on the question of affirmative action policies. Among administrators, 46 percent agree that "no one should be given special preferences," and 52 percent express opposition to the statement. Those who oppose racial preferences also report stronger opinions than those who favor them. Whereas 25 percent of administrators "strongly agree" that no one should get preferences in hiring and admission, only 10 percent "strongly disagree" with the statement.

It should come as no surprise that whites are the most likely to support the claim that no one should receive special treatment, but other groups are themselves divided. Among students, it appears that a majority of all racial groups

Table 5.11. Respondent's Assessment of "No One Should Be Given Special Preference in Jobs or College Admissions on the Basis of Their Gender or Race"

	Faculty						*Administrators*						*Students*					
	White	*Black*	*Hisp.*	*Asian*	*Other*	*Total*	*White*	*Black*	*Hisp.*	*Asian*	*Other*	*Total*	*White*	*Black*	*Hisp.*	*Asian*	*Other*	*Total*
Strongly agree	33%	18%	24%	66%	29%	34%	26%	9%	50%	36%	13%	25%	72%	46%	48%	55%	62%	67%
Moderately agree	23%	11%	18%	17%	22%	22%	21%	20%	25%	27%	13%	21%	17%	19%	21%	21%	20%	18%
Moderately disagree	33%	41%	47%	12%	31%	33%	42%	44%	25%	27%	40%	42%	7%	19%	23%	14%	13%	10%
Strongly disagree	10%	28%	12%	5%	18%	11%	9%	24%	0%	9%	27%	10%	3%	16%	8%	10%	4%	5%
Don't know	1%	3%	0%	0%	0%	1%	1%	2%	0%	0%	7%	1%	0%	0%	0%	0%	0%	0%
Total	100%	100%	100%	100%	100%	100%	100%	100%	100%	100%	100%	100%	100%	100%	100%	100%	100%	100%
n	1,420	76	17	76	51	1,640	733	45	4	11	15	808	1,228	150	61	92	69	1,600

is opposed to racial- and gender-related preferences. Similarly, among faculty and administrators, roughly a third of blacks and a majority of Asians believe that no one should receive special consideration. Because of the limited sample sizes, however, one should be cautious about generalizing our findings for minority groups of professors and administrators.

When faculty and administrators are asked to weigh trade-offs and consider the possibility that increasing diversity would require lower admission standards, both groups are again divided on the issue. Among NAASS survey respondents, 41 percent of professors and 44 percent of administrators agree that more minorities should be admitted to their institutions, even if it means relaxing normal academic standards of admission. For both groups, the majority of respondents are unwilling to relax admissions standards in order to achieve a more diverse student body. Students are less divided on the issue, with the clear majority (74 percent) indicating that they are opposed to efforts to increase campus diversity if those efforts involve lowering normal academic standards of admission.

As before, whites express the strongest opposition to lowering academic standards, while minorities are more divided. Black students are nearly evenly divided on lowering standards, while Asian students appear to be squarely opposed to reducing standards. Support among minority faculty is considerably stronger but by no means monolithic. Of all the groups listed in table 5.12, only one (black administrators) clearly supports lowering standards. Here too, the limited sample size makes it difficult to precisely estimate their level of support.

Students' negative opinions of race-based admissions policies may be attributed to several factors. First, compared to faculty and administrators, students tend to be more conservative in their political views, an issue we explore in great detail in chapter 4. Second, according to the NAASS, students are much less likely to see racial discrimination as a serious problem on their campus (see table 5.2). Hence, it is logical that they would see less need for campus policies designed to correct discriminatory practices. Perhaps most important, however, students may oppose admissions policies that give advantages to others, precisely because they recognize the competitive nature of college admissions and believe that advantages to others will create disadvantages for themselves. However, since the majority of black students also oppose lowering standards, it is difficult to attribute all opposition to racial preferences to fear of competition. Rather, black students may be concerned about negative stigmas associated with affirmative action programs. There is evidence that some minority students are aware of such stigmas and fear that their own academic performance will reinforce negative stereotypes of their racial or ethnic group (Sidanuis et al. 2008).

Table 5.12. Respondent's Assessment of "More [Minorities] Should Be Admitted Here Even If It Means Relaxing Normal Academic Standards of Admission"

	Faculty						*Administrators*						*Students*					
	White	*Black*	*Hisp.*	*Asian*	*Other*	*Total*	*White*	*Black*	*Hisp.*	*Asian*	*Other*	*Total*	*White*	*Black*	*Hisp.*	*Asian*	*Other*	*Total*
Strongly agree	9%	16%	12%	5%	18%	9%	7%	20%	0%	18%	0%	8%	5%	21%	20%	10%	9%	7%
Moderately agree	32%	32%	47%	31%	25%	32%	35%	42%	33%	27%	29%	36%	16%	23%	21%	24%	22%	18%
Moderately disagree	31%	20%	24%	34%	31%	31%	34%	22%	33%	18%	43%	33%	33%	28%	28%	29%	25%	32%
Strongly disagree	26%	24%	18%	29%	24%	26%	21%	16%	33%	36%	14%	21%	45%	27%	31%	36%	41%	42%
Don't know	2%	9%	0%	1%	2%	2%	2%	0%	0%	0%	14%	2%	1%	1%	0%	1%	3%	1%
Total	100%	100%	100%	100%	100%	100%	100%	100%	100%	100%	100%	100%	100%	100%	100%	100%	100%	100%
n	1,420	76	17	77	51	1,641	733	45	3	11	14	806	1,226	150	61	92	68	1,597

While support for relaxing admission standards is somewhat soft, faculty and administrators are still more supportive of the policy than students. However, when asked about relaxing academic requirements in professorial appointments, support among both faculty and administrators virtually collapses. Table 5.13 shows that, among respondents of both groups, approximately 80 percent disagree with relaxing academic standards in hiring, with nearly half reporting that they "strongly disagree." Three-quarters of students opposed relaxing standards for faculty hiring, roughly the same number who oppose relaxing standards for undergraduate admissions. Here, students show remarkable consistency. Again, this demonstrates that students' opposition to racial preferences is based on something other than their own fear of competition or reverse discrimination, since they are equally as likely to object to racial preferences in faculty hiring. The same cannot be said for professors and administrators. Faculty and administrators clearly believe that there is some underlying difference between relaxing standards for students and doing so for faculty. Among professors, there is surprisingly little difference between the races, with blacks expressing very similar reservations about relaxing standards as white or Asian professors. Not only does each of the groups disagree with relaxing standards for faculty hiring, but nearly half "strongly disagree." Among students, there may be some racial differences, with the limited sample of black students suggesting somewhat less opposition to differing standards for faculty appointments. Yet here too the majority of blacks tend to oppose relaxing standards in faculty appointments.[6]

Because our survey questions require respondents to consider the desirability of diversity when juxtaposed with special preferences and lower admission standards, the responses may underestimate levels of support for campus diversity initiatives. According to a follow-up question, the majority of professors, administrators, and students believe that it is possible to attract more members of minority groups without lowering academic standards. Table 5.14 shows what professors, administrators, and students believe are the results of giving special consideration to minorities in admissions and hiring. The top portion of the table shows perceptions of the impact of special admissions for students, while the bottom portion reveals perceptions of the impact of special hiring policies for faculty. The table clearly shows that professors, administrators, and students see virtually no difference between admissions and hiring. When comparing responses to both questions, the answers are virtually the same. Thus, we cannot attribute the greater support for student diversity initiatives, as compared to faculty diversity initiatives, to differences in concern for academic standards.

Table 5.13. Respondent's Assessment of "The Normal Academic Requirements Should Be Relaxed in Appointing [Minorities] to the Faculty Here"

	Faculty						*Administrators*						*Students*					
	White	*Black*	*Hisp.*	*Asian*	*Other*	*Total*	*White*	*Black*	*Hisp.*	*Asian*	*Other*	*Total*	*White*	*Black*	*Hisp.*	*Asian*	*Other*	*Total*
Strongly agree	2%	7%	12%	4%	2%	3%	1%	2%	0%	0%	0%	1%	5%	18%	10%	11%	14%	7%
Moderately agree	16%	17%	18%	16%	16%	16%	15%	15%	0%	45%	15%	16%	16%	24%	20%	28%	12%	17%
Moderately disagree	33%	23%	47%	34%	27%	32%	35%	30%	100%	27%	38%	35%	30%	27%	31%	28%	23%	29%
Strongly disagree	49%	48%	24%	46%	51%	48%	48%	49%	0%	27%	38%	48%	49%	29%	39%	34%	49%	46%
Don't know	1%	5%	0%	0%	4%	1%	0%	4%	0%	0%	8%	1%	0%	2%	0%	0%	1%	1%
Total	100%	100%	100%	100%	100%	100%	100%	100%	100%	100%	100%	100%	100%	100%	100%	100%	100%	100%
n	1,420	75	17	76	51	1,639	732	47	3	11	13	806	1,227	150	59	94	69	1,599

Table 5.14. Respondent's View of Special Admissions and Hiring Policies and Academic Standards

What impact, if any, do you think special admissions policies for minority *students* have on academic standards?

	Faculty						*Administrators*						*Students*					
	White	*Black*	*Hisp.*	*Asian*	*Other*	*Total*	*White*	*Black*	*Hisp.*	*Asian*	*Other*	*Total*	*White*	*Black*	*Hisp.*	*Asian*	*Other*	*Total*
Higher standards—much	0%	11%	6%	1%	0%	1%	0%	0%	0%	0%	0%	0%	2%	9%	2%	5%	6%	3%
Higher standards—a little	2%	5%	0%	7%	6%	2%	2%	2%	0%	0%	0%	2%	6%	12%	13%	17%	7%	7%
No real impact	56%	68%	71%	54%	63%	57%	66%	91%	33%	64%	77%	67%	53%	64%	55%	39%	54%	53%
Lower standards—a little	31%	9%	12%	24%	21%	29%	25%	6%	0%	36%	15%	24%	30%	12%	28%	29%	23%	28%
Lower standards—much lower	8%	4%	12%	9%	10%	8%	4%	0%	0%	0%	0%	3%	8%	2%	2%	7%	9%	7%
Don't know	3%	3%	0%	5%	0%	3%	3%	0%	67%	0%	8%	3%	2%	1%	0%	2%	1%	2%
Total	100%	100%	100%	100%	100%	100%	100%	100%	100%	100%	100%	100%	100%	100%	100%	100%	100%	100%

Higher standards—much	1%	11%	13%	4%	6%	2%	1%	7%	0%	0%	7%	1%	2%	9%	3%	10%	4%	4%
Higher standards—a little	4%	5%	6%	8%	0%	4%	3%	4%	0%	0%	0%	3%	8%	17%	15%	14%	18%	10%
No real impact	55%	75%	44%	61%	57%	56%	69%	80%	67%	73%	71%	70%	59%	60%	53%	47%	50%	58%
Lower standards—a little	29%	3%	13%	13%	25%	27%	21%	2%	0%	27%	7%	19%	23%	9%	22%	20%	16%	21%
Lower standards—much lower	8%	4%	19%	12%	8%	8%	4%	0%	0%	0%	0%	3%	7%	3%	7%	8%	9%	7%
Don't know	3%	3%	6%	3%	4%	3%	3%	7%	33%	0%	14%	3%	1%	1%	0%	2%	3%	1%
Total	100%	100%	100%	100%	100%	100%	100%	100%	100%	100%	100%	100%	100%	100%	100%	100%	100%	100%
n ≈	1,419	75	16	76	51	1,639	733	46	3	11	13	807	1,227	149	60	92	68	1,596

Interestingly, few respondents believe that special consideration for minority students will actually raise academic standards. While the majority believes that special admission programs have no effect on academic standards, a sizable group of respondents believes that these programs will lower academic standards. More than one-third of students believe that admissions policies that give preference to minorities actually lower academic standards.[7] Whites and students of Asian descent are the most likely to perceive this negative effect, while black students are the least likely. Similar patterns emerge among professors and administrators, with about one-third of respondents indicating that minority admission policies will lower academic standards. This appears to confirm our earlier claim that blacks and whites oppose preferential policies for different reasons. Whites are more likely to believe that such policies will actually lower standards. Blacks, possibly conscious of the stigma attached to race-based hiring and admissions policies, argue that such policies need not impact quality, either in faculty hiring or in student admissions.

Based on our findings, it appears that those within the academy believe they can have it all. While not willing to compromise academic standards to obtain political ends, the majority of professors, students, and administrators believe that their institution can enroll more minority students without compromising standards. There is some question, however, about the extent to which colleges can actually attract larger numbers of qualified minority students. While more and more minority students are attending college, the widespread desire to diversify the campus has produced tough competition for the most academically prepared. Among college-bound blacks, approximately one-quarter choose to attend HBCUs, which further limits the pool of applicants at other institutions. As such, many schools have a difficult time attracting minority students. The most prestigious names appear to fare the best. For example, Harvard University successfully enrolls 64 percent of the black students accepted to the institution. However, even highly ranked institutions like Carnegie Mellon struggle to compete. Although Carnegie Mellon admits 38 percent of black applicants, as compared to their 29 percent overall acceptance rate, fewer than 20 percent of admitted blacks choose to enroll, leaving the university on the low end of the diversity ratings (The State of Black . . . 2008).

Even universities that manage to close the deal are still faced with a limited applicant pool. For example, the University of Virginia accepts nearly 50 percent of black applicants and enrolls nearly 45 percent of those admitted. Yet this still produces a student body that comprises only 9 percent blacks. Liberal arts colleges face similar struggles. While the most successful boast student bodies of 10 percent black or more, others struggle to attract minority students, despite relatively high admittance rates. For example, Colby College enrolls 40 percent of black applicants, a rate 10 percentage points higher than its overall acceptance rate. Yet only 18 percent of admitted black students choose to attend Colby. In 2008, blacks comprised only 1.7 percent of Colby's first-year class. Even if we assume that blacks who apply to college have, in the aggregate, exactly the same grade-point averages (GPAs) and standardized test scores as whites, the fact that the admissions department must reach deeper into the black applicant pool to obtain significant numbers suggests that objective measures of standards, such as standardized test scores and high school grades, will have to be relaxed. While the usefulness of these objective measures may be up for some debate, they do factor into institutional rankings and prestige—issues that the faculty rate higher in priority than campus diversity. Similarly, if colleges were to consciously try to increase enrollment of males, veterans, or even persons who write with their left hand, the very act of issuing a greater proportion of acceptance letters to one subgroup of the population axiomatically requires a relaxation of other admissions criteria.

From a theoretical standpoint, colleges can try to meet admission targets for minorities by making a special effort to attract qualified candidates rather than reaching deeper into the existing admission pool. However, in the competitive world of college recruiting, one institution's gain is clearly another's loss. Since there are always limits on the number of highly qualified applicants in any demographic pool, if every college engages in special outreach in an effort to diversify the student body, admissions officers will be forced to either lower entrance requirements or increase the incentives for minorities to enroll. In either case, these approaches are not cost free. If a university intends to bid for the best-and-brightest minority applicants, the monetary costs can be burdensome.

Given that most institutions have identified enrollment diversity as an important goal, there is considerable competition for select groups of applicants, resulting in what some people have labeled a "bidding war" for top black candidates (Kreuzer 1993–1994). Because of the high level of competition for qualified minority applicants, as it currently stands, colleges and universities already relax admissions requirements in order to obtain a more diverse student body. There is substantial evidence that black and Latino students enter college with lower SAT scores, poorer high school grades, and fewer college preparatory courses than their white classmates. While these indicators may not be a definitive measure of potential success in college, there is no evidence that minority students overcome these differences once enrolled. In fact, researchers demonstrate that minority students often underperform when compared to white students with similar test scores and credentials (Bowen and Bok 2000; Sidanuis et al. 2008).

This is not to say that these differences in performance are inherent. The previously cited authors argue that the underperformance of minority students may be due to the college environment. Still, from an admissions perspective, it is difficult to argue that individuals with lower test scores, poorer high school grades, and less college preparatory work will outperform their peers. Far from an ideological critique of affirmative action, this is a dilemma that even the most vocal advocates of campus diversity often confront as they seek to admit larger numbers of minority applicants. According to an article in the *Journal of Blacks in Higher Education* (*JBHE*), a source that is clearly sympathetic to the needs of minorities, "major admissions advantages" would be required to admit blacks to the best universities:

> It is widely known that black students score far lower on the SAT standardized test than do white students. But data also shows that black high school students have significantly lower grade point averages and are less likely to take honors courses than are white high school students. In an academic environment where universities may be reluctant to give major admissions advantages to blacks, inferior performance in these three measures will keep many blacks from being admitted into the nation's highest-ranked colleges and universities.[8] (Black Students Come Up Short . . . 2003)

The *JBHE* article also notes that the gaps in objective achievement indicators are not small. On average, black college-bound students score two hundred points lower than white college-bound students on the SAT and are half as likely to have graduated with a grade average of A-minus or better or to have taken a calculus course. Since most colleges are not satisfied with their current minority enrollments and actively seek to attract more black and Latino students to campus, at some point they will have to further adjust admission requirements in order to realize any substantial gain in these enrollments. This market reality creates further tension between the goal of producing a diverse student body and the desire to attract better students to improve ranking and prestige. These tensions are unlikely to abate as long as minority students fall behind in achievement in secondary education and as long as national rankings systems continue to equate selectivity with quality.

The fact that such a large proportion of professors, administrators, and students support the notion of diversity while opposing special admissions and hiring policies is interesting in that it reveals an underlying tension in the values and priorities of the academy. Within the public opinion literature, it is common for researchers to find that people fail to consider tradeoffs between their preferences. For example, Americans appear to want both lower taxes and more government spending on social services (Sears and Citrin 1982; Welch 1985). Since the majority of students, professors, and administrators oppose lowering academic standards, especially in the appointment of new faculty, what will become of their simultaneous commitments to increasing diversity and maintaining standards? On the basis of the answers given in table 5.12, where respondents seemingly ranked academic standards above racial and gender preferences, one might conclude that support for diversity would weaken considerably if the debate centered not on the benefits of diversity but rather on the methods for achieving it. Yet most members of the campus community are usually not involved in the discussion of diversity at this level. Rather, students and professors often affirm the institution's commitment to diversity in broad terms by endorsing mission statements, educational philosophies, and other declarations of purpose. The campus community then assigns the task of implementing this objective to a small group of administrators and staff who view the institution's general commitment to diversity as a mandate to accomplish it by whatever means necessary. Perhaps it is as a result of this all-too-frequent pattern of specialization and delegation that the means of achieving tolerance and diversity are rarely debated within the academy. Attempts to debate the merits of specific diversity initiatives may even be viewed with suspicion among those who support the overall goals of the program. Accordingly, those who are opposed to specific measures for achieving diversity may, in fact, have the opportunity to discuss specifics but merely elect not to do so for fear that any opposition to popular diversity initiatives would jeopardize relationships with colleagues.

It is clear that most faculty members and administrators desire to both admit a diverse student body and maintain academic standards and selectivity. However, the challenge of pursuing both goals simultaneously is a difficult one. Most obvious solutions to the problem require intervention at the K–12 level that would reduce or eliminate the achievement gap between racial and ethnic groups before they entered the college admissions pool.

Impact of Diversity

Undoubtedly, efforts to increase diversity on campus have met some resistance. Admissions programs designed to benefit minorities have been challenged in the courts on the grounds that these special preferences are unfair to white applicants who are denied admission. For this reason, the main rationale offered by the higher-education community for race-based admissions policies has rested on the positive educational value that diversity has for the entire campus. In order to make this case, educational associations have produced a number of studies designed to empirically verify the benefits of exposing white students to those unlike themselves.

Because these studies are produced with the goal of defending higher-education practices, it is especially important to place them in their proper context and consider whether the conclusions are consistent with a larger body of research on group relations. There is, in fact, a great deal of debate about the educational benefits of campus diversity. However, while authors draw different conclusions from their data, we find that the data itself is rather consistent and that disagreement is due to the overgeneralization and misapplication of specific findings.

For example, a number of studies that claim to find positive benefits for diversity merely demonstrate that those within the academy *believe* diversity has positive benefits. The American Council on Education and the American Association of University Professors (2000) produced a series of three studies designed to answer the question of whether diversity makes a difference in college classrooms. All three studies, however, rely on subjective assessments from faculty members who are asked whether they believe that diversity enriches their classroom environment. While professors' assessments of their classroom environments are certainly important, we must also recognize the potential limitations of this approach to measuring the impact of diversity. In the course of the study, the researchers report that "there is substantial agreement among respondents that diversity is valued at their institutions" (13) and that "faculty believe diversity is important" (12). There is no question as to the truthfulness of either of these claims. However, the researchers ask faculty members to evaluate the impact of diversity on a number of more specific educational outcomes and conclude that these results "indicate that racial and ethnic diversity on campus provides educational benefits for all students—minority and white alike—that cannot be duplicated in a racially and ethnically homogeneous setting" (3). But the research does not demonstrate that diversity provides educational benefits. It merely demonstrates that professors *believe* that these benefits are produced. This is not surprising given the widespread commitment to the concept of "diversity" among those within the academy. We must ask whether academics' commitment to diversity is the cause of their positive evaluations or rather the effect of them.

Students also report that diversity contributes to their undergraduate experience (Bowen and Bok 2000). Using an experimental design, Meacham and colleagues (2003) demonstrate that students assign greater educational value to classrooms that have a higher percentage of minority students. This study is especially revealing since students are asked questions about hypothetical classroom situations rather than about their actual classroom experience. In other words, students are able to articulate the educational benefits of diversity without having real, direct experience of these effects. Again, this suggests that support for diversity is largely normative and not based on an objective assessment of personal experience.

Studies that focus on people's perceptions of diversity are not without value. From these, we can conclude that students and professors believe that diversity produces positive effects and that they welcome diversity in the classroom. However, researchers have often overstated these findings and confused opinion with factual evidence. Educational professionals may have a great deal of experience in the classroom, but that does not mean that they can objectively evaluate those experiences. Even highly educated individuals fall prey to the sort of motivated reasoning and biases that are well documented in the psychology literature. Bear in mind that 94 percent of professors also report that they are better than average at their jobs (Gilovich 1991).

Another body of research attempts to examine student experiences more directly. One of the most influential of these studies was produced by Patricia Gurin (1999) and offered as expert testimony in the University of Michigan cases. However, Gurin's findings have been subject to some dispute since that time. Among other things, Gurin's testimony tends to focus on students' experiences with multicultural education rather than their actual exposure to minorities. For example, she finds that students who enroll in ethnic studies courses, attend a racial awareness workshop, or socialize with those of another race have better foreign language skills and greater listening ability and score better on a number of other particular outcomes. Yet it is difficult to rule out the possibility that students who enroll in these courses are already predisposed to the general purpose of these workshops and programs. Thus, any changes observed at the end of these seminars may not apply to the student body as a whole.

Other studies provide further evidence for the effectiveness of diversity workshops and other campus experiences. Some researchers even control for precollege attitudes, helping to eliminate the concern that students who are tolerant of others self-select into these sorts of programs (Whitt et al. 2001). It is important to note that many of the observed effects are attitudinal rather than cognitive. For example, students who take ethnic studies courses are more likely to believe that they should take action to improve society and work for social justice (Laird 2005). More important, there is no indication that the demographic composition of the student body, the faculty, or the administration contributes to these effects.[9] Students at an all-white university may demonstrate the same attitudinal changes after completing similar multicultural courses or workshops.

Research on the impact of actual institutional diversity is rather limited. However, there is some evidence that increased minority enrollment leads to a number of positive social outcomes. For example, students at more racially diverse schools are more likely to have interracial friendships (Gurin 1999). To some extent, this is simply due to the fact that interracial friendships are more possible in heterogeneous environments. However, it is important to note that most of the studies on the impact of diversity search only for such positive effects. Yet, if we assume that interracial contact is always positive, then there would be little need for diversity programs and multicultural educational requirements. Leaders in higher education have argued that interracial contact is not inherently positive and that this is why valuable campus resources are devoted to promoting positive relationships. As diversity increases, there is indeed more opportunity for interracial friendship. However, there is also more opportunity for interracial conflict.

In a study of racial integration at the high school level, Goldsmith (2004) draws similar conclusions about integration increasing the likelihood that students will make friends from other racial and ethnic groups. However, the author notes that school integration also raises perceptions of conflict and that conflict increases more rapidly than friendliness:

> I find the net effect of heterogeneity on conflict to be 2.5 times stronger than its effect on friendliness. In other words, school integration does increase interracial friendliness, but it appears to produce much more interracial conflict. This finding must be interpreted cautiously, however. Because the dependent variables are ordinal and perceptual, it is not known exactly how many more friendships or conflicts are associated with changes in heterogeneity. At the very least, this study demonstrates the potential benefits of investigating both positive and negative outcomes simultaneously. (608)

Goldsmith's last point is important. Diversity creates opportunity for contact. If we search for only positive signs of that contact, we are likely to find them. However, there may very well be negative interracial exchanges occurring at the same time. If permitted to focus only on one side of the diversity equation, one could also look only to the drawbacks of integration and thus conclude that colleges should attempt to keep the races separate lest the contact foment unnecessary racial animosity. As with all political controversies, there are costs and benefits associated with every policy choice. A fair interpretation of the evidence points to both potential and risk.

A recent study by a prominent sociologist, Robert Putnam (2007), further suggests that interracial contact may have some unintended effects. In a study of community diversity, Putnam finds that diversity has a negative impact on social solidarity. Putnam concludes that many Americans are uncomfortable with diversity, a claim to which experts in multicultural education could probably attest. Yet Putnam also concludes that this discomfort causes residents of ethnically diverse communities to "hunker down" and withdraw from the community. Accordingly, they show lower levels of interpersonal trust, both for members of their own race and for others, have fewer friends, and are less inclined toward altruistic and cooperative behaviors.

Putnam's research is consistent with the results of the NAASS (see table 5.15). When campuses are broken down into thirds, depending on the percentage of the black student population, we find statistically significant differences with respondents who attend more diverse institutions being less likely to say that "most people can be trusted." The difference is most significant among students, where the difference among schools is nearly twenty percentage points. While some of this difference is a reflection of different demographics characteristics among institutions, the results are robust and consistent across students, professors, and administrators. Even when controlling for other institutional traits (per student expenditures, Carnegie classification, public or private funding) and respondent traits (age, sex, race, income), the systematic differences in trust remain (for the full regression models, see appendix 4). Again, while the relationship may not be causal, the results tend to reinforce the notion that campus diversity carries with it both costs and benefits.

Putnam's findings are somewhat consistent with the claims of those who promote diversity initiatives. Both would acknowledge that, in general, people prefer to interact largely with people who are similar to themselves. Indeed, one of the arguments for race-based admissions programs is that Americans do display some racial hostilities toward, or at least discomfort with, those unlike themselves. However, proponents of racial preferences often imply that exposure to diversity alone will overcome these tendencies and resolve interracial tensions. Yet the contact hypothesis, the idea that mere exposure and familiarity increases acceptance, has produced mixed results in the social science literature. At the very least, it is safe to say that the environment in which contact is made is important.

Based on Putnam's work and the results of the NAASS, if a prospective college student placed a premium on attending an institution with a strong sense of community, he or she would have a somewhat better chance of finding it at a more homogeneous campus. The idea that diversity makes people less comfortable and undermines a sense of community is also not limited to white institutions. A number of scholars have raised concerns about the integration of HBCUs and the effect of large white enrollments on institutional values and mission (Brown 2002; Drummond 2000; Levinson 2000). In fact, the erosion of community is significant enough that, eventually, majority students leave the campus as the number of minority students increases. In something akin to "white flight" into suburbia, many blacks stop attending HBCUs once white enrollment reaches a "tipping point" (Brown 2002).

Table 5.15. Respondent Level of Trust by Campus Diversity*

	Faculty				*Administrators*				*Students*			
	Lowest	*Middle*	*Highest*	*Total*	*Lowest*	*Middle*	*Highest*	*Total*	*Lowest*	*Middle*	*Highest*	*Total*
You can't be too careful	21%	23%	28%	24%	9%	12%	17%	12%	52%	59%	71%	61%
Most people can be trusted	79%	77%	72%	76%	91%	88%	83%	88%	48%	41%	29%	39%
Total	100%	100%	100%	100%	100%	100%	100%	100%	100%	100%	100%	100%
n	408	624	529	1,561	223	333	226	782	488	502	601	1,591

*Campus diversity is broken down roughly into thirds, with "lowest" meaning <3.4% blacks and "highest" meaning >7% black.

Within the campus community, this discomfort with diversity may cause people to self-segregate into "ethnic enclaves," associating with those like themselves and avoiding others (Broadway and Flesch 2000; Crisostomo 2001; McDermott 2002). While minority ethnic organizations tend to increase segregation for minorities, fraternities and sororities appear to have the same effect for whites, giving them social organizations that are far more homogeneous than the campus at large (Sidanuis, van Laar, Levin, and Sinclair 2004). This self-segregation has some effect on relations between members of different groups. For example, minority students' membership in ethnically oriented student organizations "increased their perceptions that ethnic groups are locked into a zero-sum competition and increased their feelings of being victims of ethnic discrimination" (Sidanuis et al. 2008, 247). For white students, membership in Greek organizations has similar effects, increasing students' opposition to campus diversity and contributing to a sense of ethnic victimization.

Thus, while there is some evidence that institutional diversity has a positive effect on interracial friendships, it is not clear whether the net effect of diversity is positive. Few researchers are willing to consider the good along with the bad and weigh them accordingly. Among those who do give honest consideration to the range of possible outcomes, the evidence appears to be mixed. Diversity has both positive and negative consequences on group relationships, with the net effect being fairly limited. In one of the more recent and thorough studies of college students' experiences with diversity, Sidanius et al. (2008) conclude that after four years of college, students show relatively little change:

> Our central goal was to assess the trajectory of college student from before college entry to graduation and provide a portrait of the impact of diversity in college on undergraduate students. At a number of junctures, however, we saw the remarkable staying power of the individual and group differences student brought with them when they entered college. In some ways, we were more struck by the continuity of students' attitudes through college than by the changes that occurred. Most notable in this regard were whites' political and racial attitudes, which seemed to be quite crystallized at college entry and were quite stable across the college years. (318)

The researchers conclude that students do gain from their experiences with diversity in that they think about their views and come away with more coherent and consistent views. However, this tends to polarize students and serves to reinforce and strengthen their precollege attitudes. This finding that college students' attitudes are fairly stable and merely continue to crystallize over their college careers is consistent with the wide range of reports that students who attend diversity workshops and take multicultural courses gain greater appreciation for diversity. However, since students self-select into these courses and experiences, what we are seeing may simply be a crystallization of existing attitudes.

The evidence on the impact of diversity on global educational outcomes is even more limited. If the net benefit of diversity on education is positive, we should see some direct effects of institutional diversity on measures like student satisfaction, graduation rates, test scores, and so on. This positive relationship has yet to be established. On the contrary, the few studies that have examined the relationship between institutional enrollment diversity and educational outcomes find either that there are no direct effects or that the effects are negative.

Astin's (1993) thorough study of college student experiences, *What Matters in College?*, is often cited as evidence in support of multicultural education. But on the issue of enrollment diversity, the author summarizes his findings as follows:

> Three percentage measures are included in the regressions to assess possible effects of the racial composition of the peer group: African-Americans, Asians, and Latinos. With few exceptions, outcomes are generally not affected by these peer measures, and in all but one case these effects are very weak and indirect. Perhaps the most interesting finding is the negative effect of the percentage of Latino students on attainment of the bachelor's degree. This finding is reminiscent of earlier research . . . indicating that Chicanos, in particular, are relatively likely to drop out of high school and college, even after controlling for their academic preparation and other background factors. One possibility is that this measure, the percentage of Latino students in the student body, may well be a crude proxy—like Outside Work—for the overall dropout rate of the institution.
>
> The only other direct effect is the negative effect of percentage Asian students on the perception of a Student-Oriented Faculty (Beta = −.21). Otherwise, none of these three measures produces any direct effects, and practically all of the indirect effects are weak. (362)

It is important to note that Patricia Gurin's (1999) work for the University of Michigan also failed to find direct positive relationships between enrollment diversity and educational outcomes. More recently, two additional studies investigate the link more directly, with different sources of data, and reach similar conclusions. Even after controlling for a wide range of variables, such as institutional selectivity, public or private classification, and student income, Rothman, Lipset, and Nevitte (2003) argue that the relationship between the percentage of blacks in the student body and students' satisfaction with their college experience is, in fact, negative. Students attending more racially diverse institutions also report less satisfaction with the quality of their education and admit to lower worker effort. While these are subjective measures, students are not merely asked to indicate whether they believe diversity has a positive effect. Rather, the actual racial composition of the institution is used to measure the impact of diversity on students' self-reported experience, absent any mention of "diversity." This eliminates the potential for students to respond on the basis of their impression of what diversity *should* produce.

Critics of Rothman et al. (2005) argued that, on methodological grounds, the analysis incorrectly modeled student attitudes and that, if properly specified, the results would be quite different. Indeed, the statistical models underlying their major findings are open for debate. The inverse relationship between overall satisfaction and diversity is rather modest. As is often the case with correlations that skirt the edge of statistical significance, the results are somewhat fragile in that modest changes in the statistical assumption underlying the model effectively eliminate the correlation altogether (see appendix 5). If true, criticisms of Rothman et al.'s statistical methodology would not prove that diversity is either useful or important. In its entirety, the Rothman et al. model purports to explain only 7 percent of the overall variance in student satisfaction. By Rothman et al.'s own figures, institutional diversity plays a minor role in overall student satisfaction. In light of the technical questions that complicate their initial findings, either diversity plays a small role in reducing overall satisfaction with college or it is irrelevant. In either case, it is an important finding that runs counter to those of the thirty national education associations whose joint statement emphatically argued just the opposite, claiming that "we now know, from experience and from a growing body of research, that engaging diversity on campus deepens students' individual learning and reaps rich dividends—in both knowledge and values—for democracy."

Like Goldsmith's findings on racial conflict in high schools, the Rothman et al. (2005) study also finds that diversity increases the chance that students will report unfair treatment. The finding may be attributed to a number of factors. More diversity simply raises the chance of interracial encounters. However, the researchers find that minorities also report more unfair treatment as diversity increases. Thus, it appears that this is due not to more encounters with people unlike oneself but rather to a change in the general climate of the institution. Still, there are multiple possible explanations. It may be the case that increases in the number of minorities lead to greater interracial tensions. It is also possible that the racial composition of the campus merely contributes to the perception of racial conflict. As we noted earlier, Astin (1993) finds that students who attend a college that promotes diversity and multiculturalism are more sensitive to race issues and, thus, perceive racism to be a bigger problem. Additionally, larger populations of minorities may lead to the creation of ethnic student organizations, which tend to contribute to perceptions of intergroup conflict and victimization (Sidanius et al. 2008). Based on the NAASS, we cannot sort out whether racial composition actually changes the environment or, rather, whether it merely changes people's perceptions of the environment.

Since the effects of institutional diversity may be limited if minority students tend to congregate in certain majors or courses, Herzog (2007) attempts to measure students' exposure to diversity more directly by looking at students' experiences within the classroom. However, even using this more precise measure, the author concludes that "compositional diversity in terms of classroom exposure to ethnic/racial minority students (excluding Asians) is mostly inconsequential to a student's final GPA, graduate school admission test scores, and likelihood to pursue a graduate education within four years of completion of an undergraduate degree" (33). Herzog also finds a negative correlation between exposure to non-Asian minorities and math scores, which he finds to be consistent with other studies that point to a "negative peer effect" (34).

It is important to note that these negative associations between compositional diversity and educational outcomes are fairly weak. For example, Rothman et al. (2005) find small correlations between enrollment diversity and students' perceptions of the educational environment. In this regard, the research findings are rather consistent. Both those who claim benefits of diversity and those who claim costs agree that the effects are small. There is no evidence that a modest increase in the number of minority students on campus will have any substantial consequence on the experience of most college students, for the better or for the worse.

Usually, such a nuanced finding would promote little controversy. After all, our claim is merely that the jury is still out on the costs and benefits of racial diversity. Such caution is usually applauded in social science research. However, this is a problematic finding for proponents of affirmative action programs, given that the U.S. Supreme Court has upheld race as a factor in college admissions on the basis of the educational benefit of diversity for all students. In its 2003 decision that upheld the University of Michigan Law School's race-based admission policy (*Grutter v. Bollinger*, 539 U.S. 306), the Supreme Court ruled that public institutions could continue to use racial classifications in their admission policies. However, as race-based policies fall under the doctrine of *strict scrutiny* (whereby laws are presumed to be unconstitutional unless a racial classification is "narrowly tailored" to advance a compelling government interest), educational institutions carried a heavy burden in proving that such policies were aimed at improving education and not simply advancing the interests of one group over another:

> As part of its goal of "assembling a class that is both exceptionally academically qualified and broadly diverse," the Law School seeks to "enroll a 'critical mass' of minority students." Brief for Respondents Bollinger et al. 13. The Law School's interest is not simply "to assure within its student body some specified percentage of a particular group merely because of its race or ethnic origin." Bakke, 438 U.S., at 307 (opinion of Powell, J.). That would amount to outright racial balancing, which is patently unconstitutional. Ibid.; Freeman v. Pitts, 503 U.S. 467, 494 (1992) ("Racial balance is not to be achieved for its own sake"); Richmond v. J. A. Croson Co., 488 U.S., at 507. Rather, the Law School's concept of critical mass is defined by reference to the educational benefits that diversity is designed to produce. (*Grutter v. Bollinger*, 539 U.S. 306)

The emerging line of research that calls into question the benefits of diverse enrollments (as opposed to required courses on diversity, multiculturalism, international studies, or study abroad) seemingly undermines the main legal justification for race-based admission at public universities. Simply as a matter of law, if race-based policies do not advance a compelling government interest, which the Supreme Court identified as the "educational benefits that diversity is designed to produce," the court may conclude that the continued use of racial classifications for admissions is unconstitutional.

The situation has led some proponents of affirmative action to engage in rather dubious research practices. For example, a new line of research from Stanford's Institute for Higher Education Research claims to find evidence that exposure to racial diversity improves students' cognitive skills (Antonio et al. 2004). However, the researchers' findings are far from conclusive, despite the fact that many have heralded their findings as evidence of the benefits of diversity. For starters, the researchers claim that previous research on the benefits of diversity fails to account for the self-selection problem. Hence, they logically argue that an experimental design is more appropriate since it allows them to randomly assign participants to various conditions and measure actual effects. Yet when the researchers fail to find a statistically significant relationship between the race of one's discussion partner and one's integrative complexity on a postdiscussion essay, they do not consider the possibility that this refutes their hypothesis. Rather, they search for additional measures of exposure to diversity, eventually abandoning the experimental manipulation and turning to self-reported measures of diverse social contacts—the very sort of self-reported measures the experimental design is intended to eliminate. The researchers then conclude that "participants who reported more racially diverse social contacts in their everyday lives exhibited higher complexity in their post-discussion essays compared to those reporting more racially homogenous contacts."[10] While the researchers do find some secondary experimental effects, including the fact that people who are exposed to other *opinions* show greater cognitive complexity, they never adequately address the insignificance of their main experimental manipulation; students who are exposed to racially diverse discussion partners show no greater cognitive complexity on a postdiscussion essay than those who had racially homogeneous discussion partners. Had the finding been positive, this would most certainly have been presented as evidence that exposure to diversity leads to more complex thinking. Yet the null finding should be considered among the body of evidence. In this way, research on diversity in higher education has become nonfalsifiable, with only positive results entering the discussion.

In fairness to Antonio and his colleagues, the study measures change in cognitive skill over a very short time frame. It is possible that, over the course of four years, exposure to diversity would have more measurable effects. Yet, even if we concede this point, conclusions about the benefits of racial diversity on cognitive ability are still premature, given the mix of evidence. For example, other studies conclude that racially diverse discussion partners may actually limit cognitive function. For example, a number of studies in social psychology and neuroscience conclude that interracial interactions can have a negative effect on postinteraction cognitive tasks for both blacks and whites (Richeson and Shelton 2003; Richeson and Trawalter 2005; Richeson et al. 2003; Trawalter and Richeson 2006). This decline in cognitive function appears to be the result of "resource depletion." That is, the self-monitoring involved in interracial interactions appears to exhaust certain cognitive abilities that are reduced in subsequent tasks. While this research does not suggest that races be kept separate in order to prevent this depletion of cognitive skill, the point is that evidence on these effects is often more complicated that those in the higher-education community recognize. In fact, this fairly large body of work from prominent psychologists is routinely ignored by the higher education associations who report on racial diversity (see, e.g., Milem, Chang, and Antonio's 2005 review of the literature for the AAC&U), despite its obvious contribution to our understanding of race relations on campus. One promising extension of Richeson and colleagues' work is to consider whether repeated exposure to racial diversity increases or decreases the sensitivities and effects the researchers observe. It is quite possible that the "resource depletion" effects decrease over time, which could be an argument in favor of campus diversity initiatives. However, it is also possible that negative interracial exchanges or campus diversity initiatives themselves heighten sensitivity to race in a way that enhances these effects over time.

In another example of contentious and overlooked research findings, a research team investigated the underrepresentation of blacks in academic careers (Cole and Barber 2003). The researchers concluded that one of the explanations for low numbers of blacks in PhD programs is that affirmative action programs create a mismatch between black and white college students such that blacks fail to graduate at the top of their class and are, thus, less likely to pursue advanced degrees. Since releasing their findings, the authors report that they have been under intense scrutiny and that the Andrew W. Mellon Foundation, which funded the research, has distanced itself from the work (see Wilson 2003).

It is no surprise that social science is susceptible to bias- and agenda-driven claims. However, this becomes much more apparent when social science research becomes so crucial to real policy debates. With stakes this high, it is difficult to find objective research reports. People on both sides of the affirmative action debate claim to have evidence to support their position. This is not to say that researchers are intentionally misleading the public. Rather, one's motivation to arrive at a particular conclusion may have more subtle effects on the search for evidence and the interpretation of the findings. In fact, we suspect that one's motivations will likely influence the read of this chapter. People are more willing to accept findings that appear to support their policy objectives while subjecting contradictory evidence to a high degree of scrutiny (Kunda 1990; Lord, Ross, and Lepper 1979). In analyzing the research, we find that there are some areas that appear to offer consistent evidence. For example, most professors and students believe that diversity has education benefits. However, researchers have not adequately demonstrated the real educational benefits of diversity, and one should be suspicious of any reports that draw premature conclusions about our understanding of this complex problem. College administrators frequently cite studies that report positive learning outcomes for enrollment diversity. Admittedly, we do not discuss all these studies. However, we have addressed some of the most frequently cited in an effort to demonstrate that the findings are less conclusive and more nuanced than commonly reported. We also demonstrate that there are competing claims and evidence that warrant some consideration, as is the case in any area of social science. Many of these findings are either intentionally or unintentionally overlooked in summary reports produced by higher education organizations, thus leading campus administrators and faculty to mistakenly believe that all campus efforts to restructure students' social and racial experiences will be universally positive.

CONCLUSION

We started this chapter with a discussion of the context of the debate over diversity in higher education. This is a politically charged, emotion-laden issue. Undoubtedly, some of our readers will find our discussion to be difficult and emotionally unsettling. We question some of the commonly cited findings about diversity in higher education with the goal of demonstrating that the jury is not yet in and that the issue is likely to produce additional conflict for higher education. However, the higher-education community is now in the position of defending admissions policies such that it has engaged in a one-sided search for evidence that allows little room for discussion of competing evidence. This has the unfortunate effect of distracting researchers from the task of identifying the specific conditions under which racial and ethnic diversity might produce either positive or negative outcomes. It also fails to prepare institutions for some of the problems and difficulties that may accompany demographic changes on campus. As such, those who are genuinely interested in understanding race relations on campus will need to move beyond reports produced by the higher-education community and delve into the more complex literature in social psychology—literature produced with the goal of understanding complicated dynamics rather than justifying policy positions.

For the most part, we find that members of the academic community view the environment for women, minorities, homosexuals, and religious groups to be quite positive. Few individuals believe that they have been the victims of harassment or other forms of unfair treatment. With that said, there are some significant areas of disagreement that are likely to affect relationships and dialogue on campus. For example, contrary to our findings in other chapters, on this issue students appear to have the most positive view of their educational environment, and administrators have the most negative assessments. As a result, administrators are likely to dedicate campus resources to addressing issues of diversity and discrimination. Students may believe that their colleges should apply those resources elsewhere. Additionally, we see significant disagreement about faculty hiring. Racial minorities believe that they face a disadvantage in the hiring process, while whites believe that the tables have turned and that white men face the most difficult time getting hired. For this reason, we expect that campus efforts to hire more minority faculty will be fairly divisive. More important, this finding demonstrates that perceptions of the campus climate differ between groups. These differences most likely apply to interpretations of other events, such as tenure decisions and promotions. On both sides, those who are denied awards may attribute their circumstances to their own groups' disadvantage.

On the issue of affirmative action and race-based preferences, the academy is very much divided. It is important to recognize, however, that the disagreement within the academy is not about increased diversity in and of itself. Opponents of the diversity movement do not object to colleges enrolling or hiring larger numbers of qualified minorities. Rather, the contention appears to be over the methods by which colleges attempt to achieve this goal. When forced to contemplate the trade-off between diversity and standards, members of the academic community appear to place a higher emphasis on standards. We find widespread opposition to racial preferences among college students in regard to both student admissions and faculty hiring. Students believe that people should not receive special consideration because of their race or sex, and they are unwilling to lower academic standards in order to obtain minority students and professors. Surprisingly, the majority of minority students also support this view, although they appear to do so for different reasons than whites. While white students fear that racial preferences will lower academic standards, black students do not agree. Among faculty, we see a great divide. While professors are evenly split on the issue of preferences and lowering admission standards in student admissions, they are considerably less likely to support lowering standards for faculty hiring. Students are far more consistent and apply the same standards to both faculty hiring and student admissions.

Although the majority of students, professors, and administrators do not believe that special admissions or hiring policies will actually lower academic standards overall, there is some disconnect between people's perceptions and the factual evidence. We provide evidence from proponents of affirmative action programs that standards do need to be adjusted to increase diversity, at least when diversity is defined in terms of black/Latino populations. Additionally, the evidence to date is that, once enrolled, black and Latino students do not perform better than white students but, rather, worse (Allen 1992; Bowen and Bok 2000; Cole and Barber 2003; Sidanuis et al. 2008). This may explain why so many institutions have aimed to achieve "diversity" by other means, specifically by increasing the number of international students and Asian students, who are more similar to whites in terms of their academic preparation and test scores. If the only motivation for diversity is to expose students to different ideas and teach them to appreciate other cultures, then increasing the number of international students would likely produce the best outcomes, and this would be a valid approach. However, if higher education views its role as one of correcting social imbalances and providing opportunities for members of historically disadvantaged groups by admitting them to more prestigious institutions than test scores and grades would otherwise permit, then it becomes more difficult to balance diversity and academic standards. Hence, values within the academy come into conflict with one another, forcing tough decisions and trade-offs.

We find that professors and administrators demonstrate support for racial diversity but not when this threatens longstanding commitments to meritocracy. Professors also rank poor student quality and lack of preparation for college as one of the most important problems facing higher education. Another possible method for achieving a more diverse student population would simply be to lower tuition and make education more accessible for members of disadvantaged groups. Yet, as we argue in chapter 2, administrators and professors do not share the public's concerns over tuition costs and believe that, if anything, they need more resources to achieve their objectives. While campuses may be able to offer scholarships to offset the cost of tuition for select groups of students, for many institutions this will have the effect of raising tuition overall and constricting rather than enlarging the applicant pool. These trade-offs raise questions about the objective costs and benefits of various alternatives. Yet these are difficult things to objectively measure. Research that tends to downplay the objective educational benefits of diversity appears to generate the most virulent criticism, perhaps because, if true, these findings seriously undermine the legal justifications for preferences based on race, ethnicity, sex, or other measures of difference. But the evidence to date fails to demonstrate a positive relationship between institutional diversity and global educational outcomes. Still, it is important to note that this does not mean that diversity is incapable of producing positive results. Nor do findings of negative consequences mean that diversity will inherently produce these effects. Rather, the environment in which people are introduced to diversity is important, and our findings may indicate that higher education has simply not gotten its formula right.

Colleges' efforts to increase diversity may be partially to blame for lack of positive results. Our research shows widespread student opposition to race-based admissions policies. Universities that openly implement such policies may inadvertently increase racial tensions among students and stigmatize minority students. Even if admissions officers can keep such policies under wrap, aggressive racial preferences appear to produce a mismatch between white and black students that causes blacks to underperform compared to their white peers and even compared to their white peers with similar test scores and academic preparation. This mismatch can reinforce negative stereotypes about blacks and create greater division on campus. Minority student performance may be further jeopardized by the fear that their poor performance will reinforce negative stereotypes about their racial group (Sidanius et al. 2008). Hence, the unintended effects of aggressive race-based preferences may be to undermine the benefits that a more naturally occurring diversity might produce.

Chapter Six

Academic Freedom, Tenure, and the Free Exchange of Ideas

We have argued, up to this point, that higher education is beset with conflict, both within and between the various groups of people who claim to have a stake in the institution. Yet conflict is not inherently bad and may, in fact, be useful if different ideas lead to fruitful dialogue about what is best for society. The university is, ideally, a place for the free and open exchange of ideas.

But the modern American university serves a number of different, sometimes competing, functions, not all of which necessitate or even allow the unhindered exchange of ideas. Obviously, the university exists to transmit knowledge and skills from one generation to the next in order to prepare the future workforce. According to Ladd and Lipset (1975), the transmission of information and values was the primary function of American higher education until the last part of the nineteenth century. Thus, early colleges and universities were "apolitical or conservative," and college professors were merely teachers who rarely challenged the conventional wisdom they imparted on their students. The modern university continues to serve as an agent of socialization, introducing students to the ideas of previous generations.

Yet the American system of higher education, like that in most Western cultures, changed remarkably in the latter part of the nineteenth century. American universities became centers for research and scientific discovery. While larger universities often appear to operate first and foremost as research centers, even small liberal arts colleges have now adopted the perspective that college professors are both teachers and scholars. As such, they offer rewards to faculty members who produce original scholarship, with those who publish most earning tenure, promotion, pay increases, and other benefits.

While a professor's commitment to original scholarship certainly varies across disciplines and institutions, there is clearly some expectation that at least a portion of the academy be engaged in scholarship. In this way, universities have the potential to become quite political. In their role as scholars, college professors may challenge and reject conventional wisdom, placing them at odds with government, religious institutions, and other sectors of society. Accordingly, universities, professors, and the professional organizations that represent them have taken measures to provide academics with the freedom to research and to teach without fear of retribution. At least in theory, scholars ought to be able to follow the evidence, even if it leads them to form unpopular conclusions.

Since the early part of the twentieth century, the American Association of University Professors (AAUP) has served as the foremost authority on matters related to academic freedom. Although the term "academic freedom" encompasses a number of meanings, including the right of a university to be free from government interference, the AAUP's *1940 Statement of Principles on Academic Freedom and Tenure* defines academic freedom as an individual right guaranteed to college professors. According to the AAUP statement, institutions of higher education advance the common good, which requires the "free search for truth and its free exposition." As such, teachers are "entitled to full freedom in research and in the publication of the results, subject to the adequate performance of their other academic duties." They are also "entitled to freedom in the classroom in discussing their subject, but they should be careful not to introduce into their teaching controversial matter which has no relation to their subject." It is important to note that the AAUP statement does not merely protect original scholarship. It also grants freedom of inquiry and expression in the classroom. If teaching merely involved the transference of accepted, conventional wisdom, this protection would be unnecessary.

It is one thing for institutions of higher education and professional organizations to argue for the rights and privileges to their own members. It is quite another for those privileges to be recognized by outside entities and government institutions. In 1957, the U.S. Supreme Court argued that academic freedom, for both students and teachers, is essential to the mission of higher education and the future of a democratic nation:

> The essentiality of freedom in the community of American universities is almost self-evident. No one should underestimate the vital role in a democracy that is played by those who guide and train our youth. To impose any strait jacket upon the intellectual leaders in our colleges and universities would imperil the future of our Nation. No field of education is so thoroughly comprehended by man that new discoveries cannot yet be made. Particularly is that true in the social sciences, where few, if any, principles are accepted as absolutes. Scholarship cannot flourish in an atmosphere of suspicion and distrust. Teachers and students must always remain free to inquire, to study and to evaluate, to gain new matu-

> rity and understanding; otherwise our civilization will stagnate and die. (*Sweezy v. New Hampshire*, 354 U.S. 234, 250 [1957])

A decade later, Justice Brennan argued that academic freedom is rooted in the First Amendment of the Constitution:

> Our Nation is deeply committed to safeguarding academic freedom, which is of transcendent value to all of us and not merely to the teachers concerned. That freedom is therefore a special concern of the First Amendment, which does not tolerate laws that cast a pall of orthodoxy over the classroom. (*Keyishian v. Board of Regents*, 385 U.S. 589, 603 [1967])

While legal scholars disagree about the interpretation of these rulings and the justices' understanding of academic freedom, the fact that the nation's highest court has defended the concept certainly gives it some legitimacy outside of academic circles. In fact, even the most vocal critics of the academy appear to accept the basic argument that the university ought to encourage the free exchange of ideas. What remains open for debate, however, is whether the modern university actually lives up to this mission.

THE POLITICS OF ACADEMIC FREEDOM

In testimony before the Pennsylvania House of Representatives in 2006, David French, president of the Foundation for Individuals Rights in Education (FIRE), articulated his support for the university's central mission and the concept of academic freedom while arguing that this goal has been compromised by campus speech codes and other efforts to control discourse:

> The goal of the university is to create a place, a marketplace where you can debate and you can discuss, you can disagree, and you can even offend in the goal of exchanging ideas and the goal of advancing human knowledge and the goal of advancing our culture. Unfortunately, our universities across this country . . . have to a large degree abdicated that responsibility. (French 2006)

Other critics of higher education take the claim even further, arguing not only that colleges and universities are abdicating their responsibilities but also that they are deliberately agents of ideological indoctrination, offering a one-sided view of social and political issues to which students and faculty members must conform. In the preface to his book *Indoctrination U*, David Horowitz (2007b) argues that members of the faculty have "intruded a political agenda into the academic curriculum and have sought to close down intellectual discussion and prevent open-minded inquiries into 'sensitive' subjects" (p. xi).

Although the evidence for the indoctrination thesis is largely anecdotal, the Horowitz critique has received a great deal of attention, in part because it is consistent with what we do know about the political climate in higher education. As we demonstrate in chapter 4, college professors are not a representative cross section of the public. Rather, they tend to hold views that are considerably to the left of the general public. A number of other studies confirm this finding, which appears to hold true whether the researchers measure faculty politics in terms of ideology, party affiliation, voting behavior, or specific policy positions (see, for example, Gross and Simmons 2007; Klein and Stern 2005; Klein and Western 2004–2005; Ladd and Lipset 1975; Rothman, Lichter, and Nevitte 2005). Without evidence to the contrary, it is natural to question whether conservative viewpoints receive a fair hearing in this environment. Even if we assume that college professors are surprisingly tolerant of those who disagree with their core values, opposing viewpoints may simply be absent from the campus, at least within specific disciplines.

In his proposal for an "Academic Bill of Rights," Horowitz (2008) claims that this ideological imbalance is a threat to the concept of academic freedom, denying students the right to hear and contemplate conservative ideas. He argues that campuses should promote "intellectual pluralism" and "organizational neutrality" to ensure that all valid points of view are considered. The Academic Bill of Rights has had some success, prompting legislative inquiries and encouraging some universities to adopt statements concerning students' rights.

Yet critics of the university continue to cite a number of recent incidents on college campuses to demonstrate that conservative ideas are not welcome in academic discourse. For example, when Harvard president Larry Summers suggested that one possible explanation for the lack of women in science fields might be attributed to differences in intrinsic aptitude, the reaction from segments of the Harvard faculty was swift and severe. After a great deal of media attention, a vote of "no confidence" from the Faculty of Arts and Sciences, and reports that the board was scheduled to replace him, Summers resigned from his position, stating that "rifts between me and segments of the arts and sciences faculty make it infeasible for me to advance the agenda of renewal that I see as crucial to Harvard's future" (quoted in Jaschik 2006). While Summers's statement about women in science was clearly not the beginning of the rift between him and segments of the Harvard faculty, the incident provided his critics with some heavy ammunition. More important, the incident provided media personalities on the right with further evidence that the university was inhospitable to certain ideas.

Faculty protests against conservatives have made headlines at other institutions. According to an article in the *New York Times*, the Hoover Institution's decision to appoint Donald Rumsfeld, former defense secretary, as a visiting fellow drew "fierce protests from faculty members and students at Stanford University" (Glater 2007). In other incidents, conservative commentator Ann Coulter was struck with a pie during a speech at the University of Arizona and was unable to complete her speech at the University of Connecticut because of audience protests (*US News & World Report* 2007).

These incidents appear to portray a campus environment that is hostile to unpopular ideas, a charge that has been gaining steam since the 1980s. A 1983 article in the *New York Times* reported that the American Council on Education, the AAUP, the National Coalition of Independent College and University Students, and two other student organizations endorsed a statement to address the disruption of speakers on college campuses. Their effort followed protests against Jeane J. Kirkpatrick, U.S. delegate to the United Nations, and several other campus speakers (Maeroff 1983). Three years later, the AAUP created a panel to study academic freedom and issued a statement condemning the censorship of textbooks and library holdings, including Mark Twain's *Huckleberry Finn*, which had been criticized for promoting racial stereotypes (Vobeda 1986).

In the early 1990s, the dominant critique of American higher education focused on the "lunacies of the Political Correctness regime now dominating American universities" (Krauthammer 1991, A18). Critics took aim at campus speech codes, designed to restrict speech that might offend the sensibilities of others, especially related to race, gender, and sexual preference. The National Association for Scholars (NAS), an organization founded in 1987 to "foster intellectual freedom and to sustain the tradition of reasoned scholarship and civil debate in America's colleges and universities," found itself in conflict with the AAUP, an organization that, in principle, supports the same freedoms. Yet the AAUP and the NAS have frequently disagreed about what constitutes intellectual freedom and civil debate.

Although the AAUP has historically been concerned with threats to academic freedom from government, outside entities, and administrative ranks, the organization has not been sympathetic to more recent charges that members of the professoriate are guilty of similar offenses. For this reason, critics of the AAUP have argued that the organization is committed only to fending off attacks on the professoriate and that it has failed to recognize the threat to academic freedom from campus orthodoxy (Wilson 2007). Yet the AAUP charges that accusations of political correctness are unjustified attacks on the faculty and that these accusations have the effect of chilling speech on campus and constitute the real threat to academic freedom. In fact, the AAUP recently released a report, "Freedom in the Classroom," defending a professor's right to cover material that others might view to be overly political or inappropriate.

In a detailed, point-by-point response to the report, the NAS has charged that this position is a departure from the original 1940 statement of principles. Among their more pointed critiques, the NAS argues that the AAUP has redefined "truth" as whatever the members of the academy decide it to be. Thus, academics are justified in presenting one-sided views of controversial issues as long as there is some consensus within the academy that their particular viewpoint is the correct one (National Association of Scholars 2007).

The debate over campus speech codes, censorship, and political intolerance has not been restricted to a few critics and defenders of higher education or to the professional organizations designed to confront these issues. Rather, it has filled the airwaves and newspapers with countless reports and editorials that cite a wide range of examples. *Newsweek* ran a cover story on the "tyranny of PC" (Adler 1990). Several popular books on the topic reached mass audiences, including Allan Bloom's highly influential work, *The Closing of the American Mind* (1987), which stayed on the *New York Times* best-seller list for four months and alerted half a million readers to what Bloom saw as the failures of American higher education. Other books followed, including David Kimball's (1990) *Tenured Radicals*, now in its third edition; Dinesh D'Souza's (1991) *Illiberal Education*; and Alan Kors and Harvey Silverglate's (1998) *The Shadow University: The Betrayal of Liberty on America's Campuses*. Even the president of the United States, George H. W. Bush, warned of the danger to free speech on college campuses. During a 1991 commencement speech at the University of Michigan, whose campus speech code had recently been struck down by the courts, the president stated,

> The notion of political correctness has ignited controversy across the land, and although the movement arises from the laudable desire to sweep away the debris of racism and sexism and hatred, it replaces old prejudice with new ones. . . . It declares certain topics off limits, certain expressions off limits, even certain gestures off limits. What began as a crusade for civility has soured into a cause of conflict and even censorship. Disputants treat sheer force, getting their foes punished or expelled for instance, as a substitute for the power of ideas. They've invited people to look for an insult in every word, gesture, action. (quoted in Innerst 1991, A1)

As accusations of political correctness intensified, the academic community launched several counteroffensives. Stanley Fish, a distinguished English professor at Duke University, helped to organize Teachers for a Democratic Culture, a group that condemned the use of the term "political correctness," arguing that it was an attempt to undermine positive campus initiatives like affirmative action. The group organized a conference at the University of Michigan titled "The P.C. Frame-Up: What's behind the Attack?" (DePalma 1991). Others also argued that the debate about political correctness was an unfounded, conservative attack on higher education. For example, in his book *The Myth of Political Correctness: The Conservative Attack on Higher Education*, John K. Wilson (1995) argues that conservatives created the myth of political correctness in order to portray all objectionable social policies as a vast leftist conspiracy.

By the mid-1990s, the campus "PC wars" were in full swing. According to one college president, "Scarcely a day goes by in the life of a college president that does not include new charges of political correctness" (quoted in Dye 1995, R20). Other organizations formed to tackle the problem as they saw it. In 1995, former National Endowment for the Humanities chairman Lynne V. Cheney launched the American Council of Trustees and Alumni (formerly the National Alumni Forum) in an effort to organize alumni and trustees to confront political intolerance and challenges to academic freedom on college campuses. Four years later, Alan Kors and Harvey Silverglate launched the Foundation for Individual Rights in Education (FIRE). According to its website, FIRE was a response to the "hundreds of communications and pleas for help" they had received from people who had read *The Shadow University* (FIRE 2004). Since its founding, the organization has coordinated a number of successful lawsuits against public universities for free speech violations related to speech codes and has exerted pressure on a number of other institutions that, in response, have changed their own speech codes.

While conservatives have been citing cases of political intolerance and censorship on campus for the past two decades, the September 11, 2001, terrorist attacks altered the campus environment and led those on the left to lament the "war on academic freedom" (McNeil 2002). A number of academics, especially those who study the Middle East, found that the post-9/11 political environment was not receptive to their interpretations of U.S. foreign policy. A report in the National Education Association's *Higher Education Journal* lists several examples of this "chilling of speech on campus":

> In 2002, the North Carolina House of Representative moved to cut the budget of University of North Carolina because a fall reading list for first year students included a book about the Koran. In the same year, the governor of Colorado and state legislators denounced the University of Colorado for inviting Hanan Ashrawi, a Palestinian spokesperson and educator, to speak on campus. The legislature in Missouri sought to cut funding in 2002 from the University of Missouri's budget because the director of the public television station located on the Columbia campus decided that personnel should not wear flag pins on camera. A year after the September 11th attacks, a Philadelphia think tank established a website to monitor professors and institutions that were critical of U.S. actions in the Middle East. Individual academics were listed on the website as

"hostile" to America; as a result, the professors identified were spammed with thousands of angry e-mails. (Tierney and Lechuga 2005, 13)

The perception that academic freedom was in jeopardy following the September 11 attacks was widespread in the academic community. John K. Wilson (2007) published another book on academic culture, claiming to find evidence of "patriotic correctness," an intolerance for any criticism of the Bush administration or its war on terror. The AAUP believed that the threat was substantial enough to warrant the creation of a "Special Committee on Academic Freedom and National Security in a Time of Crisis." The committee issued a lengthy report, outlining a significant number of incidents on college campuses, including an episode at Rockford College, where audience members chanted "God Bless America" over a commencement speaker who had referred to the United States as an "occupying force" in Iraq. The report also detailed several incidents of legislatures, alumni, and citizen groups calling for resignations of academics who spoke against the Iraq War, in the defense of terrorists, or against the state of Israel (American Association of University Professors 2003).

The most public incident involved Ward Churchill at the University of Colorado (see discussion in chapter 4). In this case, the AAUP perceived the public's response to Churchill and demands for his resignation as threats to his academic freedom and issued a statement defending his right to speak freely, while making it clear that the AAUP did not endorse his specific remarks (American Association of University Professors 2005). For many, this episode demonstrated the power that external forces can exert on the university. While Churchill was ultimately fired for research misconduct and for falsifying his credentials, it was clear that his statements about the causes of 9/11 were the trigger for the investigation. Had Bill O'Reilly and other prominent conservatives not put pressure on the University of Colorado, it is likely that Churchill would still hold his tenured position.

While both sides in the political culture wars claim that the other side routinely violates academic freedom and represses free debate, there is a noticeable difference in their claims. Based on the examples they cite, it appears that one's perception as to the source of the threat differs according to political ideology. As the minority group within the academic community, conservatives perceive that the threat to academic freedom comes from within the university itself. Those who attempt to espouse controversial, conservative views within the academy find themselves in conflict with the faculty, the administration, and the student body. According to this view, the university is guilty of violating its mission to support the search for truth and the free exchange of ideas.

As the majority group in academia, liberals perceive relatively little threat from their conservative colleagues. Yet, as the minority group in the larger society, they perceive a threat from hostile external critics, citing examples of intrusion from the government, the media, and the public. According to the American Federation of Teachers (AFT), "Some conservatives advocate government intervention to control professors in the name of academic freedom, which is ironic to say the least . . . academic freedom requires the defeat of government intrusion, or any external intrusion, into curriculum, teaching, hiring and student assessment" (America Federation of Teachers 2007, 15). The AAUP points specifically to David Horowitz's efforts to promote academic freedom as part of the problem, stating that the Academic Bill of Rights undermines academic freedom because it "threatens to impose administrative and legislative oversight on the professional judgment of faculty" and deprives professors of the "authority necessary for teaching" (American Association of University Professors 2003).

OTHER SOURCES OF THREAT

It is important to note that the perception that academic freedom is in jeopardy precedes current political controversies. In 1955, Richard Hofstadter and Walter P. Metzger published *The Development of Academic Freedom in the United States*, which concludes with a rather ominous warning about the "slender thread by which it hangs" (506). Since its inception, the AAUP has been asked to rule on cases involving perceived violations of academic freedom and has voted to censure forty-five administrations as a result. Often, these cases involve employment issues and do not appear to be directly related to national politics.

In their report, *Academic Freedom in the 21st-Century College and University*, the AFT (2007) outlines four additional threats to academic freedom: increased emphasis on vocational training, reductions in state funding, corporate-style management practices, and the increase in non-tenure-track faculty. In fact, the AFT sees this last concern as the "greatest threat to academic freedom today" (2).

These other threats to academic freedom have been developing for the past quarter of a century. College students and their parents show increased concern for acquiring marketable skills as opposed to general knowledge. Students see little purpose in taking costly courses that appear unrelated to their future career goals. According to Derek Bok (2006), this difference in perspective is growing, with students placing less emphasis on the acquisition of knowledge and faculty resisting the move toward technical education. This divide may create pressure on administrations to alter course requirements and take the curriculum out of the hands of the faculty.

Financial pressures also contribute to the use of part-time faculty, who accept lower wages, or contingent faculty, whose flexible status allows the institution to have greater budget flexibility. Many voices in higher education have expressed concerns that these changes in employment practices reduce professorial power not only for the individual faculty members involved but for the faculty body as a whole. Often, these nontraditional faculty members are not actively involved in faculty governance, which means that fewer faculty members are free to actively participate in institutional decision making. Accordingly, managerial styles in higher education have also changed in the past quarter of a century, favoring stronger administrations and weaker faculty bodies.

Finally, as student satisfaction and retention become more important to the bottom line, institutions place greater emphasis on student evaluations of professors. According to the AFT, peer evaluation is one of the key processes that secure academic freedom. The principle that academics are best able to judge the competency of their peers is the justification for faculty committees on tenure and promotion. Yet colleges and universities appear to place increased emphasis on students' evaluations of faculty. Robert Haskell (1997) argues that the use of student evaluations has a number of negative effects on academic freedom; they introduce administrative control over teaching, they reward faculty who lower standards and inflate grading to earn high evaluations, and they discourage open discussion by punishing faculty who offend students' sensibilities.

It may be the case that those faculty members who are concerned about academic freedom are not concerned about the intrusion of political agendas into their research and teaching but rather are concerned about administrative control of their teaching and evaluation. The decline in tenure-track positions alone may alarm some members of the academy who believe that tenure is necessary to maintain academic freedom.

PERCEPTIONS OF ACADEMIC FREEDOM

The NAASS was administered in 1999. The timing has some advantages and disadvantages. On the one hand, this places the survey before the 9/11 terrorist attacks. Thus, it is possible that the events changed the campus culture in a meaningful way that we cannot capture in our analysis. However, as we demonstrate in our discussion, the campus culture wars were well under way prior to the attacks. While the post-9/11 environment may have been unusually hostile to liberal ideas and attacks on the president, the effect was relatively short lived. By the close of Bush's second term, public support for the president was exceedingly low, American opinion on the Iraq War was fairly negative, and Americans had elected a staunch critic of the war, Barack Obama, as the new president. Even Republican candidates for office in 2008 felt it necessary to distance themselves from the unpopular president and his policies. In fact, some of the most negative advertisements of the 2008 campaign attacked the Republican nominee, John McCain, by comparing him to George W. Bush. If Congress, the media, and higher education "accepted the Bush Administration plans, often without debate or inquiry" as John K. Wilson (2005) suggests, it is obvious that this "patriotic correctness" has dissipated. If there was any question as to whether support for Bush had eroded, students and faculty at Brigham Young University, a conservative Christian institution, made the case when they protested the selection of Vice President Dick Cheney as commencement speaker. Protesters held signs that read, "You lied. They died" (Berkes 2008).

But the Cheney incident is rare in recent years in that it was triggered by controversy over the war in Iraq. The debate over campus speech has now returned to discussions of political correctness, censorship, and speech codes. Even protests against campus speakers have shifted to other policy concerns, with recent protests aimed at those who oppose illegal immigration, homosexuality, or race and gender preferences (*US News & World Report* 2007). The AAUP and other professional associations continue to warn that allegations of political bias and indoctrination are unwarranted attacks on the university and on the rights of college teachers. In other words, things have returned to normal.

The NAASS was completed in the midst of the political correctness culture wars, the same year that *The Shadow University* was published and FIRE was founded. At this time, the debates over the "politically correct" university had been circulating in the mass media continuously for ten years, with both sides claiming that the other was threatening the principles of academic freedom and hampering campus discourse. Based on the media reports and the political dialogue, academic freedom was in crisis.

Yet, according to the NAASS, those within the academy show mild concern about the future of the academy. While academics do not express the same intensity as those in the media, there does appear to be some concern over the security of academic freedom, with notable differences between administrators and members of the faculty (see table 6.1). When asked about the state of academic freedom in higher education in general, only 18 percent of professors believe that academic freedom is "very secure," compared to 38 percent of administrators. While the most common response from both groups is that academic freedom is "somewhat secure," a sizable group is less optimistic. Approximately 32 percent of college professors and 14 percent of administrators believe that academic freedom is either "somewhat" or "very" insecure.

This portrait is somewhat more optimistic when respondents consider the state of academic freedom on their own campuses. Among administrators, there is great confidence in academic freedom on campus. The overwhelming majority, 67 percent, report that academic freedom on their campus is "very secure," while 27 percent report that it is "somewhat secure." Professors are also more positive about the environment on their own campuses. Again, they are less confident in the security of academic freedom than are their administrators, with 36 percent arguing that academic freedom on their campus is "very secure," 45 percent indicating that it is "somewhat secure," and 19 percent indicating that it is either "somewhat" or "very" insecure.

It would appear that academics' perceptions of academic freedom are somewhat unrelated to their personal observations about their own campuses. This may suggest that actual violations are relatively uncommon, providing individual faculty members with little cause for concern. Yet a few high-profile cases may lead to the perception that the problem is more widespread at other universities. It is also possible that people simply trust their own colleagues and administrators more than they trust the institution of higher education. Researchers have noted similar incongruence between people's ratings of Congress and their approval of their own representatives. In short, people often believe that institutions are filled with scoundrels but that their own representatives are the exception. Academics may, perhaps foolishly, trust their own colleagues and administrators to support and defend their interests.

Among administrators, we see no statistical difference between Republicans and Democrats in their perceptions of threats to academic freedom, either for higher education as a whole or for their own campuses (see table 6.2). Among

Table 6.1. How Secure Is Academic Freedom?

	Faculty		*Administrators*	
	In General	*Your Campus*	*In General*	*Your Campus*
Very secure	18%	36%	38%	67%
Somewhat secure	50%	45%	48%	27%
Somewhat insecure	28%	16%	13%	5%
Very insecure	4%	3%	1%	1%
Total	100%	100%	100%	100%
n	1,640	1,638	805	807

Table 6.2. How Secure Is Academic Freedom by Party Identification?

	Faculty				*Administrators*			
	Democrat	*Independent*	*Republican*	*Total*	*Democrat*	*Independent*	*Republican*	*Total*
In General								
Very secure	16%	17%	26%	18%	35%	38%	51%	38%
Somewhat secure	51%	52%	46%	51%	49%	51%	38%	48%
Somewhat insecure	29%	28%	25%	28%	15%	10%	10%	13%
Very insecure	5%	3%	3%	4%	1%	2%	1%	1%
Total	100%	100%	100%	100%	100%	100%	100%	100%
n	821	546	178	1,545	400	293	99	792
Your Campus								
Very secure	35%	36%	43%	36%	67%	67%	69%	67%
Somewhat secure	46%	45%	42%	45%	27%	27%	24%	27%
Somewhat insecure	15%	17%	12%	15%	5%	6%	6%	5%
Very insecure	3%	2%	3%	3%	1%	1%	1%	1%
Total	100%	100%	100%	100%	100%	100%	100%	100%
n	818	547	176	1,541	399	292	100	791

faculty, we do see a small difference between the parties, with Republicans reporting that academic freedom is secure, more so than their Democratic colleagues. However, the data demonstrate that people on both sides of the political spectrum perceive some threat. Further analysis of the data suggests that threats to academic freedom may not be political in nature.

Those respondents who report that academic freedom is "somewhat" or "very" insecure, either in general or on their own campuses, answered a follow-up question about the source of the threat (see table 6.3). For faculty, the most common response is that the administration constitutes a threat to academic freedom. Since faculty and administrators have similar ideological viewpoints, it is difficult to argue that this is a reaction to administrators' politics. A fair number of faculty also point to the government as the source of threat. Among administrators, the most commonly identified threats to academic freedom are the government and the general public. A handful of faculty and administrators specifically identify political ideologies as the primary source of threat, with responses balanced between "the left" and "the right." While some offer that religion is a source of threat, presumably a threat from the right, an equal number of both groups identify political correctness as a threat. However, the number of people who identify any of these political sources is still relatively small.

Table 6.3. If There Is a Threat to Academic Freedom, Where Is It Coming From?

			Faculty Party Identification		
	Administrators	*Faculty*	*Democrat*	*Independent*	*Republican*
Government	23%	22%	21%	25%	23%
Administration	17%	35%	35%	30%	44%
Business	7%	8%	9%	7%	0%
General public	21%	6%	5%	8%	4%
Religion	6%	6%	7%	5%	2%
Within the faculty	5%	6%	4%	8%	6%
Financial reasons	7%	4%	6%	2%	2%
Political correctness	6%	5%	1%	9%	12%
The right	2%	3%	4%	1%	2%
Attack on tenure	3%	4%	6%	2%	2%
The left	4%	1%	1%	2%	4%
Nowhere	1%	0%	0%	0%	0%
Total	100%	100%	100%	100%	100%
n	107	527	267	170	52

The fact that faculty most commonly identify administrators as the threat to academic freedom while administrators identify external threats is not surprising. When external constituencies are dissatisfied with higher education, they hold administrators responsible. Administrators respond to these external demands by placing demands on the faculty. As we noted in chapter 4, administrators responded to legislative inquiries during the McCarthy era by launching their own assault on their faculties, requiring them to take loyalty oaths or firing controversial members (Shrecker 1986; Thelin 2004). More recently, administrators are under considerable pressure to make higher education more accountable to government agencies. As a result, they spend a good deal of time discussing measures of institutional "assessment." The faculty is often distrusting of such efforts and may view them as infringements on their freedom and autonomy in the classroom.

Earlier, we hypothesized that political orientation appears to affect whether one believes the threat to academic freedom comes from within the university or from external sources. When faculty members identify sources of threat to academic freedom, we see what might constitute small differences between Democrats and Republicans, although the limited number of observations constrains our ability to draw precise conclusions about the results.[1] As we predict, Republicans are more likely than Democrats to identify forces operating within the university, including the administration, the faculty, and political correctness. Democrats are more likely to identify sources outside the university, such as business, religion, and the attack on tenure. It is important to note, however, that these differences are not overwhelming. Few respondents identify politics directly, although 16 percent of Republicans point to the political left or political correctness, and 26 percent of Democrats point to sources that might reflect conservative criticisms of the academy: religion, the right, business, and attacks on tenure. Surprisingly, Republicans are as likely or slightly more likely to identify "the government" as the source of the threat. The fact that Republicans share this concern suggests that perceptions of government threat are not based on legislative inquiries into political correctness or liberal indoctrination, nor would they, in 1999, be based on the Patriot Act or other security measures. Rather, perceptions of government intrusion on academic freedom may be more practical and reflect concerns about the increased dependence of higher education on government funding for both teaching and research.

The fact that both Democrats and Republicans identify government and campus administrators as the largest threats to academic freedom does not necessarily mean that political correctness is absent from the campus, nor does it mean that external criticism is harmless. It is still possible that either of these forces—or both of them—presents a threat to academic freedom.

However, it appears that the majority of faculty either has not received the message or is not persuaded by the evidence.

SUPPORT FOR TENURE

The concept of academic freedom is widely embraced by both the academic community and its external critics. According to the AAUP, academic tenure is the means by which the academy grants freedom in teaching and research. Following a probationary period, academics are provided with "permanent or continuous tenure," which can be terminated only for "adequate cause," "extraordinary circumstances," or "financial exigencies." This job security is designed to allow professors to freely exchange controversial ideas, without fear of reprisal. Yet critics of the academy are less supportive of tenure and cite this as an example of the luxuries awarded to college faculty, often while making claims that academics are underworked and overpaid. David Horowitz (2007b) writes,

> Virtually alone among workers in America, academics are entitled to four months paid vacation, and every seven years are awarded a sabbatical leave that provides them with ten months off at full or half pay. To crown these privileges, they alone among America's public employees—with the exception of Supreme Court Justices—have lifetime jobs. (61)

Like tenure for Supreme Court justices, tenure for academics is conditioned on good behavior. Administrators can fire tenured professors with adequate cause. But more often than not, tenure does mean lifetime employment. Violations of this norm often involve costly legal battles, negative publicity, and the threat of censure from the AAUP. It is these controversial cases that tend to make the headlines and help to form public perceptions of tenure. It is not surprising, therefore, to see academics referred to as "tenured radicals" (Kimball 1990) or to hear political pundits blame the tenure system for higher education's failings. In response, academics and the institutions that represent them often launch a rigorous defense of tenure, claiming that it is essential to the mission of higher education and that it encourages the brightest minds to enter the profession.

Given the premise that tenure is a privilege designed to protect those within the academy, one might expect to find almost unanimous support for the tenure system among college faculty. Yet there are those within the academy who question the merits of tenure. As we noted in our discussion of academic freedom, employment practices in higher education are changing. An increasing number of academics are employed through non-tenure-track appointments.

While this is often a matter of institutional design or financial necessity, some members of the faculty claim that there are benefits to a non-tenure-track appointment, citing the lack of publication pressure and the freedom to focus on teaching as inducements. Others argue that, rather than encourage debate and academic freedom, the tenure system actually stifles debate, forcing new members of the academy to take a vow of silence for the first seven years of their careers, lest they offend someone in a position to vote on their tenure review. A 1999–2000 survey of graduate students finds that nearly one-quarter would consider accepting a non-tenure-track position in exchange for other perks, such as a more prestigious university or a more favorable geographic location (Trower 2001). This appears to represent a decline in the importance placed on tenure. The question remains, does this mean that academics, as a whole, have begun to question the merits of the tenure system, or is it merely less important to a new generation of academics?

According to the NAASS, as an institution, tenure enjoys widespread support among the universities' various constituencies (see table 6.4). Among professors, one-third responded that tenure is "essential," while another third rate it as "very important."[2] Although they show less enthusiasm for tenure, administrators are also generally supportive of the practice, with 16 percent indicating that it is "essential" and 32 percent reporting that it is "very important" overall. While the faculty/administrative commitment to tenure is, itself, important, there are deep divisions within these groups that reveal an important philosophical difference on the role of tenure in protecting academic freedom.

If tenure protects academic freedom and allows faculty to investigate controversial ideas, as is commonly argued, then we should expect that tenure

Table 6.4. On Balance, Do You Think Academic Tenure Today Is . . .

	Faculty			
	Social Science and Humanities	*Sciences, Professional, and Other*	*All*	*Administrators*
Essential	41%	27%	34%	16%
Very important	33%	34%	34%	32%
Somewhat important	18%	27%	23%	34%
Not very important	5%	8%	7%	13%
Not important at all	2%	3%	2%	5%
Don't know	0%	0%	0%	0%
Total	100%	100%	100%	100%
n	814	830	1,644	807

would be more important to people in subjective fields, such as the social sciences and humanities, and less important to faculty in the professional studies and sciences. Indeed, support for tenure is stronger among those in the more subjective/political disciplines, with 41 percent of professors in the social sciences and humanities rating tenure as "essential," compared to 27 percent of the professors in professional fields, natural sciences, or others. Yet even outside the more subjective arena of academic inquiry, a strong majority of the professors regard tenure as "very important," suggesting that, while tenure may help secure academic freedom, this freedom is not limited to political expression. Rather, academic freedom includes the right to challenge administrators on matters of campus policy. Given recent growths in administrative ranks and more top-down managerial styles, faculty in all disciplines may recognize the need for tenure such that they may freely participate in faculty governance without fear of job loss.

Interestingly, the NAASS does reveal that support for the tenure system is declining with each career cohort. Those who have entered the academic profession most recently believe that tenure is less important than do their more experienced colleagues (see figure 6.1). Whereas newer faculty, on average, rated the importance of tenure at about a 3.7 (where 3 is "somewhat important," 4 is "very important," and 5 is "essential"), their more senior colleagues consistently rated the importance of tenure at around a 4.3. The change is not dramatic from year to year, but the differences are rather consistent as a function of time. It is unclear whether this is truly a cohort change or, rather, a generational change. In other words, it is possible that as these new academics spend more time in the academy, they will change their assessment of tenure and rate it higher in importance. However, we believe that this is more likely to represent a permanent difference between cohorts, one that reflects employment changes in higher education. As more people find employment off the tenure track, it becomes a more acceptable practice. Young academics may even engage in motivated reasoning (Kunda 1990). With fewer tenure-track jobs available, it is useful to seriously consider the benefits of other forms of employment.

We also consider whether support for tenure differs according to professors' political affiliations. Critics of the tenure system often claim that permanent employment status protects people with radical, liberal views. The Ward Churchill case feeds into this critique, demonstrating the lengths to which a university must go to terminate the employment of a controversial or unfit scholar. In this view, it would appear that tenure protects liberal academics from external, conservative critics. However, historian and retired professor Thomas C. Reeves (2005) argues that tenure, once achieved, serves as a greater benefit to conservatives in academia:

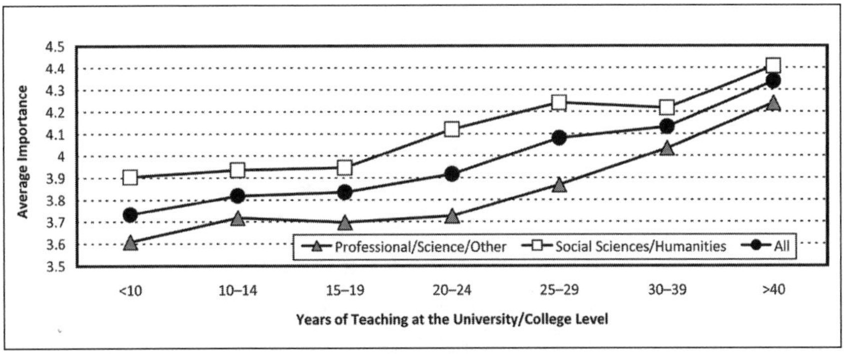

Figure 6.1. Importance of Tenure among Faculty by Years of Service (3.5 = Somewhat Important, 4 = Very Important, 4.5 = Essential/Very Important)

> Today, on campus, conservatives are heretics, often challenging the established principles of orthodox leftist ideology with scholarship and bold thinking. It is a dangerous business, for the people who talk the most about diversity and tolerance are rarely in the mood to welcome dissent. As an abundance of literature shows, and experience verifies, conservatives are often persecuted on campus. They must sometimes mask their beliefs in order to be hired. But tenure, once achieved, protects them. Eliminate that protection and watch conservative heads roll, both at the hands of administrators and fellow faculty members.

Yet, notwithstanding its potential benefits to the conservative professoriate, the NAASS clearly demonstrates that both Democratic faculty and administrators see tenure as a higher priority than do their Republican counterparts (see table 6.5). While Republican professors do generally support tenure, they do so to a lesser extent than their Democratic peers, who are twice as likely to rate tenure as "essential." It turns out that, independent of their partisanship, social liberals tend to support tenure more than social conservatives (for more details on the independent impact of partisanship and ideology, see appendix 6). This seems to imply that, at least from their own perspective, Democrats and liberals find greater protection in the tenure system than do Republicans and conservatives. It may be the case that, as noted previously, the tenure system actually has the effect of silencing dissent in the years before review. Some have also argued that tenure does not actually ensure academic freedom. Professors are dependent on their colleagues' approval for many things, including pay increases, committee assignments, faculty grant awards, and promotion to full professor. If conservatives find that they cannot speak freely on campus, even with tenure, they may become skeptical of its actual value. Remember, however, that Repub-

Table 6.5. On Balance, Do You Think Academic Tenure Today Is . . .

	Faculty Party Identification				*Administrators' Party Identification*			
	Democrat	*Independent*	*Republican*	*All*	*Democrat*	*Independent*	*Republican*	*All*
Essential	39%	30%	20%	34%	20%	14%	7%	16%
Very important	34%	34%	34%	34%	33%	33%	25%	32%
Somewhat important	20%	25%	30%	23%	33%	34%	40%	34%
Not very important	5%	8%	13%	7%	11%	16%	14%	13%
Not important at all	1%	3%	3%	2%	4%	3%	13%	5%
Don't know	0%	0%	1%	0%	0%	0%	0%	0%
Total	100%	100%	100%	100%	100%	100%	100%	100%
n	823	549	179	1,551	400	294	99	793
	*Faculty Liberal Social Views**				*Administrators' Liberal Social Views*			
	3	2	0–1	All	3	2	0–1	All
Essential	39%	28%	27%	34%	19%	12%	14%	16%
Very important	34%	35%	32%	34%	33%	35%	27%	32%
Somewhat important	20%	25%	27%	23%	32%	37%	35%	34%
Not very important	5%	9%	9%	7%	13%	11%	15%	13%
Not important at all	2%	2%	4%	2%	3%	5%	9%	5%
Don't know	0%	0%	0%	0%	0%	0%	1%	0%
Total	100%	100%	100%	100%	100%	100%	100%	100%
n	967	318	358	1,643	452	187	170	809

* 3-point Social Liberal Scale includes support for abortion, cohabitation, and homosexuality.

licans in our sample actually rated academic freedom as more secure than did the Democrats.

It is worth noting that, with one exception, each of the aforementioned factors is an independent predictor of a professor's support for tenure. In other words, it is not that Republicans, who are less supportive of tenure, also happen to think academia is secure and avoid working in the humanities. Rather, each of these attitudes has its own impact on support for tenure. When these factors are placed together in a statistical model, we find that the most important predictor of support for tenure is a professor's general assessment of academic freedom, followed by partisan leanings, years of teaching, and field of study. The only factor that seems to have no real influence on support for tenure is a professor's assessment of academic freedom at his or her own institution. While assessment of academic freedom at their own school is correlated with support for tenure, the regression model shows that the real driving influence is a more general assessment of academic freedom in the academy at large (see appendix 6).

Finally, although professors and administrators show general support for the tenure system, significant numbers in both groups do recognize that there are potential drawbacks to the system (see table 6.6). When asked if institutions should be able to get rid of faculty who are "deadwood," even if they have tenure, 69 percent of professors and 85 percent of administrators answer "yes." Among professors, Republicans are more likely to support firing "deadwood" than are Democrats, again suggesting that they place less importance on this protection, despite their minority position in the academy.

FREE EXPRESSION ON CAMPUS

Given that both professors and administrators believe that academic freedom is fairly secure, we might expect there to be a free and open exchange of ideas on the college campus. Yet, as we have seen from the political discourse on this topic, people on both sides of the political culture wars claim that this is not the case. Conservatives claim that professors and students are stifled by political correctness, while liberals claim that professors and students are stifled by false accusation of political correctness. The NAASS asked professors, students, and administrators about their willingness to express viewpoints to others. Faculty and students responded to questions about withholding views because of fear of faculty reactions and because of concern for students' reactions. Administrators were asked only the question about concern for faculty reactions.

Table 6.6. Do You Think Your Institution Ought to Be Able to Get Rid of Such [Deadwood], Even If They Have Tenure?

	Faculty				*Administrators*			
	Democrat	*Independent*	*Republican*	*Total*	*Democrat*	*Independent*	*Republican*	*Total*
Yes, should be able to get rid of "deadwood"	65%	72%	82%	69%	82%	86%	92%	85%
No, should not	30%	25%	17%	26%	16%	13%	4%	13%
Don't know	5%	4%	1%	4%	3%	1%	4%	2%
Total	100%	100%	100%	100%	100%	100%	100%	100%
n	822	548	179	1,549	400	294	100	794

Faculty Expression

The majority of college professors surveyed claim that they rarely or never avoid expressing particular points of view for fear of a negative reaction from other faculty. Similarly, the majority of faculty also report that they rarely or never avoid expressing points of view because they expect a negative student reaction. With that said, a substantial group of faculty do report some self-censorship, with 31 percent indicating that they sometimes or frequently withhold views because they anticipate a negative reaction from other faculty and 34 percent indicating that they do so to avoid negative reactions from students. Interestingly, faculty members' perceptions of the campus speech environment are more pessimistic when they are asked to evaluate other people's behaviors. When asked whether they think other members of the faculty avoid expressing their views, 67 percent report that this occurs frequently or sometimes.

When professors are divided by partisan affiliation, we see small differences between Democrats and Republicans, with Democrats reporting slightly more self-censoring than Republicans. When asked if they avoid expressing particular points of view because they expect a negative student reaction, 36 percent of Democrats and 29 percent of Republicans report that they sometimes or frequently avoid expressing opinions. When asked if they avoid expressing viewpoints because of reactions from other members of the faculty, Republicans again appear to self-censor less than Democrats, with 23 percent of Republicans and 30 percent of Democrats indicating that they sometimes or frequently avoid expressing opinions (see table 6.7).

Oddly enough, when it comes to self-censoring out of a concern for faculty reactions, the political independents seem to fair the worst, with 35 percent indicating that they avoid expressing a particular point of view compared to 30 percent for Democrats and 23 percent for Republicans. It is difficult to sort out the causal connections in this case since we cannot say for sure if independents feel they need to be careful not to offend colleagues or, rather, if a person who is generally concerned about offending colleagues tends to gravitate toward the political center. Identification as an "Independent" may, itself, be an indication that one avoids taking positions. Nonetheless, this pattern, shown in figure 6.2, tends to hold when one examines each of the major fields of study.[3] With the exception of the sciences, where Democratic professors tend to self-censor in higher numbers, self-identified independents tend to censor in relatively high numbers.

In a follow-up question, those faculty members who claim that they avoid expressing views because they anticipate a negative student reaction are asked to clarify their concerns. As with table 6.3, the differences between Republi-

Table 6.7. How Often, if at All, Did the *Faculty* Respondent Avoid Expressing Any Particular Points of View Because of . . .

	Democrat	*Independent*	*Republican*	*Total*
A Negative Reaction from Other Faculty				
Frequently	6%	7%	6%	6%
Sometimes	24%	28%	17%	25%
Rarely	37%	32%	39%	35%
Never	33%	33%	37%	34%
Total	100%	100%	100%	100%
n	821	546	180	1,547
A Negative Reaction from Students				
Frequently	6%	7%	6%	6%
Sometimes	30%	27%	23%	28%
Rarely	35%	35%	39%	35%
Never	29%	31%	32%	30%
Total	100%	100%	100%	100%
n	817	547	179	1,543

cans and Democrats shown in table 6.8 must be interpreted with additional caution since the questionnaire includes only those faculty who, in the prior question, reported that they had "sometimes" or "frequently" avoided expressing themselves. Approximately one-half of professors who self-censor say that they avoid expressing views because they are concerned about hurting students' feelings or confusing students. Democrats and Independents are more likely to cite this as a concern than are Republicans. If sensitivity to "hurt feelings" is a measure of political correctness, it is interesting to note that this appears to censor faculty on the left of the political scale more so than those on the right. This may be an indication that faculty on the left are simply more concerned with offending students' sensibilities, a claim that is consistent with conservative critiques of the politically correct campus environment. However, we have yet to hear anyone suggest that the problem on campus is that liberals, because of their concern for students' feelings, are self-censoring their own speech. This may, in fact, be the case. The question remains, which views are they withholding? Are they sensitive to the feelings of conservative students with whom they may disagree, or are they being especially vigilant not to offend the groups of people who are typically offered protection under campus speech codes? It is possible that Democrats are simply exercising the oversensitivity and restraint that conservatives claim they require of others.

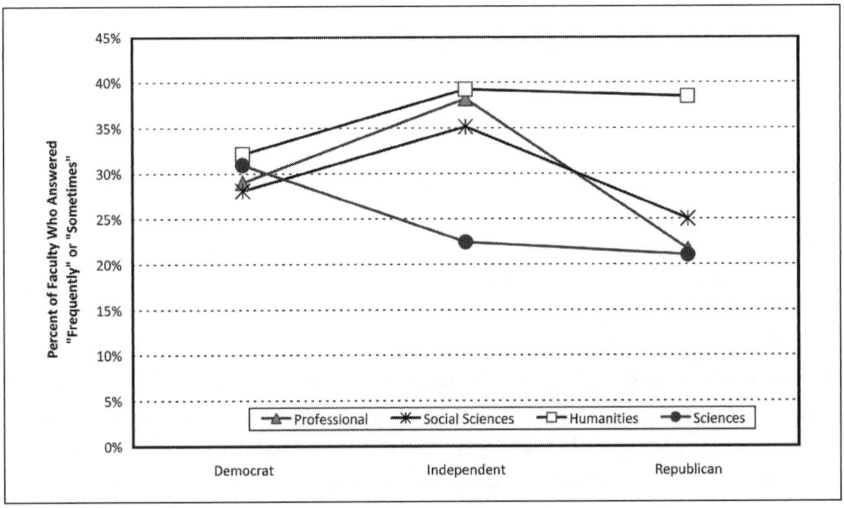

Figure 6.2. Faculty Member "Frequently" or "Sometimes" Avoids Expressing Any Particular Points of View Because of Reactions from Other Faculty

Table 6.8. Faculty Avoided Expressing Points of View because Worried about Student Reaction (First Response)

	Democrat	*Independent*	*Republican*	*Total*
Hurt feelings/confuse students	47%	50%	38%	47%
Complaints to administration	21%	19%	24%	21%
Other	13%	10%	18%	12%
Poor student evaluations	11%	10%	6%	10%
Don't know	6%	9%	12%	8%
Lower enrollment in class	2%	2%	3%	2%
Total	100%	100%	100%	100%
n	373	236	68	677

The second most common reason that faculty members give for withholding views from students is that they are concerned that students will complain to the administration. Recognizing the limited sample size, there is no meaningful difference between Republican members of the faculty and Democrats. The fact that Democrats are about as likely to state this as a concern raises questions as to the nature of this response. It is possible that students of both political persuasions complain when faculty offer opinions that contradict their own. However, if political sensitivities do stifle debate, it appears to affect members of both political parties.

A small but significant number of professors, 10 percent of those who withhold viewpoints, openly admit that they avoid expressing opinions in order to avoid negative student evaluations. While this is not a large percentage of the faculty, the survey question is open ended and asks faculty members to volunteer their concerns. It is possible that those who cite concern for hurting students' feelings are also concerned with how this affects their teaching evaluations. Also, faculty members may alter other aspects of their course in order to improve teaching evaluations. As Haskell (1997) has argued, faculty may adjust grading standards, rigor, teaching style, and course content under the assumption that these things affect student satisfaction with the course.

Perhaps one of the most revealing findings from the NAASS, relating to faculty partisanship and academic freedom, comes from a pair of questions intended to gauge the prevalence of discrimination within the university. Nested with a series of questions about the prevalence of discrimination against women, minorities, homosexuals, and religious groups, the survey included two queries about the seriousness of discrimination against those with "left-wing political views" and "right-wing political views." Overall, only 7 percent of professors reported that persons with "left-wing political views" faced "fairly serious" or "very serious" discrimination. Only 5 percent of professors concluded that persons with "right-wing political views" faced "fairly serious" or "very serious" discrimination. Figure 6.3 breaks these results down by the professor's party affiliation. Indeed, Republican professors tend to see discrimination against their favored group as more serious than against the opposite point of view. Even within the left-dominated academic environment, Democratic professors tend to see "left-wing" discrimination as more serious than "right-wing" discrimination. Furthermore, within all three groups, a very small percentage of the professors felt that political discrimination of any kind was a "fairly serious" or "very serious" problem.

Looking at party affiliation in general, these results raise some interesting questions. We do not find that Republicans are more reluctant to express their views on a college campus. One must be careful in interpreting this result. This does not necessarily mean that Republicans are treated fairly or that their colleagues are respectful of their opinions. Rather, it merely suggests that Republicans do not hold their tongues simply because they are in the minority. Republicans who choose to enter academia do so with the knowledge that they will encounter opposition to their views. Those who are squeamish about controversy may self-select out of the profession, leaving the academy with a small group of particularly outspoken Republicans. It is also important to note that the opinions that faculty are withholding may not be related to politics at all but, rather, could have more to do with campus policies, student performance, or other issues. Professors may withhold opinions about their

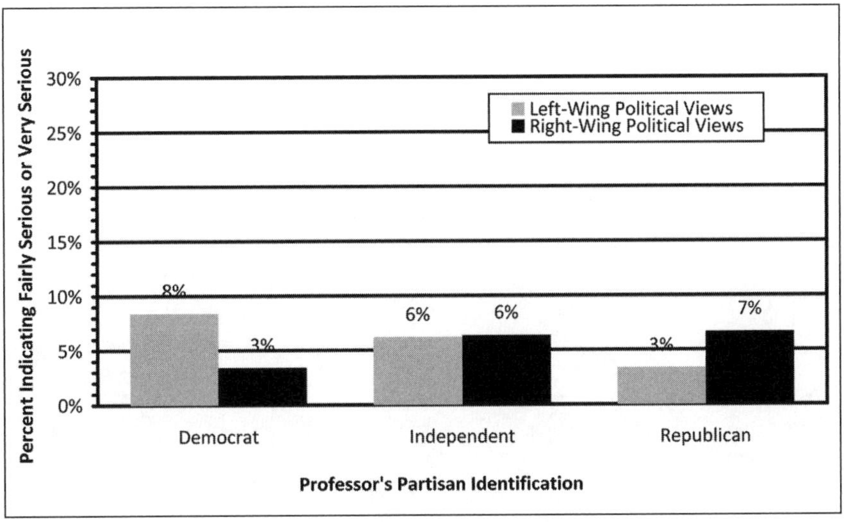

Figure 6.3. Seriousness of Discrimination against People with Left- or Right-Wing Viewpoints

colleagues or campus administrators. Professors may also withhold opinions about a students' aptitude or performance. In conversations with colleagues, professors may refrain from criticizing committee decisions, course proposals, and other matters of faculty governance, especially if they perceive their position to be unpopular and do not want to expend social capital to fight a losing battle. Often, these institutional battles divide the faculty along lines unrelated to political orientation.

We also considered whether the willingness to express viewpoints is related to a professor's academic rank. We find, as one might expect, that assistant professors, who are unlikely to be tenured, are most likely to self-censor. However, we were surprised to find that associate professors behave more like assistant professors than they do full professors. It would appear, based on the results in table 6.9, that tenure and promotion to associate professor do not create the free exchange of ideas that one might expect. Full professors, however, do behave differently, as they are significantly more likely to report that they "never" avoid expressing views for fear of faculty or student reactions. Our findings are consistent with those of Ceci, Williams, and Mueller-Johnson (2006), who also find that assistant and associate professors behave similarly. They conclude that tenure does not provide the sort of academic freedom it promises. Associate professors still depend on positive reviews from their colleagues for further promotion, committee appointments, merit pay, and other benefits.

Table 6.9. How Often, if at All, Did the *Faculty* Respondent Avoid Expressing Any Particular Points of View because of . . .

	Assistant Professor	*Associate Professor*	*Full Professor*	*Total*
A Negative Reaction from Other Faculty				
Frequently	8%	7%	6%	7%
Sometimes	34%	28%	16%	24%
Rarely	32%	34%	37%	35%
Never	26%	32%	41%	35%
Total	100%	100%	100%	100%
n	400	494	668	1,562
A Negative Reaction from Students				
Frequently	8%	7%	5%	6%
Sometimes	34%	33%	22%	28%
Rarely	32%	33%	37%	35%
Never	26%	27%	37%	31%
Total	100%	100%	100%	100%
n	402	493	666	1,561

Student Expression

Students in our survey also responded to questions about whether they avoid expressing views because of the reactions of professors or other students (see table 6.10). Several observations are useful. First, students are slightly less likely to self-censor than are college professors. Second, they are more likely to withhold opinions because of other students' reactions than they are because of faculty reactions. While 30 percent of students claim that they frequently or sometimes avoid expressing views because of student reactions, only 23 percent avoid expressing views because of faculty reactions. This may be true simply because students have greater interaction and more conversations with other students, so the frequency of self-censoring may be a function of the number of opportunities for disagreement. Students do not differ in their willingness to express opinions according to party affiliation.

Our findings are consistent with the results of a large-scale survey of students conducted at the University of Georgia (Bason 2008). According to the survey of over 15,000 students in the Georgia state university system, students believe that their professors are more respectful of others' opinions than are their peers. The results from the Georgia survey are also similar to ours in terms of the number of students who believe there is a problem with free expression in the classroom. According to the students surveyed in Georgia,

Table 6.10. How Often, if at All, Did the *Student* Respondent Avoid Expressing Any Particular Points of View because of . . .

	Democrat	*Independent*	*Republican*	*Total*
A Negative Reaction from Faculty				
Frequently	5%	5%	3%	4%
Sometimes	18%	19%	22%	19%
Rarely	37%	33%	38%	36%
Never	41%	44%	38%	41%
Total	100%	100%	100%	100%
n	495	556	415	1,466
A Negative Reaction from Other Students				
Frequently	6%	4%	5%	5%
Sometimes	24%	25%	27%	25%
Rarely	37%	33%	38%	36%
Never	33%	37%	31%	34%
Total	100%	100%	100%	100%
n	495	556	415	1,466

66 percent feel that they can freely discuss important public issues in class, without fear that their professor will criticize them. There is a small difference between Republicans and Democrats on this question, with 64 percent of Republican students feeling free to discuss issues and 74 percent of Democrats feeling the same. Students in the Georgia state system are even less willing to discuss religious issues in class, with Republicans, again, falling below the Democrats.

While the majority of students feel free to discuss their viewpoints most of the time, the fact that a sizable group does not feel so inclined may still raise some important questions about the discourse in higher education. As college professors lament the lack of student participation in class discussion or students' disinterest in the political process, perhaps they should be concerned that nearly a quarter of their students have viewpoints they are unwilling to share because of a fear that the professor will respond negatively. In fact, one of the standard items on student evaluation forms is a question measuring the extent to which the professor encouraged students to share their own viewpoints, under the assumption that higher scores on this scale measure better teaching. It is important to recognize that students' fears about others' reactions may be unfounded. However, professors bear the responsibility of setting the tone of discourse in their classes and may be able to reduce such fears by actively encouraging disagreement and demonstrating an appreciation for counterarguments.

Administrator Expression

One of our more striking findings, shown in table 6.11, is that college administrators report the greatest amount of self-censoring. When administrators are asked to estimate how often they avoid expressing views to avoid a negative reaction from faculty, 39 percent respond that they do so frequently or sometimes. This is significantly higher than the number of students who fear a faculty reaction (23 percent) or the number of faculty who fear their colleagues' reactions (31 percent). Republican administrators were slightly more likely to self-censor than were their Democratic counterparts, but the difference between the groups is relatively small.

More important, table 6.12 reveals that administrators who "usually agree" with their faculty are more likely to express their viewpoints than are administrators who only "sometimes agree" with their faculty. Among administrators who only sometimes agree with the faculty about the direction of the institution, half say that they frequently or sometimes avoid expressing their viewpoints. Again, this raises some question about the climate for dialogue on college campuses. A fair number of administrators appear to be concerned that expressing their honest viewpoints will jeopardize collegial relationships with faculty. In general, administrators suffer more public scrutiny because of their leadership roles and position as representatives of the institution. They may simply be more careful about what they say in general. However, the question wording does reveal that there is some concern not merely for public perception but also for the specific reactions of faculty members. These findings also seem to suggest that many administrators do not trust that the fac-

Table 6.11. How Often, if at All, Did the Administrator Respondent Avoid Expressing Any Particular Points of View because of a Negative Reaction from the Faculty?

	Administrators					
	Democrat	*Independent*	*Republican*	*Total*	*Faculty*	*Students*
Frequently	6%	5%	3%	6%	6%	4%
Sometimes	33%	32%	40%	34%	25%	19%
Rarely	39%	38%	34%	38%	35%	36%
Never	22%	25%	22%	23%	34%	41%
Total	100%	100%	100%	100%	100%	100%
n	400	292	99	791	1,547	1,466

Table 6.12. Administrator Avoids Expression versus Agrees with Faculty

		When it comes to the direction your institution is going, does administrator respondent usually agree with their faculty?					
		Always Agree	*Usually Agree*	*Sometimes Agree*	*Usually Disagree*	*Always Disagree*	*Total*
How often did administrator avoid expressing a particular point of view because he or she expected a negative reaction from their faculty?	Frequently	0%	4%	10%	0%	—	6%
	Sometimes	20%	31%	39%	17%	—	33%
	Rarely	20%	39%	36%	50%	—	38%
	Never	60%	25%	15%	33%	—	23%
	Total	100%	100%	100%	100%	—	100%
	n	5	562	228	6	0	801

ulty will respond well to disagreement, at least when it comes from administrative ranks. College professors appear to either be less concerned about maintaining collegial relationships among themselves or else place greater faith in their ability to politely disagree with one another.

SPIRAL OF SILENCE?

For all three campus constituent groups, we find little or no difference between Democrats and Republicans in their willingness to express viewpoints. Among professors, Republicans seem to be slightly less concerned about reactions from their colleagues than are Democrats. This is a perplexing finding given that a number of studies conclude that willingness to express viewpoints is related to the perception that one's views are supported by others. This is especially true in environments that involve close personal networks. One is more likely to disagree with a stranger than with a friend, family member, or other close acquaintance. Accordingly, we should expect that Republicans speak less freely in an academic environment given the overwhelming evidence that their perspective places them in the minority. Why is this not the case?

According to the spiral of silence theory (Noelle-Newman 1974), people are less likely to express views when they perceive those views to be in the minority for fear of social isolation. However, people's perceptions of agreement with others are not always accurate. For example, those in the minority may underestimate the number of people who agree with them. This further suppresses their willingness to voice opposition to the majority, which contributes to others misjudging the strength of the opposition as well.

The NAASS asked professors, administrators, and students to judge their political orientation relative to that of the faculty body. When we measure people's political orientations in terms of their perceived relation to others, we do see a connection between political isolation and willingness to express viewpoints. Among all three groups of survey respondents in figure 6.4, individuals who believe that their political orientation differs from the faculty are more likely to report that they withhold viewpoints because they expect a negative reaction from the faculty. The relationship is strongest among students. Of those students who believe professors are similar to them, only 9 percent report that they frequently or sometimes avoid expressing their viewpoints out of concern for faculty reaction. Among those who believe that professors are very much to the left of themselves, 47 percent avoid expressing views. When professors are perceived to be far to the right of the student, 38 percent hold back views. Among professors, we see a similar pattern, although the self-censoring occurs slightly more often when the professor believes that colleagues are to the right. The pattern holds for administrators, but the differences are not as substantial. Also, few administrators report that the faculty is "very much" different from themselves, so we have too few cases to examine what occurs when the perception of difference is substantial.

Given that one's perception of ideological distance from the faculty does predict one's willingness to express viewpoints, it is surprising to find little

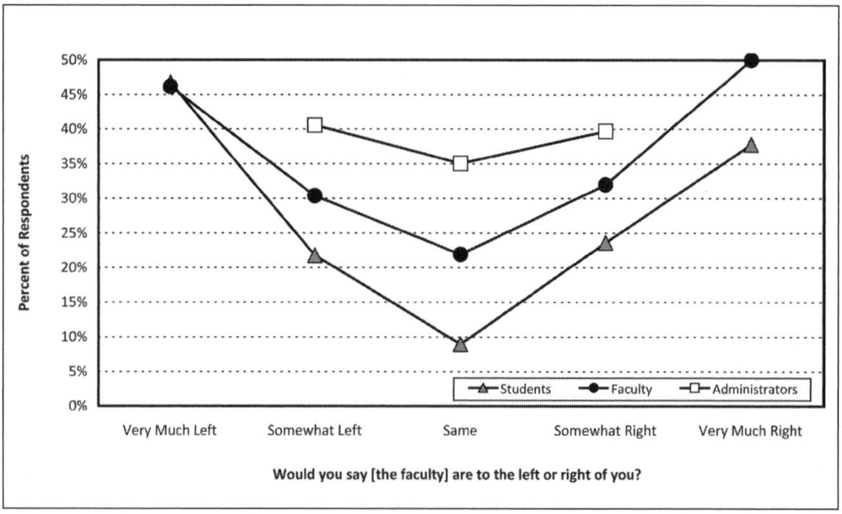

Figure 6.4. Frequently or Sometimes Avoid Expressing Particular Point of View Because You Expect Negative Reaction from Faculty

relationship between party affiliation and expression of views. Presumably, Republicans would know that they are in the minority and would respond accordingly.

After reviewing surveys on faculty politics, it is difficult to imagine how anyone within the academy could perceive it to be a conservative environment. Yet perception is relative. Those who fall toward the far left end of the political scale will find the campus to be conservative relative to their own views, even if it is liberal compared to the environment outside the academy. For example, feminist scholars continue to charge that the academy is hostile to feminist scholarship. Hart (2006) argues that the academy is "entrenched in the power of patriarchy." The author reviews the major journals in higher education and concludes that, despite the influx of women into the academy, "academic culture has changed very little. There is a paucity of explicitly feminist scholarship in the journals under investigation." In *Anti-Feminism in the Academy* (Clark et al., 1996), a number of authors outline what they perceive to be a backlash against feminist thought within the academy, affecting scholarship, teaching, and hiring decisions (also see Superson and Cudd 2002). Hart observes that the feminist scholarship that does get published tends to be "liberal feminism," which she regards as a traditional, mainstream form of feminism. In calling for a wider acceptance of more radical feminism, Hart demonstrates that there are competing pressures on the academy. At the same time that conservatives criticize the academy for being left of center, which the survey data supports, those who are even farther to the left claim that the academy is not open to their ideas. As such, perceptions of political solidarity vary, and, as we see in our analysis, it is this perception of isolation that stifles discourse on the college campus.

CONCLUSION

In their mission to create and interpret art, culture, and science, academics require a certain degree of autonomy from outside interference. While the public debate on academic freedom often centers on tolerance for political diversity, we find that a number of other threats, both from outside the university and from within, are of greater concern among professors and administrators. In our efforts to understand the state of academic freedom at the turn of the century, we examined the debate from the broadest possible perspective, considering a number of important factors that pertain to academic freedom. These include various constituencies' perceptions of the threat to academic freedom, the importance of tenure, perceptions of discrimination against various political orientations, and the impact of others on free expression.

Perhaps not surprisingly, there is a great deal of agreement among academics about the state of free expression within the academy, with both professors and administrators in agreement that academic freedom is generally secure. Consistently, respondents are inclined to see academic freedom as more secure at their own campus when compared to higher education in the abstract. Predictably, administrators are consistently more sanguine about the status of academic freedom than are their counterparts among the faculty. While professors and administrators of all political persuasions tend to think of academic freedom as either "very" or "somewhat" secure, Republican academics report more confidence in the state of academic freedom than do their Democratic counterparts.

When faculty and administrators are asked to identify the threats to academic freedom, the results are somewhat surprising. Among the faculty, Republicans, Independents, and Democrats alike do not focus on the government, which is often portrayed as a major threat to scholarly autonomy, but rather on their own administrators as the principal threat to academic freedom. Concerns about the government are the second most identified source of threat, followed by business, the public, religion, and the faculty itself. Among the limited number of administrators who actually perceived there to be some threat to academic freedom, the sources of threat are evenly divided among the government, the public, and, astoundingly, the administration.

Tenure, often criticized by those outside of academia as contributing to radicalism, sloth, and mediocrity, is supported by both faculty and administrators alike. For the most part, there is widespread support for the practice among those employed by the university. Whereas relatively few faculty and administrators elect to characterize tenure as unimportant, faculty are consistently more enthusiastic about the practice, identifying it as "essential" 34 percent of the time compared to a mere 16 percent of administrators. However, the most striking difference on the importance of tenure occurs among members of the faculty themselves, wherein we identify at least four distinct factors that contribute to a professor's view of tenure. These factors include one's general perceptions of the threat to academic freedom, one's partisan leanings, one's length of service as a professor, and one's general field of study. Yet, despite academics' strong support for the concept of security, when pressed, a vast majority of respondents felt that institutions should have the right to oust professors whom they characterize as "deadwood," even if they had previously been awarded tenure. This is a powerful indication that, among academics, tenure is not so much about job security as a protection for those who remain active and productive as members of the faculty.

Overall, faculty, students, and administrators claim that they feel free to express their personal viewpoints. Among the professors in the study, Republicans are the least likely to report that they "frequently" or "sometimes" avoid expressing opinions, fearing the reaction of others, while political Independents express the most concerns. Again, running counter to widespread claims of ideological persecution in academia, relatively few professors believe that political discrimination is a serious problem on their campus.

It should come as no surprise that full professors engage in less self-censorship than do their junior colleagues. However, the most dramatic difference is not between assistant professors and associate professors but rather between associate professors and full professors. While the reasons for this difference may be complex, these results seem to suggest that, as far as freeing academics to express themselves freely, the security provided by tenure may be less important than seniority itself. Even after winning tenure, many academics may be playing it safe in an effort to improve their standing among those who will continue to judge their service and employment.

Students, too, seem to feel relatively free to express themselves, indicating that they engaged in self-censorship "rarely" or "never." However, unlike the faculty, students do not seem to guard their remarks on the basis of their politics. Roughly the same percentage of Democrats and Republicans state that they "sometimes" or "frequently" avoid remarks because they fear the reaction of students or faculty, with concern about other students' reactions being more common than fear about faculty reactions.

The segment of the academy that engages in the most frequent self-censorship is the administration. Some 40 percent of administrators claim that they "sometimes" or "frequently" avoid remarks because they are concerned about the reaction of the faculty. Again, self-identified Republican administrators express only slightly higher levels of caution as compared to Democrats, perhaps indicating that, whatever the basis of their restraint, it is probably unrelated to the traditional ideological divides that often polarize public debates elsewhere.

Perhaps the most interesting finding pertaining to self-censorship concerns how people perceive themselves relative to others. While we find little difference in rates of self-censorship on the basis of political affiliation, each of the university's chief constituencies seems to limit their remarks less frequently when they perceive that faculty members share their beliefs. This self-censoring occurs on both sides of the political divide and demonstrates that academia operates much like other social environments, with people placing greater emphasis on social acceptance and collegiality than on the honest search for truth. The fact that people refrain from expression when they perceive themselves to be in the minority is especially problematic in an environment that is meant to foster new ideas. This finding appears to give some credence to Klein and Stern's (2009) argument that academia is prone to "groupthink."

Overall, data from the NAASS reveal that, as of the turn of the century, members of the academy remained relatively confident in their academic freedoms. With that said, we do find some cause for concern. Although it appears to be unrelated to party affiliation, a fair number of those within the academy report that they sometimes withhold viewpoints because of concerns that others will react negatively. While defenders of the university will be quick to point out that this is a minority, one must ask what level of opinion suppression is acceptable in the free marketplace of ideas. One-quarter of students and even greater numbers of faculty and administrators believe that others will react negatively to disagreement, and, as a result, they avoid sharing their ideas. While this may not be cause for alarm, it does suggest that there is considerable room for improvement.

Chapter Seven

Conclusion

The American system of higher education has undergone significant changes since the founding of the first colonial colleges. Whereas a college education was once reserved for the wealthy and elite, higher education has become a highly prized public utility. The American people clearly regard advanced education as the gateway to individual success and the engine of national prosperity. For the most part, the public holds America's colleges and universities in high esteem. Public opinion polls show that Americans have greater confidence in their institutions of higher education than they do in their government institutions, religious organizations, or the media (Gross and Simmons 2006). Yet public criticism of higher education does appear to be on the rise, leading policy analysts to conclude that "the bloom is off the rose" (National Center for Public Policy and Higher Education 2008).

In the past two decades, some rather harsh critiques of America's colleges and universities have garnered a significant amount of public attention. Published under such provocative titles as *Tenured Radicals* (Kimball 1990), *Freefall of the American University* (Black 2004), *Brainwashed* (Shapiro 2004), *The Shadow University* (Kors and Silverglate 1998), and *The Closing of the American Mind* (Bloom 1987), a continuous stream of books lament the crises of American higher education. Criticism from conservative political corners tends to be the most pointed, with charges that the academy is a haven for liberal radicalism and that educational goals have given way to social and political agendas.

Yet criticisms of the academy are not limited to political pundits and conservative gadflies. Rather, difficult questions about higher education have permeated public policy debates and Washington culture, resulting in the formation of organizations dedicated to exposing inadequacies in higher education and demanding institutional change. Examples of these institutions include the National Association of Scholars, the American Council of Trustees and Alumni, and the Foundation for Individual Rights in Education. Policymakers and government officials have taken note of the critiques offered by these organizations as well as the growing public dissatisfaction with the cost of higher education. As a result, state and federal officials have expanded their review of education beyond primary and secondary education. In 2006, a national panel created by Secretary of Education Margaret Spellings sent a shock wave through the higher-education community when the members declared in their report that U.S. higher education requires "urgent reform." The Spellings Commission report received a great deal of criticism from the higher-education community, both for its specific recommendations about educational reform and for the general expansion of government involvement in the workings of the academy. In general, the higher-education community's response to the report reflected a common complaint among academics that those on the outside fail to appreciate the culture, practices, and goals of the academy. For example, the Association of American Colleges and Universities (AAC&U) criticized the report for focusing on the narrow goal of workforce preparation, which fails to appreciate the academy's broad educational goals and commitment to liberal education. The AAC&U also criticized the report's recommendation that student progress be measured through standardized testing, which may not account for the differences in students' learning experiences or capture broad gains in critical thinking, cognitive development, and values clarification (Association of American Colleges and Universities 2006).

The academy appears to be more receptive to critiques offered by insiders, who express the same basic values and can speak in terms familiar to academics. Yet even insiders have offered compelling arguments that American colleges and universities are underperforming and could be doing better (see Bok 2006). Whether or not academics agree on the challenges facing higher education, there does appear to be some consensus that changes in the system are necessary in order for the nation's universities to remain competitive. According to the AAC&U, higher education must adapt and respond to changing demographics, new enrollment patterns, increased regulation, cuts in state funding, and other external factors that place new demands on our colleges and universities. It is not change, per se, that the academy resists. However, those within the academy often disagree with one another or with the general public on the direction that change should take.

Citizens have very different views concerning the main purpose of American's colleges and universities. For some, college is nothing more than a gateway to a career, providing a credential required of most employers to get a good job. Others view the institution as a center for research and discovery, an engine for the arts, literature, and science. Some even regard academia as an important agent of socialization, charged with disseminating important social values to the leaders of the next generation. As such, demands on the university often tug on it from different directions. While some call for the depoliticization of what they perceive to be a radical political environment, others argue that the real problem with higher education is that people discuss political matters too infrequently (see Smith, Mayer, and Fritschler 2008). While the Obama administration calls on colleges to provide practical career training, others lament trends toward vocational training in higher education. While government institutions and accreditation agencies demand objective assessment indicators, others view government intrusion into the university as a disruptive force. Regardless of its institutional trajectory, the future of higher education will likely involve considerable controversy.

Even as the public debates the competing proposals to reform America's colleges and universities, constituencies within the academy battle to shape higher education on their own terms. Faculty members, administrators, and students all place their own demands on the institution. Occasionally, we find that these groups agree on the basic goals of the university, but more often, we find that those within the university bring different values and assumptions to the table, making productive dialogue difficult. Even when the internal constituents appear to be in general agreement on the goals of the academy, we find that their shared assumptions conflict with those of the general public.

Disagreement within the university is not inherently harmful. Nor is the difference in perspective between the academy and external stakeholders always a liability. In fact, the exchange of competing ideas, at least in theory, has the potential to generate productive discussion and reflection on the mission and goals of the university. Research on group deliberation concludes that disagreement within the group enhances the quality of decision making (Schulz-Hardt et al. 2006). However, our analysis demonstrates that there are some serious obstacles to meaningful deliberation on the future of higher education. In order for debate and deliberation to have positive effects, the actors engaged must agree on the terms of debate, value one another's perspectives, and be willing to work together to find solutions. As is, we find that the various actors often do not agree on the interpretation of the facts before them, let alone on the problem and its solutions. Differences in agendas, core assumptions, and values will make dialogue difficult on many of the issues currently facing the academy. An understanding of how competing perspectives influence university culture should help to inform any discussion of American higher education.

ACCESS AND AFFORDABILITY

On the surface, institutions of higher education, policymakers, and the public all agree on the basic goals of expanding educational opportunity and making college more affordable. The issues of access and affordability are key components of the Spellings Commission report, which concludes that "too many students are either discouraged from attending college by rising costs, or take on worrisome debt burdens in order to do so." Educational associations and university presidents agree that tuition costs are rising but contend that since instructional costs are fixed, tuition increases are required to offset cuts in state funding (Fong 2005; National Education Association 2003). Yet the Spellings Commission's recommendations for improving affordability are a stark contrast to those who demand more student loans and government subsidies. According to the Spellings Commission report, the current financing system provides little incentive for universities to improve efficiency and productivity. Rather, public subsidies tend to "insulate" colleges and universities from "the consequences of their own spending decisions." As such, the commission recommended a "focused program of cost cutting and productivity improvements" in order to make college more affordable.

While colleges and universities are correct to point out that most students do not pay the full tuition price, the public continues to express sticker shock, citing tuition costs as their number one concern about higher education. When asked about the major problems facing the university, students appear to respond much like the general public, citing rising costs as their primary area of concern. Professors and administrators appear to be out of touch with the demands of their students, policymakers, and the public. Data from the North American Academic Study Survey (NAASS) demonstrates that professors and administrators are not concerned about tuition costs. Rather, they are concerned about their institution's lack of financial resources. While the public believes that colleges and universities could do more or the same with less, administrators believe that spending cuts would sacrifice educational quality and student services. In fact, both professors and administrators believe that college education is still a good value. Indeed, the NAASS provides evidence that professors, students, and administrators alike perceive quality to be better at colleges with higher per-student expenditures. However, the relationship is not as strong as one might expect, with minor differences in quality ratings between schools with radical differences in expenditures. Additionally, it is not clear whether more objective measures of educational quality would show the same relationship, nor can we establish the causal direction of the relationship. It is quite possible that a university's reputation generates financial resources rather than the other way around. Still, professors and administrators cite lack of funding as a primary concern, indicating that they believe they could do a better job of educating students if they had more money to spend. Whether or not this is objectively the case, the perception is important. The gap between the public perception and the views of those within the academy is most apparent in times of economic hardship. In response to a drop in revenue created by a recession or other economic hardship, state legislatures typically trim government spending, often placing heavy burdens on publicly funded colleges. In an attempt to offset the decline in public financing, many colleges and universities elect to raise student tuition and fees rather than to cut operating costs (Mincer 2008). In the midst of hard economic times, these sudden increases in tuition often generate a public backlash. These ill-timed tuition hikes also tend to anger state legislatures that demand that public universities justify their actions (Martin 2009).

Several real life examples illustrate the tension surrounding financing for higher education. As state governments make efforts to lower educational costs, colleges and universities seek additional revenue. The situation came to a head in 2009, when Pennsylvania's governor, Ed Rendell, cited his lack of control over tuition increases and operating costs as one of his reasons for excluding Penn State University and three other state-affiliated institutions from his plans to spend the state's allocated federal stimulus money (Schackner 2009a). In response, the university issued several press releases, informing students and others that the lack of stimulus money would force the university to raise tuition by nearly 10 percent rather than 4.5 percent (Schackner 2009b). By appealing to public concerns about tuition costs, the university was able to mount a political offensive. The majority of Pennsylvania's congressional delegation petitioned the Department of Education, which subsequently instructed the governor to resubmit his spending proposal to include funding for Penn State and the three other state-related universities. Given the competitive nature of college admissions, it is unlikely that colleges and universities will make voluntary cuts to expenditures. If anything, budget restraints serve to help curtail an arms race of spending, with institutions competing to provide the best facilities and most attractive student services.

Yet some institutions attempt to reconcile these seemingly competing priorities by offering lower tuition costs as an incentive to expand their applicant pool and, by extension, the number of highly qualified students who seek admission to the school. A focus on thrift provides some schools with a unique opportunity to attract the best among cost-conscious educational consumers. However, lowering or simply constraining tuition in the service of educational quality has it limits. Presuming that college admission officers take full advantage of lower tuition in attracting better students, the professoriate are then left to make do with less, providing fewer financial resources for infrastructure, equipment, teaching, and research. Paradoxically, even if some colleges manage to raise admission standards by holding the line on costs, the decline in tuition revenue may make it more difficult to educate students once they arrive, with fewer resources for infrastructure, equipment, teaching, and research. However, this is open for some debate. While those within the academy believe that lack of resources hinders educational outcomes, the public believes that more can be done with less, a concept echoed by some educational reformers.

Apart from their desire to constrain the growing cost of higher education, politicians have consistently sought to expand educational opportunities in higher education, providing an ever-growing number of Americans the opportunity to attend college. While professors and administrators hardly resist the public's interest in expanding educational opportunities (particularly when it comes at public expense), the drive for universal access to higher education tends to marginalize the central priority of faculty and administrators, namely, educational quality. If President Obama's vision of every American obtaining some college education is realized, institutions of higher education will be called on to educate an ever broader cross section of the public, many of whom are ill prepared for the demands of higher education. Inevitably, as a college education becomes more common, the overall quality of students entering the academy will decline. This educational transformation has important consequences for the university as a whole, one of which is to create greater differences between elite institutions and those that aim to serve the masses.

While American colleges and universities have always been stratified, based on students' aptitude and financial resources, these differences will continue to be exaggerated as mass education becomes universal education. Already, there is evidence that the achievement gap between institutions is growing, with top students migrating to a handful of elite institutions, more so than was previously the case (Cook and Frank 1993; Ehrenberg 2000). Hence, while more Americans may be attending college, all college degrees do not carry the same weight in a competitive job market. According to Ehrenberg (2000), large companies aim their recruitment efforts at elite, private institutions, making these institutions even more attractive to the top applicants. Debates about access to a college education will likely begin to resemble those centered on primary and secondary education, focusing not on basic accessibility but rather on differences in educational quality and opportunity available to various groups of students.

ACCOUNTABILITY AND ASSESSMENT

With greater public interest in higher education and growing concern over tuition prices, policymakers have attempted to make colleges and universities more accountable. According to the AAC&U, "Many campuses have found creative and sophisticated ways to gather evidence of student learning." The assessment movement aims to demonstrate that college education produces something of real value. Colleges and universities strive to demonstrate that they have met their goals and objectives: educating students and achieving institutional goals and missions.

The assessment movement, however, is not without controversy. On most every campus, some faculty members express reservation about how success and learning are measured. The concern is often that many of the broad learning goals of liberal education are not easily measured. As institutions rewrite their objectives, some skeptics charge that they define student learning according to their ability to measure it rather than on more principled discussions of the skills and abilities students ought to acquire. More important, those outside the academy often view the function of the university differently than those on the inside. If members of each group measure institutional effectiveness based on their own views about the purpose of higher education, they are likely to reach substantially different conclusions about how well our institutions are performing.

Within the university, we find broad support for the notion that universities exist to foster the exchange and creation of ideas. The NAASS finds that the vast majority of students, professors, and administrators believe that the primary role of the university is to encourage the exploration of new ideas. In this regard, the major actors within the university have a shared commitment to academic freedom and the basic components of a broad, liberal education. From the perspective of those on the inside, America's four-year colleges and universities are places of intellectual discovery first and foremost, and specific career training is a secondary goal at best.

Agreement within the university on the basic purpose of higher education is certainly an advantage for institutional decision making and strategic planning. However, colleges often have a difficult time articulating these goals to an outside audience. Faculty members in the liberal arts often field questions from concerned parents about the job opportunities that would be available to their son or daughter after graduating from college. In fact, the general public holds views and expectations of higher education that are in conflict with those of academics.

From a public perspective, universities exist primarily to train young people for work after college or even for a particular career. This difference in perspective means that much of the activity valued and rewarded within higher education is viewed with some skepticism by the outside world, which demands that faculty spend more time teaching and less time on their own research and professional development. If anything, the trend in higher education, even among small colleges, appears to be toward increasing faculty research and professional development. Many colleges have reduced teaching loads in recent years in order to encourage faculty scholarship. Professors are rewarded for securing outside research grants, and they perceive that research and publications have greater importance in tenure and promotion decisions than was once the case (Schuster and Finkelstein 2006). Academics tend to see professional activity as something that enhances their teaching, making them better all-around scholars. At the very least, faculty publications tend to enhance the reputation of the college or university, which leads to higher placement in reputational rankings and thus serves to attract better students. Yet concerns over the rising costs of higher education encourage those on the outside to question the use of tuition and tax dollars to fund activities that, on the surface, have no direct relationship to the workforce preparation they expect universities to provide.

While the assessment movement has caught on in higher-education circles, the academy has not yet come to terms with what it is the public demands. Most colleges and universities have begun to articulate learning objectives and make an effort to measure students' progress on these goals. However, the assessment of education is often instituted to satisfy policymakers and accreditation agencies rather than to meet some immediate educational objective. Accordingly, since assessment itself is often engineered to satisfy public concerns over the cost of skyrocketing tuition rather than to improve the quality overall, it is unclear whether the efforts to measure students' educational progress will ultimately bear fruit. Even if the academy can demonstrate that students have made tremendous academic progress over the course of their college careers, much of the public will nevertheless conclude that, given the high cost of tuition, the education could have been delivered more efficiently. To the extent that assessment is a response to public concerns over college affordability and efficiency, those colleges with higher price tags will need to offer some evidence that students gain proportionally more than their peers at less costly institutions.

Administrators, who can foresee this inevitable next step in the assessment movement and strive to demonstrate efficiency rather than mere learning, may be able to move their institutions into a more competitive position in the marketplace. Again, this presumes that the public is even aware of the assessment measurements and are making decisions on the basis of assessment results rather than on a school's community outreach and long-standing reputation.

Given their commitment to educational quality, a great many academics will cringe at the thought of promoting educational "efficiency." Yet the fact remains that students and parents are already informally making these cost–benefit calculations. Provided that the movement toward assessment in higher education continues, policymakers will most likely demand that universities readily disseminate this information, allowing students and parents to make more informed choices. Given Governor Rendell's efforts to divert local and national resources away from Penn State University (siphoning the proceeds to Pennsylvania's cheaper state schools and community colleges), it seems likely that other policymakers will seek to selectively fund those institutions that they deem to be both excellent and economically efficient.

Given the public's concerns about costs, the implementation of educational assessment procedures may continue for the foreseeable future. Nevertheless, it does not logically follow that such policies are automatically in the best interest of the academy. If the success of a university is measured in terms of student outcomes alone, many functions of the modern university may suffer. Research activities will likely come under assault unless the academy can demonstrate and articulate the value of these programs directly to their students. While graduate schools may have little difficulty justifying their research expenses, undergraduate programs, particularly in the humanities and social sciences, may find that the public regards their research activities as nonessential. Programs that produce community outcomes will also be difficult to fund unless they provide measurable direct benefits to students. The higher-education community clearly views its worth in terms that extend beyond vocational training. Colleges and universities aim to foster community development, facilitate social change, and encourage the creation of knowledge. However, the institution has, as a general rule, failed to effectively communicate this broad vision of purpose to the outside world.

SOCIAL CHANGE

One of the more controversial goals of higher education is that of fostering social and political change. The commitment to this goal varies from university to university and even from one college major to the next. However, it is relatively easy to find evidence of this commitment in college mission statements and on the websites of higher-education associations, which frequently discuss the importance of college education for expanding "social justice" and an appreciation for "diversity." The higher-education community is so committed to these issues that it frequently asserts them as a universal truth or basic human right.

The concept of social justice, however, is not universally valued in political circles. While some individuals understand social justice as a drive for basic human rights and legal protections, to others the concept is synonymous with a radical ideological agenda, inexorably tied to left-leaning social and economic policies.

The academy's flirtation with social justice is complicated by the fact that there is no clear, universal application of the term. For example, in the fight to seek social justice for America's underclass, advocates of social justice could take diametrically opposing positions on President Clinton's 1995 welfare reform. Arguing that the reforms successfully moved millions of Americans from welfare to work, supporters might claim that the program benefited the poor and therefore served to advance social justice. Conversely, opponents of the welfare reform could argue that restricting needy citizens' access to government assistance only worsened the effects of poverty on the most vulnerable Americans, thus making social justice more difficult to achieve. Critics like Friedrich Hayek (1976) refer to social justice as a "mirage," concluding that "the people who habitually employ the phrase simply do not know themselves what they mean by it and just use it as an assertion that a claim is justified without giving a reason for it" (xi). Indeed, philosophers have continually argued about the use and application of the concept (see Miller 1999), making it unlikely that an undergraduate student would clearly understand its meaning.

While a working definition of social justice remains elusive, on college campuses the term is more often than not associated with redistributive policies and government programs designed to help various groups of disadvantaged people (the poor, women, minorities, homosexuals, and so on). Since the means of achieving social justice typically involves the implementation of left-leaning social programs, it is inevitable that faculty, students, and administrators will view the university's role in its pursuit differently, depending on their ideological disposition.

Those who advocate incorporating social justice into the academy's mission often fail to recognize that there may be a legitimate alternative point of view. Yet surveys of the faculty, students, and administrators reveal several areas of contention over social justice and related issues. For example, while *equality* is clearly an important component of social justice, two-thirds of faculty, students, and administrators in our survey believe that ultimately *freedom* is a more important value. If programs aimed at fostering social justice are framed in terms of trade-offs between equality and freedom—a trade-off commonly invoked in debates on distributional policy—many of those within the academy may find reasons for concern. Nevertheless, the overwhelming majority of academics believe it is the government's role to reduce income inequality, a position that places the academy at odds with the general public. Again, the notion of social justice, in and of itself, may not be controversial to the majority of Americans, depending on how one defines the elusive concept. Yet actual efforts to promote social justice will likely raise more specific policy objections, especially in cases where the application of social justice involves redistribution of resources. To the extent that leaders in higher education promote the university as a vanguard of programmatic social justice, they will continue to clash with constituencies both inside and beyond the walls of the academy.

One of the most internally contentious issues relating to the academy and the promotion of social justice centers on race. Many within higher education believe that the academy has a role to play in reducing racial conflict and creating a more equal society. Indeed, fostering diverse learning environments is frequently listed as one of the primary objectives of universities and educational associations. As we argue in chapter 5, however, the academic community often fails to recognize that there is still some debate about the actual value of institutional diversity for learning and race relations. To say that people disagree on the issue of "diversity" is misleading, however, in that few people within the academy would argue that qualified blacks and other minorities should be kept out of predominantly white colleges and universities. Thus, it is not the goal of obtaining diversity, in and of itself, that is so controversial. Rather, the chief point of contention centers on the methods by which colleges and universities promote racial and ethnic diversity.

Given a limited pool of highly qualified blacks and the fact that many of them choose to attend a historically black college or university, administrators have argued that preferential admissions policies are necessary to admit more black and Latino students. It is this policy of preferential admissions that generates conflict not only among the university's internal constituents but also between the academy, the general public, policymakers, and the courts.

The majority of students are opposed to racial preferences in higher education both for student admissions and for faculty hiring. Students' views on issues of race appear to be closely aligned with those of the general public, with both groups being overwhelmingly opposed to race-based policies that would lower admissions and hiring standards. Professors and administrators are more supportive of racial preferences than students, but when asked to consider the trade-offs between diversity and admission standards, the majority of professors and administrators do not believe that more minorities should be admitted to their institutions if this would result in lower standards of admission. Clearly, many academics place a higher value on institutional reputation and student quality than they do on institutional diversity. So why do campuses appear to be overwhelmingly committed to increasing the diversity of the student body? In short, professors and administrators do not acknowledge that there is a conflict between obtaining a more diverse student body and maintaining current admissions standards, asserting that affirmative action policies have no substantive impact on academic quality.

The widely held belief that affirmative action policies will not impact academic quality is at a variance with much of the research on admission rates, minority yield, and student performance. Indeed, efforts to diversify campuses by admitting a higher proportion of racial and ethnic minorities come with a cost. As we discuss in chapter 5, minority students on campus enter with lower test scores, fewer college preparatory classes, and lower high school grade-point averages. Furthermore, these differences in preparation are not overcome during the course of four years but rather are exaggerated. The stigma of being the weakest students on campus may further impede academic success for some minority students.

Yet college professors are rarely asked to confront these complicated relationships. Although they weigh in on institutional goals and mission statements, they are not engaged in the specific policies or admissions decisions that are necessary to achieve their objectives, nor do they engage in a systematic evaluation of how different groups of students are faring academically. For this reason, it is fairly easy for many college professors to express support for the university's mission of obtaining a more diverse student body without having to surrender their commitment to academic selectivity and student quality.

University efforts to increase diversity on campus are further complicated by widespread public resistance to affirmative action policies, which are rooted in both an ideological opposition to its implementation and more pragmatic concerns about the cost of implementing such initiatives. Colleges and universities that aim to increase diversity are thus caught in a catch-22. If they lower admission standards to achieve diversity, they run the risk of suffering in institutional rankings that include measures of selectivity, student test scores, and graduation rates. If admissions standards for minority applicants are radically different than those for white applicants, the university also runs the risk of being dragged into public debates and legal action, as whites who are denied admission raise objections to their treatment. If schools do not lower admissions standards, then efforts to attract more minorities involve recruiting efforts, scholarships, and other costly solutions. In this case, efforts to increase diversity are juxtaposed to the public's most vocal demand that colleges and universities strive to contain costs.

Despite the difficulties associated with achieving diversity, college administrators remain staunchly committed to affirmative action policies. Beyond their belief that diversity is an essential component of higher education, it appears as though a commitment to activism and social justice contributes to administrators' continued support for difficult and often controversial policies.

Institutions of higher education have often been arenas for social change. The impetus for change, however, has shifted, from student-led protests to faculty and administrative initiatives. College campuses are not the same environments they were during the days of the student revolutions. In fact, many professors lament the lack of student interest in social issues and political causes. Thus, the push for social change is now driven from the top down.

On the issue of race and gender discrimination, we find that students perceive the college environment to be positive. This is true despite the fact that students are as likely as professors and administrators to report that America is a racist society. This suggests that students are not simply oblivious to issues of discrimination, as they perceive them to be present elsewhere. Yet students report little direct experience with discrimination and harassment and perceive these issues to be minor problems on campus. Professors are much more likely to perceive there to be a problem with racism, sexism, and other forms of discrimination. To put this in some perspective, it is worth noting that white professors believe racism on campus to be a bigger problem than do black students. This explains why professors and administrators are more likely than students to support efforts to increase student diversity in the name of social change. In chapter 5, we argue that there is actually considerable debate about the benefits of campus diversity for student relationships and racial attitudes. In fact, the evidence suggests that students' political and social attitudes are fairly constant across four years of college.

Consistent with other studies (Kelly-Woessner and Woessner 2006; Woessner and Kelly-Woessner, 2009a; Mariani and Hewitt 2008; Smith et al. 2008), we find no evidence to support the theory of mass political indoctrination. This does not mean that academics are always professional and neutral in their presentation of material. However, direct examination of undergraduate attitudes suggests that students are fairly resilient in their political orientations and that they tend to scrutinize or tune out information that challenges their preexisting beliefs (Kelly-Woessner and Woessner 2006; Woessner and Kelly-Woessner 2009a). The NAASS does suggest some difference in attitudes between first-year students and those in their senior year, with small gains in acceptance of homosexuality. However, juniors and seniors in the survey were almost 10 percent less likely than freshman to argue that government should work to reduce the gap between the rich and the poor. Other researchers do show a small shift to the left, with students associating more with the Democratic Party after four years of college, but note that the change is not large enough to constitute a major problem (Mariani and Hewitt 2008; Woessner and Kelly-Woessner 2009a).

In some cases, however, we see that different standards are used to measure attitude change, depending on the motivations of the researchers. When defending higher education from charges of ideological indoctrination, researchers conclude that a nine-percentage-point change in opinion is of little consequence. Yet when defending higher education's race-based admissions practices, researchers are quick to point to much smaller changes in students' racial attitudes as signs of program effectiveness. We conclude that, in both cases, students are fairly resistant to attitudinal change and that they, most often, leave campus with similar attitudes to those they brought with them. This is good news for the academy on the political indoctrination question but presents a problem for the future of race-based admissions policies.

This is not to say that discussion of values on campus is unimportant. Even if students do not move from one attitudinal position to another, it appears that discussion of their views can lead to clarification of values and deeper contemplation of competing issues. This may have the effect of polarizing students, as those on each side of the debate become more capable of articulating and defending their positions. Yet some cognitive skill may be gained from these deliberations. It is not clear from the existing evidence, however, that the proportion of blacks or other groups on campus have net positive effects on learning. While several researchers have made the claim, their motivations to arrive at this particular conclusion have led them to overstate their findings and/or ignore evidence to the contrary (see discussion in chapter 5). At the very least, it is safe to say that the evidence is mixed and, at this time, inconclusive.

However, in an effort to satisfy the U.S. Supreme Court's conditions for race-based admission policies, leaders in higher education have declared the debate closed, asserting that the evidence for educational benefits is undeniable. We argue that this position, while useful in defending university admissions policies, has grave consequences for our understanding of race relations on campus. Researchers tend to search only for positive benefits of institutional diversity, ignoring complicated effects of intergroup relations. Even when honest researchers do attempt to answer difficult questions about racial diversity, others tend to interpret their findings to suit their own needs, pointing to evidence that supports their agenda while ignoring contradictory evidence. On the issue of campus diversity, we find that honest dialogue and consideration of the evidence is difficult within the higher-education community. Given that students and the public perceive racial issues on campus to be of relatively minor concern, at least compared to the more pressing issue of college costs, the question the higher-education community will have to address is not merely whether diversity initiatives produce some benefits for students but, rather, whether the benefits they produce warrant the expense. The Supreme Court adds to the burden, requiring that universities demonstrate that the value of racial preferences to student learning is significant enough to override the Constitution's color-blind imperative.

It is understandable that institutions of higher education would attempt to protect their current practices from external influence. However, the fact that higher-educational associations have prematurely declared a consensus on this issue makes it difficult to trust their assessment of the evidence in the future. If leaders within higher education were truly motivated to understand intergroup relationships for the purpose of addressing them on campus, they would be well advised to spend some time considering the large body of research in social psychology on race relations rather than relying on reports produced by institutes charged with promoting and defending the rights and privileges of the academy.

POLITICS AND IDEOLOGY IN AMERICAN HIGHER EDUCATION

The ideological dominance of the left in academia is an interesting but perhaps an overly emphasized feature of American higher education. While the reasons for the left's dominance in the academy are numerous and fairly complex (Woessner and Kelly-Woessner 2009b), the importance of this ideological hegemony is open for considerable debate. Whereas prominent conservative thinkers like David Horowitz and Dennis Prager portray the university as an institution steeped in bitter ideological conflict, the results of the NAASS suggest otherwise.

In assessing the overall importance of politics in academia, it is important to acknowledge that ideology does play in important role in shaping opinions within the academy. On many of the key questions posed in the NAASS, the participants' partisan affiliation stood out as an important predictor of their response. Knowing if a professor is a Republican or a Democrat was very helpful in guessing what answer he or she would give on a point of controversy. These differences are not surprising when asking respondents to assess political questions dealing with the environment, abortion, and affirmative action. Beyond politics, the underlying philosophical differences that help to shape respondents' views of policy controversies also appear to play a role in their assessment of the university itself. Among Democratic faculty, 75 percent stated that the main purpose of the university is "to encourage exploration of new ideas." By contrast, only 54 percent of Republicans felt the same way. The perception of campus climate appears to be tied to politics as well, with substantially more Democratic faculty identifying discrimination based on race, sex, sexual orientation, and religion as a problem on their campus. Even the perception of academic freedom is linked to the respondents' partisan disposition, with Republican faculty and administrators more apt to characterize academic freedom as "very secure." Clearly partisanship/ideology is an important dividing line on most of the major issues that confront the university.

Lost in the discussion of political schisms, however, are important differences that exist among respondents based on nonideological attributes. On many of the large philosophical questions that confront the academy, there are deeply rooted differences between respondents based on sex, race, and academic disciplines. In most instances, the differences are not dramatic, but more often than not, these fault lines are clear and predictable. For example, among the professoriate, the value of tenure varies predictably by the sensitivity of their work and research. In the social sciences and humanities, 41 percent of respondents described tenure as "essential" to academic freedom, whereas 27 percent of those in the professional and natural science majors agreed. On the issue of race, most professors do not regard discrimination as a serious problem. As one might expect, however, women and minorities consistently rate concerns over discrimination and harassment as more important than their counterparts, even though a vast majority of respondents have never personally been the victim of discrimination. Perhaps the most interesting line of conflict within the institution arises between faculty and administrators. On most abstract political questions (the main exception being affirmative action), faculty and administrators look much the same. On any question related to the state of their campus or higher education, administrators are wildly optimistic compared to professors. Recognizing that ideology does play an important role in shaping higher education, scholars should not lose sight of the myriad of schisms that help to define conflict within the university. On a day-to-day basis, a typical professor's support for abstract political causes like military spending, universal health care, and abortion is probably less important than his or her view of concrete educational issues like curricular reform, faculty governance, and assessment.

The fact that ideology is but one of many competing points of conflict among faculty, students, and administrators becomes even more obvious when respondents are asked whether they have ever been treated unfairly as a result of "race, ethnicity, gender, sexual orientation, religious beliefs, or political views." Roughly 15 percent of respondents answered in the affirmative, citing mostly complaints about race or gender. Of the more than 1,500 faculty in the survey, only thirty-one individuals claimed that they had been treated unfairly because of their political beliefs, and of those, only nine professors felt that the unfair treatment constituted harassment. Students and administrators fared even better with just over 1 percent indicating that they had suffered unfair treatment because of their political beliefs. Lest one conclude that complaints about politics were infrequent because of the relatively few conservatives in the NAASS sample, it is worth noting that of the thirty-one faculty who reported mistreatment as a result of their politics, only three reported that they were Republicans.

Beyond the fact that very few professors expressed concern about their treatment resulting from their political beliefs, it is worth noting that Republican professors appear to be satisfied with their careers. When asked, "If you were to begin your career again, would you still want to be a college professor?," Republicans and Democrats gave virtually the same answer. For decades social scientists have observed that, on a variety of dimensions, Republicans tend to be happier than Democrats (Taylor 2008; Taylor, Funk, and Craighill 2006). This underling contentment means that researchers should be cautious not to assume, on the basis of their similar levels of career satisfaction, that Republicans and conservatives have exactly the same challenges and difficulties within the academy. Still, the relatively positive feedback given by Republicans in the NAASS suggests that, at least among those who choose to enter the academy, Republicans are satisfied with their experiences. Other studies demonstrate that the same is true of students. Republican students actually report the same satisfaction with their college careers than do Democrats, although they do tend to be less satisfied with courses in the humanities and social sciences (Woessner and Kelly-Woessner 2009b). It is also possible that Republican professors find themselves at institutions that are more sympathetic toward conservative perspectives. In fact, Rothman and Lichter (2009) find that conservatives are represented in lower proportions at select, elite universities.

Consistent with the findings of Rothman, Lichter, and Nevitte (2005), we do find evidence that, controlling for various measures of professional success, socially liberal professors tend to work at slightly more prestigious institutions than their socially conservative counterparts. The observed discrepancy is relatively small, but the results are consistent across a variety of statistical models. In light of the fact that a similar prestige gap can be observed among women and blacks, it is difficult to know if the discrepancy is the byproduct of discrimination or social choice. Indeed, there is evidence to suggest that, like women and blacks, social conservatives may be less motivated to seek out positions based largely on institutional prestige. Nevertheless, to the extent that this modest prestige gap among women and blacks is a cause for concern, administrators should be mindful of the possible impact of ideology in the recruitment and promotion process. Even the possibility of favoritism based on factors other than academic productivity raises questions about the fairness of the academy as a whole.

The fact that ideological conflicts do not appear to dominate the academy does not preclude the possibly that, in selective instances, faculty, students, and administrators fall victim to political mistreatment at the hands of their colleagues or superiors, just as the low reports of discrimination found in the NAASS results do not preclude the occasional episode of racial discrimination. One of the challenges for conservatives, much like those for any minority, is trying to determine which mistreatment is motivated by ideology and which mistreatment is caused by normal human interaction. The evidence simply does not support claims that politics and ideology play a pivotal role the quality of campus life for most professors, students, or administrators. However, people's perceptions of political isolation do have some impact on self-expression, though this is true on both sides of the political spectrum. Faculty appear to measure their support in relative terms, such that even liberal faculty may feel isolated if their views are left of the campus median.

Hidden within the NAASS is one potentially important fact that, along with other surveys of academic politics, has important implications for the academy. Aside from the fact that members of the Republican Party are seriously underrepresented within the academy, those who do serve as professors and administrators hardly embody the views of a typical Republican, whether we compare professors to Republicans in government or in the general population. Just over half of Republican professors can fairly be characterized as pro-choice. Nearly two-thirds expressed a desire for more environmental regulations. Nearly four in ten Republican professors believe that the government needs to work to reduce the gap between the rich and the poor. Beyond the shortage of self-identified Republicans, those who do work in academia appear to come from the more liberal wing of the party, are moderate on social issues, and are willing to embrace a greater role for the government in the economy. Particularly in the social sciences, where researchers consider important questions related to politics and policy, the absence of conservative-leaning scholars in the academy may mean that right-leaning ideological perspectives are not being thoroughly explored and that left-leaning ideas are not being vigorously challenged. Maranto, Redding, and Hess (2009) argue that, whatever the cause, the ideological imbalance in academia "limits the questions we ask and the phenomena we study, retarding our pursuit of knowledge and our ability to serve society" (5).

CAMPUS DIALOGUE

The results of the NAASS show that, on most questions, students, faculty, and administrators have markedly different views on issues of importance to the academy. Perhaps not surprisingly, on issues ranging from affirmative action to control of the curriculum, students tend to be outliers. Whereas faculty and administrators hold fairly similar views on a wide range of issues, significant and persistent differences emerge that have important implications for campus dialogue and shared governance.

For the most part, administrators perceive their institutions and higher education in more favorable terms than the faculty. This alone presents some challenge for dialogue. Faculty members who are critical of institutional practices or question educational quality are likely to find that their voices fall on deaf ears.

Similar to research on other organizational settings, we find evidence that one's position in the institutional hierarchy impacts one's willingness to express unpopular opinions. For students and professors, perception of ideological camaraderie appears to have some effect, with people self-censoring communication more often when they believe that others are ideologically different from themselves. With that said, the self-censorship rate among students is fairly low. For the most part, students perceive the campus to be a place for open dialogue. Surprisingly, administrators report the most self-censoring because of concerns for faculty reactions. Yet administrators and professors agree that, compared to the faculty, the administration has a great deal of influence in institutional policy. So what does administrative self-censorship really mean? We find that administrators' willingness to communicate viewpoints is based not on their ideological distance (i.e., liberal vs. conservative) from the faculty but rather on their perception that they disagree with the faculty on institutional goals. This would suggest that administrators simply elect to avoid conflict and debate with the faculty yet maintain control of campus decision. This view is supported by the faculty survey, which shows that faculty members who disagree with the administration perceive themselves to have less voice in institutional matters than agreeable faculty members. Hence, self-censorship among administrators appears to reduce faculty voice and input rather than administrative voice. This finding is consistent with some studies in organizational communication that show that managers may discourage upward dissent from employees. Without overstating the problem, we conclude that there are forces at work in the academy that discourage the free and open exchange of competing perspectives. While there is evidence that students and faculty are less likely to express themselves when they perceive they are a political minority, not all censorship is attributed to ideological difference. Rather, professors and administrators often disagree about institutional goals, objectives, spending priorities, and the daily operations of the institution. In an effort to move the institutional agenda forward without getting bogged down in unnecessary conflict, administrators may simply choose to communicate with those who agree with their objectives, electing to work with ad hoc committees rather than with faculty governance and more representative bodies. This may make institutional decision making more efficient. However, it also has the potential to reduce deliberation and may lead to institutional groupthink and the devaluation of those who are critical of administrative objectives.

In our analysis, we highlight some areas of contention and demonstrate that different groups of people enter the dialogue with their own values, perspectives, and agendas. While the NAASS data are based on surveys of students, professors, and administrators, we also compare the survey responses and perspectives with those of the public as measured by a number of opinion polls. Yet these are not the only forces at work within the contemporary university. Alumni, for example, are an important source of revenue for the university and, hence, may be given a great deal of voice in university matters. We also have not considered the role of trustees in determining the future and direction of higher education, nor do we know whether large donors have some voice in institutional affairs. In short, the processes at work to shape institutional policy and structure are complicated and difficult to capture in a large-scale study of the academy. Nonetheless, it is clear that there are multiple and sometimes competing demands on the academy. Thus, while change is inevitable, it is not clear what direction some of these changes will take. Given the variety of perspectives about American higher education, any institutional change will produce both winners and losers. Those who endeavor to influence such change should have some basic understanding of the values, priorities, and relationships within the academy that contribute to its ongoing evolution.

Appendix 1

List of Questions Used in the NAASS Survey

1. VIEWS OF HIGHER EDUCATION/QUALITY ISSUES

Question 1.1a

Faculty/Administrator Question: In general, how satisfied are you with your career? Let's use a scale from 1 to 7, where 1 means you are "very dissatisfied" and 7 means you are "very satisfied." You may use any number between 1 and 7 to describe your overall satisfaction with your career.

Student Question: In general, how satisfied are you with your university experience? Let's use a scale of 1 to 7, where 1 means you are "very dissatisfied" and 7 means you are "very satisfied." You may use any number between 1 and 7 to describe your overall satisfaction with your university experience.

Responses

(1) Very Satisfied – (7) Very Dissatisfied

Question 1.1b

Faculty Question: If you were to begin your career again, would you still want to be a college professor?

(1) Definitely yes
(2) Probably yes
(3) Probably no
(4) Definitely no
(9) DK, etc.

Question 1.2

Faculty/Student/Administrator Question: What would you describe as the most pressing problem confronting (American/Canadian) colleges and universities today?

(1) Quality—General/Declining
(2) Quality—Students' skills
(3) Quality—Teachers
(4) Courses/Curriculum
(5) Bureaucracy/Administration
(6) Funding/Need more $
(7) Tuition fees
(8) Other—Specify: __
(9) DK, etc.

Question 1.3

Faculty/Student/Administrator Question: Compared to other industrialized democracies, would you say the (American/Canadian) higher-education system is one of the very best in the world, better than most, more or less average, worse than most, or one of the very worst?

(1) One of very best
(2) Better than most
(3) More or less average
(4) Worse than most
(5) One of very worst
(9) DK, etc.

Question 1.4

Faculty/Student/Administrator Question: Overall, do you think your university (college) does (READ LIST) job of educating students?

(1) An excellent
(2) A good
(3) A fair
(4) Or poor
(9) DK, etc.

Question 1.5a

Faculty Question: What proportion of the students in your classes are academically prepared to be in your class? Almost all, most, only some, or almost none?

(1) Almost all
(2) Most
(3) Only some
(4) Almost none
(9) DK, etc.

Administrator Question: What proportion of the students at your university (college) are academically prepared to be there? Almost all, most, only some, or almost none?
(1) Almost all
(2) Most
(3) Only some
(4) Almost none
(9) DK, etc.

Question 1.5b

Student Question: How well did your own high school education prepare you for your university (college) work?
(1) Very well
(2) Fairly well
(3) Not very well
(4) Not well at all
(9) DK, etc.

2. PROFESSIONS' RANKINGS

Question 2.1

Faculty/Administrator/Student Question

(From SR's Elite Study/Verba?—Business, Media, Women, Religious Leaders—All Other Items Here Added to Elite Q Version.)

Now we would like to know how much influence you think various groups have over (American/Canadian) life. Think of a scale from 1 to 7, where 1 represents "very little influence" and 7 represents " a great deal of influence." Where on this 7-point scale would you place

Items

a) Business leaders
b) The news media

c) Women
d) Religious leaders
e) Union leaders
f) Ethnic and racial minorities
g) University professors

Responses

(1) Very little influence – (7) Great deal of influence with (9) DK, etc.

Question 2.2

Faculty/Administrator/Student Question: Going over this list again and using the same 7-point scale, where 1 represents “very little influence” and 7 represents “ a great deal of influence,” please tell me how much influence you would like each group to have over (American/Canadian) life. Where on this 7-point scale would you place (READ ITEM—RANDOMIZE ORDER)

Items

a) Business leaders
b) The news media
c) Women
d) Religious leaders
e) Union leaders
f) Ethnic and racial minorities
g) University professors

Responses

(1) Very little influence – (7) Great deal of influence with (9) DK, etc.

Question 2.3

Faculty/Administrator/Student Question: How much respect do you personally have for each of the following professions? Please use a scale of 1 to 7, where 1 means you have “very little respect” for that profession and 7 means you have “very high respect.” Of course, you may choose any number between 1 and 7. What about (READ ITEM—RANDOMIZE ORDER OF A THRU F. ALWAYS ASK G LAST)

Items

a) Lawyers

b) Politicians
c) Corporate executives
d) Journalists
e) Military officers
f) Members of the clergy
(ALWAYS ASK LAST:)
g) University professors

Responses

(1) Very little respect – (7) Very high respect with (9) DK, etc.

3. PURPOSE/CURRICULUM

Question 3.1a

Faculty/Administrator Question: Using a scale from 1 to 7, where 1 is "not important at all" and 7 is "essential," how would you rate the importance of each of the following goals of higher education? Choose any number between 1 and 7 to describe the importance of these goals. What about (READ ITEM—RANDOMIZE)?

Items

a) Provide a broad, general education
b) Prepare students for employment after graduation
c) Learn about the classic works of Western civilization
d) Learn about the importance of non-Western cultures

Responses

(1) Not important at all – (7) Essential with (9) DK, etc.

Question 3.3

Faculty/Administrator/Student Question: Overall, do you think that all undergraduates should be required to take "a common core" of courses in literature, the humanities, social sciences, and natural sciences?

(1) Yes, should
(2) No, should not
(9) DK, etc.

Question 3.4

Faculty/Administrator/Student Question: Thinking about courses on (INSERT ITEM—ROTATE A AND B. ALWAYS ASK C LAST). For undergraduates, should these be *required* courses, *encouraged* courses, made *available* for those interested, or *not offered at all*? What about (NEXT ITEM)? For undergraduates, should these courses be (READ RESPONSES)

Items

a) The experience of women
b) The experience of gays and lesbians
c) The experience of racial minorities

Responses

(1) Required
(2) Encouraged
(3) Made available
(4) Not offered at all
(9) DK, etc.

4. POWER ISSUES

Let's turn now to another topic.

Question 4.1

Faculty Question: When it comes to the direction your institution is going, do you (READ LIST) with the views of your administration?
(1) Always agree
(2) Usually agree
(3) Sometimes agree
(4) Usually disagree
(5) Always disagree
(9) DK, etc.

Administrator Question: When it comes to the direction your institution is going, do you (READ LIST) with the views of your faculty?
(1) Always agree
(2) Usually agree
(3) Sometimes agree

(4) Usually disagree
(5) Always disagree
(9) DK, etc.

Question 4.2

Faculty/Administrator Question: In your view, compared to administrators, how much say do professors have in how this institution is run?

(1) A great deal
(2) Some
(3) A little
(4) Hardly any
(9) DK, etc.

6. CLIMATE ON CAMPUS/FAIR TREATMENT

Question 6.1a

Faculty Question: Since you have become a faculty member here, have you ever *personally* been treated unfairly because of your race, ethnicity, gender, sexual orientation, religious beliefs, or political views?

Administrator Question: Since you have joined the administration here, have you ever *personally* been treated unfairly because of your race, ethnicity, gender, sexual orientation, religious beliefs, or political views?

Student Question: Since you have been a university student here, have you ever *personally* been treated unfairly because of your race, ethnicity, gender, sexual orientation, religious beliefs, or political views?

(1) Yes
(2) No
(9) DK, etc.
(IF "YES" AT Q.6.1A CONTINUE. OTHERS SKIP TO Q.6.2)

Question 6.1b

Faculty/Administrator/Student Question: In what way? (PROMPT FOR SPECIFIC GROUNDS—RACE, ETHNICITY, GENDER, POLITICAL, etc.)

1. ____________________________
2. ____________________________
3. ____________________________

FOR EACH GROUNDS NAMED AT Q6.1.B, ASK Q6.1.C AND 6.1.D CONSECUTIVELY

Question 6.1c

Faculty/Administrator/Student Question: Thinking of the unfair treatment you've experienced due to (GROUNDS NAMED AT Q6.1.B), was this an isolated incident or an ongoing problem?

1. ____________	2. ____________	3. ____________
(1) Isolated	(1) Isolated	(1) Isolated
(2) Ongoing	(2) Ongoing	(2) Ongoing
(3) (Happened occasionally) (VOLUNTEERED)	(3) (Happened occasionally) (VOLUNTEERED)	(3) (Happened occasionally) (VOLUNTEERED)
(9) DK, etc.	(9) DK, etc.	(9) DK, etc.

(FOR EACH GROUNDS NAMED AT Q.6.1B, ASK:)

Question 6.1d

Faculty/Administrator/Student Question: Do you consider this as actual harassment or was it not quite as serious as that?

1. ____________	2. ____________	3. ____________
(1) Yes, harassed	(1) Yes, harassed	(1) Yes, harassed
(2) No	(2) No	(2) No
(9) DK, etc.	(9) DK, etc.	(9) DK, etc.

Question 6.2

Faculty/Administrator Question: Here's a list of issues. Please tell me to what extent each of these is or is not a problem on your campus. What about (READ ITEM—RANDOMIZE)? Is that a problem on your campus? (IF YES: How serious would you say it is—not very serious, fairly serious, or very serious? (REPEAT FOR EACH ITEM)

Items

a) Sexual harassment
b) Racial discrimination
c) Discrimination against gays and lesbians
e) Discrimination against people with left-wing political views
f) Discrimination against people with right-wing political views

Student Question: Here's a list of issues. Please tell me to what extent each of these is or is not a problem on your campus. What about (READ ITEM—RANDOMIZE)? Is that a problem on your campus? (IF YES: How serious would you say it is—not very serious, fairly serious, or very serious? (REPEAT FOR EACH ITEM)

Items

a) Sexual harassment
b) Racial discrimination
c) Discrimination against gays and lesbians
e) Discrimination against people with left-wing political views
f) Discrimination against people with right-wing political views
h) Drug and alcohol abuse

Responses

(1) No, not a problem
(2) Yes, not very serious
(3) Yes, fairly serious
(4) Yes, very serious
(9) DK, etc

7. TENURE

Question 7.1

Faculty/Administrator Question: People debate the merits and drawbacks of tenure. On balance, do you think academic tenure today is . . . ?
(1) Essential
(2) Very important
(3) Somewhat important
(4) Not very important
(5) Not important at all
(9) DK, etc.

Question 7.2

Faculty/Administrator Question: What, in your view, is the *main benefit* of academic tenure? (DO NOT READ LIST—RECORD UP TO TWO RESPONSES)
(1) Academic freedom—general

(2) Job security for prof's
(3) Protect from government
(4) Protect from administration
(5) Help universities choose professors
(6) Helps avoid mediocrity
(7) None—no benefits
(8) Other—Specify: __
(9) DK, etc.

Question 7.4

Faculty/Administrator Question: Every institution has some "deadwood." Do you think your institution ought to be able to get rid of such faculty, even if they have tenure?
(1) Yes, should
(2) No, should not
(9) DK, etc.

8. ACADEMIC FREEDOM

Now, thinking about academic freedom . . .

Question 8.1a

Faculty/Administrator Question: In higher education today in this country, do you think academic freedom is very secure, somewhat secure, somewhat insecure, or very insecure?
(1) Very secure
(2) Somewhat secure
(3) Somewhat insecure
(4) Very insecure
(9) DK, etc.

Question 8.1b

Faculty/Administrator Question: How about on your campus? Is academic freedom very secure, somewhat secure, somewhat insecure, or very insecure?
(1) Very secure
(2) Somewhat secure
(3) Somewhat insecure
(4) Very insecure
(9) DK, etc.

(IF RESPONDENT CHOSE SOMEWHAT OR VERY INSECURE AT Q.8.1A OR Q.8.1B, ASK Q.8.2)

Question 8.2

Faculty/Administrator Question: If there is a threat to academic freedom, where is it coming from? (RECORD RESPONSE)

____

____

____

Question 8.3a

Faculty Question: How often, if at all, have you avoided expressing any particular points of view because you expected a negative student reaction?

Student Question: How often, if at all, have you avoided expressing a particular point of view on an issue because you expected a negative reaction from other students?

(1) Frequently
(2) Sometimes
(3) Rarely
(4) Never
(9) DK, etc.
(IF EVER AT Q.8.3A, ASK:)

Question 8.3b

Faculty/Student Question: When this has happened, what kind of student reaction were you most worried about? (DO NOT READ LIST. ACCEPT UP TO THREE MENTIONS)

(1) Complaints to administration
(2) Poor student evaluations
(3) Lower enrollment in class
(4) Hurt feelings/confuse students
(5) Other—SPECIFY:
(9) DK, etc.

Question 8.4

Faculty Question: And how often, if at all, have you avoided expressing a particular point of view because you expected a negative reaction from other faculty?

Administrator Question: How often, if at all, have you avoided expressing any particular points of view because you expected a negative reaction from faculty?

Student Question: And how often, if at all, have you avoided expressing any particular points of view because you expected a negative reaction from faculty?

(1) Frequently
(2) Sometimes
(3) Rarely
(4) Never
(9) DK, etc.

Question 8.5

Faculty Question: And how often, if at all, do you think other faculty have avoided expressing a particular viewpoint because they expected negative reaction from other faculty or students?

Administrator Question: And how often, if at all, do you think other administrators have avoided expressing any particular viewpoints because they expected negative reaction from faculty?

Student Question: And how often, if at all, do you think other students have avoided expressing any particular viewpoints because they expected negative reaction from faculty or other students?

(1) Frequently
(2) Sometimes
(3) Rarely
(4) Never
(9) DK, etc.

9. ATTITUDES ON ACADEMIC ISSUES—SERIES A

Question 9

Now, please tell me if you strongly agree, moderately agree, moderately disagree or strongly disagree with each of the following statements. (RANDOMIZE STATEMENTS) (REPEAT RESPONSE SCALE EVERY 3 OR 4 STATEMENTS)

Items

Question 9.1a

Faculty/Administrator/Student Question: Higher education should concentrate on challenging the brightest students to do their very best, even if that means leaving some students behind.

Question 9.1b

Faculty/Administrator Question: Collective bargaining is important to protect the interests of the faculty.

*(Split sample for items [d] and [e])

Question 9.1d*

Faculty/Administrator Question: People who donate money to endow a chair have a right to participate in the selection of the chairholder.

Question 9.1e*

Faculty/Administrator Question: Corporations that donate money to endow a chair have a right to participate in the selection of the chairholder.

Question 9.1f

Faculty/Administrator Question: Students get their money's worth for their education at this university.

Question 9.1h

Faculty/Administrator Question: Faculty are the best judges of the educational needs of students.

Question 9.1i

Faculty/Administrator Question: Students should be free to choose whatever courses they want for their degree programs.

Responses

(1) Strongly agree
(2) Moderately agree
(3) Moderately disagree
(4) Strongly disagree
(9) DK, etc.

10. DIVERSITY ISSUES

Thank you. Switching topics now . . .

Question 10

Please tell me if you strongly agree, agree with reservations, disagree with reservations, or strongly disagree with the following statements:

Question 10.1

Faculty/Administrator/Student Question: More minority group undergraduates should be admitted here even if it means relaxing normal academic standards of admission.

Question 10.2

Faculty/Administrator/Student Question: The normal academic requirements should be relaxed in appointing members of minority groups to the faculty here.

Responses

(1) Strongly agree
(2) Agree with reservations
(3) Disagree with reservations
(4) Strongly disagree
(9) DK, etc.
(Q10.3 IS U.S. ONLY:)

Question 10.3

Faculty/Administrator/Student Question: What impact, if any, do you think special admissions policies for minority students have on academic standards? Do such policies mean higher academic standards, lower academic standards, or do they have no real impact? (IF HIGHER: would you say these admissions policies mean much higher or just a little higher academic standards? IF LOWER: would you say these admissions policies mean much lower or just a little lower academic standards?)

(1) Higher standards—much
(2) Higher standards—a little
(3) Lower standards—much
(4) Lower standards—a little
(5) No real impact
(9) DK, etc.

Question 10.4

Faculty/Administrator/Student Question: What impact, if any, do you think special hiring policies for minority faculty have on academic standards? Do such policies mean higher academic standards, lower academic standards, or do they have no real impact? (IF HIGHER: would you say these hiring policies mean much higher or just a little higher academic standards? IF LOWER: would you say these hiring policies mean much lower or just a little lower academic standards?)

(1) Higher standards—much
(2) Higher standards—a little
(3) Lower standards—much
(4) Lower standards—a little
(5) No real impact
(9) DK, etc.

Question 10.5a

Faculty/Administrator: Overall, would you say that female faculty are treated better, worse, or about the same as male faculty at your university (college)?

(1) Better
(2) Worse
(3) Same
(4) (Depends on other characteristics) (VOLUNTEERED)
(9) DK, etc.

Question 10.5b

Faculty/Administrator/Student Question: Overall, would you say that female students are treated better, worse, or about the same as male students at your university (college)?

(1) Better
(2) Worse
(3) Same
(4) (Depends on other characteristics) (VOLUNTEERED)
(9) DK, etc

Question 10.7

Faculty/Administrator Question: From the following four groups, who do you think faces the toughest time getting hired for a faculty position at the average (U.S./Canadian) university? (READ 4 ITEMS IN ORDER) (ONE ONLY)

(1) White females
(2) Minority females
(3) Minority males
(4) White males
(5) (No Difference—VOLUNTEERED)
(9) DK, etc.

11. ATTITUDES ON ACADEMIC ISSUES—SERIES B (DIVERSITY ISSUES)

11.1 Please tell me if you strongly agree, moderately agree, moderately disagree or strongly disagree with each of the following statements. (RANDOMIZE STATEMENTS)

Question 11.1e

Faculty/Administrator/Student Question: This university pays too much attention to minority issues.

Question 11.1f

Faculty/Administrator/Student Question: No one should be given special preference in jobs or college admissions on the basis of their gender or race.

Responses

(1) Strongly agree
(2) Moderately agree
(3) Moderately disagree
(4) Strongly disagree
(9) DK, etc.

12. CHARACTER TRAITS

Faculty/Administrator/Student Question: Thinking about the *professors* at your university (college) . . . (RANDOMIZE ITEMS A, B, AND C).

Question 12.2a

Please rate professors on a 7-point scale where 1 means very lazy and 7 means very hardworking.
(1) Very lazy – (7) Very hardworking with (9) DK, etc.

Question 12.2b

Please rate professors on a 7-point scale where 1 means not approachable for students at all and 7 means very approachable for students.

(INTERVIEWER NOTE: For each item, if respondent is unsure or says "it depends," say: "Of course there's all different kinds of professors, but we're just looking for a generalization of the professors at your school.")

Question 12.2c

Faculty/Administrator/Student Question: Please rate professors on a 7-point scale where 1 means very underpaid and 7 means very overpaid.
(1) Very underpaid – (7) Very overpaid with (9) DK, etc.

Question 12.3a

Faculty/Administrator Question: Thinking about the *administrators* at your university (college) . . . (RANDOMIZE A, B, AND C). Please rate administrators on a 7-point scale where 1 means very lazy and 7 means very hardworking.
(1) Very lazy – (7) Very hardworking with (9) DK, etc.

(INTERVIEWER NOTE: For each item, if respondent is unsure or says "it depends," say: "Of course there's all different kinds of administrators, but we're just looking for a generalization of the administrators at your school.")

Question 12.3b

Faculty/Administrator Question: Please rate administrators on a 7-point scale where 1 means very underpaid and 7 means very overpaid.
(1) Very underpaid – (7) Very overpaid with (9) DK, etc.

Question 12.3c

Faculty/Administrator Question: Please rate administrators on a 7-point scale where 1 means very creative at problem solving and 7 means very rigid.

13. VIEWS ON BROADER SOCIAL ISSUES

Here is a series of different statements about some broader social issues. For each one, please tell me if you strongly agree, somewhat agree, somewhat disagree, or strongly disagree. (RANDOMIZE ITEMS) (REPEAT RESPONSE OPTIONS EVERY 3 OR 4 ITEMS)

Items

(Diversity)

Question 13.1a

Faculty/Administrator/Student Question: Traditional standards of merit for jobs and school admissions are basically affirmative action for white males.

(Politics/Left-Right)

Question 13.1c

Faculty/Administrator/Student Question: The government should work to ensure that everyone has a job.

Question 13.1d

Faculty/Administrator/Student Question: The government should work to reduce the income gap between rich and poor.

Question 13.1e

Faculty/Administrator/Student Question: The less government regulation of business the better.

Question 13.1f

Faculty/Administrator/Student Question: With hard work and perseverance, anyone can succeed in this country.

Question 13.1g

Faculty/Administrator/Student Question: Competition is harmful. It brings out the worst in people.

(Sexuality/Abortion/Sex Roles)

Question 13.1h

Faculty/Administrator/Student Question: Homosexuality is as acceptable a lifestyle as heterosexuality.

Question 13.1i

Faculty/Administrator/Student Question: It is a woman's right to decide whether or not to have an abortion.

Question 13.1j

Faculty/Administrator/Student Question: It is alright for a couple to live together without intending to get married.

(Miscellaneous)

Question 13.1k

Faculty/Administrator/Student Question: When changes occur in my life, I welcome the possibility that something new is beginning.

Question 13.1m

Faculty/Administrator/Student Question: (America/Canada/Québec) is a racist society.

Responses

(1) Strongly agree
(2) Somewhat agree
(3) Somewhat disagree
(4) Strongly disagree
(9) DK, etc.

Question 13.2

Faculty/Administrator/Student Question: Which do you think is more important: (ROTATE STATEMENTS)

Freedom so that everyone can live and develop without hindrance OR

Equality so that nobody is underprivileged and social class differences are not so strong?

(1) Freedom
(2) Equality
(9) DK, etc.

Question 13.3

Faculty/Administrator/Student Question: Generally speaking, would you say that most people can be trusted, or that you can't be too careful in dealing with people?

(1) Most people can be trusted
(2) You can't be too careful
(3) (It depends) (VOLUNTEERED)
(9) DK, etc.

14. POLITICS

Turning now to politics briefly.

(Source: WVS—Modified for telephone)
(IF YES TO Q.14.1A, ASK Q.14.1B:)

Question 14.2

Faculty/Administrator/Student Question: And what about professors as a whole? Politically, would you say they are to the left or right of you? (Very much or somewhat left/right?)

(1) Very much left
(2) Somewhat left
(3) Somewhat right
(4) Very much right
(5) (Same—VOLUNTEERED)
(9) DK, etc.
(Q.14.3A & B IS U.S. ONLY:)

Question 14.3a

Faculty/Administrator/Student Question: Generally speaking, do you think of yourself as a Republican, a Democrat, an Independent, or do you have some other political affiliation? (IF VOLUNTEERS "NOT AMERICAN," ASK TO CLASSIFY ANYWAY, OR THEN ACCEPT DK)

(1) Republican

(2) Democrat
(3) Independent
(4) Other
(9) DK, etc.

15. RELIGION

And now just a few questions about religion . . .

Question 15.1

Faculty/Administrator/Student Question: How important is religion in your life? Is it . . .

(1) Very important
(2) Somewhat important
(3) Not at all important
(9) DK, etc.

Question 15.2

Faculty/Administrator/Student Question: How often do you attend religious services? Is it . . .

(1) More than once a week
(2) Once a week
(3) Almost weekly
(4) Once or twice a month
(5) A few times a year
(6) Seldom or never
(9) DK, etc.

Question 15.3

Faculty/Administrator/Student Question: What is your religious preference? Is it Protestant, Catholic, Jewish, some other religion, or no religion?

(1) Protestant
(2) Catholic
(3) Jewish
(4) Other—SPECIFY:______________________________
(5) No religion
(9) DK, etc.

16. CLASSIFICATION/DEMO QUESTIONS/MISCELLANEOUS

Now, just a final series of questions for classification purposes. Let me again assure you of complete confidentiality.

Question 16.1a

Faculty Question: All things considered, what percentage of your working time would you say you spend on: research, on administration, and on teaching? These three percentages should add to 100%. (INTERVIEWER: ALLOW RESPONDENT TO THINK FOR A MOMENT. PERCENTAGES SHOULD ADD TO 100%.)

Research: ___________%
Administration: _______%
Teaching: ___________%

Question 16.1b

Faculty Question: Thinking now of what you would like to spend your time on, what percentage of your time would you like to spend doing research, on administration, and what percentage would you like to spend on teaching? These three percentages should add to 100%. (ALLOW RESPONDENT TO THINK. PERCENTAGES SHOULD ADD TO 100%.)

Research: ___________%
Administration: _______%
Teaching: ___________%

Question 16.3a

Faculty/Administrator Question: What is the highest academic degree you have earned? (RECORD CAREFULLY.)

____

Question 16.3b

Faculty/Administrator Question: In what discipline?

____

Question 16.3c

Faculty/Administrator Question: At what school did you earn that degree? (IF ANY DOUBT THAT SCHOOL IS IN CANADA/THE U.S., PROBE FOR COUNTRY.)

____

Question 16.5

Faculty/Administrator Question: How many years have you been teaching at the university (college) level?

#: ______________________

Question 16.6a

Faculty Question: Are you tenured, in a tenure track, or do you hold another kind of appointment?

(1) Tenure
(2) Tenure track
(3) Other appointment
(4) DK, etc.

Question 16.6b

Faculty Question: Do you now hold, or have you ever held, an administration position within your institution?

(1) Yes
(2) No
(9) DK, etc.

Question 16.8a

Faculty Question: Within the past five years, and counting anything now in press, how many articles, if any, have you published in refereed journals, or as chapters in academic books? (PROBE FOR BEST GUESS IF UNCERTAIN)

#: ______________________

Question 16.8b

Faculty Question: Again, within the past five years, and counting anything now in press, how many books, if any, have you authored or coauthored?

#: ______________________

Question 16.8c

Faculty Question: Have you served on the editorial board of an academic journal?

(1) Yes

(2) No
(9) DK, etc.

Question 16.9b

Faculty Question: And what about international meetings?
(1) Frequently
(2) Sometimes
(3) Rarely
(4) Never
(9) DK, etc.

17. DEMOGRAPHICS

Question 17.1

Faculty/Administration/Student Question: Gender (RECORDED, NOT ASKED DIRECTLY).
(1) Male
(2) Female

Question 17.2

Faculty/Administration/Student Question: In what year were you born?
19____________________

Question 17.3b

Faculty/Administration/Student Question: Of what country are you a citizen? (RECORD UP TO TWO IF APPLICABLE)
(1) U.S.
(2) Canada
(3) Other—SPECIFY: ______________________________
(9) DK, etc.

Question 17.4a

Faculty/Administration/Student Question: Now, a few questions for data analysis purposes. In terms of your racial background, would you describe yourself as white (US: African American/Canada: black), Hispanic, Asian, or something else?

(1) White
(2) Black/African American
(3) Hispanic
(4) Asian
(5) Something else—SPECIFY: ______________________
(9) DK, etc.

Question 17.4b

Faculty/Administration/Student Question: Do you think of yourself as belonging to a particular ethnic group? (IF YES: Which?)
(1) Yes—SPECIFY: ______________________
(2) No
(9) DK, etc.
(Q.17.5 IS CANADA ONLY:)

Question 17.5

Faculty/Administration/Student Question: What is your mother tongue? That is, the language you first learned as a child and still understand?
(1) English
(2) French
(3) Other
(9) DK, etc.

Question 17.6

Faculty/Administration/Student Question: And, just for data analysis purposes, we'd like to be able to classify respondents who belong to the gay and lesbian community. Would that include you or not?
(1) Yes, gay
(2) No
(9) DK, etc.

Question 17.7

Faculty/Administration/Student Question: What is your marital status: are you single, married, divorced, separated, or living with someone?
(1) Single
(2) Married
(3) Divorced

(4) Separated
(5) Living with someone
(9) DK, etc.

Question 17.10

Faculty Question: And what was your total combined household income before taxes last year? (READ CATEGORIES)

Administrator Question: And what was your total combined household income before taxes last year? (READ CATEGORIES)

Student Question: And, thinking of your parents' household, what was the total combined household income before taxes last year? (READ CATEGORIES)

(1) Under $40,000
(2) Over $40,000 but under $50,000
(3) Over $50,000 but under $60,000
(4) Over $60,000 but under $70,000
(5) Over $70,000 but under $80,000
(6) Over $80,000 but under $90,000
(7) Over $90,000 but under $100,000
(8) Over $100,000 but under $110,000
(9) Over $110,000 but under $120,000
(10) Over $120,000 but under $130,000
(11) Over $130,000 but under $140,000
(12) Over $140,000 but under $150,000
(13) Over $150,000 but under $160,000
(14) Over $160,000 but under $170,000
(15) Over $170,000 but under $180,000
(16) Over $180,000 but under $190,000
(17) Over $190,000 but under $200,000
(18) Over $200,000
(99) DK, etc.

Appendix 2

Professor's Assessment of Institutional Success in Educating Students

A professor's assessment of educational success is statistically linked with a number of factors, the most important of which is the institution's expenditures per student. It is worth noting that research expenditures per student are negatively correlated with assessment of education. However, this finding holds only for schools classified as "master's-level" institutions. Among baccalaureate institutions and doctoral institutions, research expenditures are not related to education.

The regression model shows that after expenditures, the professor's religiosity is the next best predictor of educational rating, with more religious faculty indicating that their colleges are not doing as well at educating students as their more secular counterparts.

Professors in the social sciences and humanities tend to think that their institutions are not doing as well in preparing students as those in the professional majors and the sciences. Faculty at doctoral institutions tend to think that their schools are not preparing students as well as those at baccalaureate institutions.

It is important to note that the model's adjusted R^2 is a mere 0.057, indicating that there is a great deal of variance yet to be explained.

Model of Professor's Assessment of How Well His/Her University Educates Students

Independent Variables	b	*Standard Error*	*Standardized Coefficients*	t	*Significance*
(Constant)	1.950	6.169		0.316	0.752
Sex	0.016	0.044	0.010	0.365	0.715
Age	0.001	0.003	0.007	0.160	0.873
Does professor teach at doctoral institution?	−0.097	0.039	−0.073	−2.476	0.013
Does professor teach at baccalaureate institution?	0.168	0.078	0.059	2.150	0.032
Is professor in the social sciences or the humanities?	−0.102	0.037	−0.076	−2.737	0.006
Percent of the time professor would prefer teaching	0.013	0.011	0.036	1.230	0.219
Number of articles or book chapters published in past five years	0.009	0.013	0.020	0.634	0.526
Years teaching at college level	0.007	0.017	0.019	0.397	0.691
Professor's rank	0.033	0.032	0.040	1.031	0.303
Party identification	−0.052	0.027	−0.054	−1.938	0.053
How often professor attends religious services	−0.040	0.010	−0.107	−3.867	0.000
Research expenditures per student	0.000	0.000	−0.216	−3.422	0.001
General expenditures per student	0.000	0.000	0.404	6.402	0.000
Adjusted R^2	0.057				
$n \approx$	1,400				

Appendix 3

University Rankings by Tier

The *US News & World Report* divides its rankings into two groups (national rankings and regional rankings), both with four tiers. The best colleges and universities are classified into national rankings. Schools that are not nationally ranked are ranked within their respective region. The NAASS tiers are based on modified *US News* rankings with the nationally ranked institutions ranked as tiers 1 through 4 and all the regionally ranked institutions falling into tiers 5 through 8. Although *US News* reports that some of the criteria used for the national institutions' rankings are somewhat distinctive from those ranked regionally, within the NAASS data set these measures are combined into a single eight-point ranking.[1] The schools are listed by tier in the following manner:

TIER 1 SCHOOLS

Boston College, Bowdoin College, Brandeis University, Brown University, Carnegie-Mellon University, Colgate University, College of William and Mary, Cornell University, Dartmouth College, Duke University, Franklin and Marshall College, Johns Hopkins University, Lehigh University, Massachusetts Institute of Technology, Northwestern University, Pennsylvania State University–Main Campus, Princeton University, Rensselaer Polytechnic Institute, Rice University, Stanford University, Syracuse University, Tufts University, Tulane University, University of California–Berkeley, University of California–Los Angeles, University of California–Santa Barbara, University of Chicago, University of Michigan–Ann Arbor, University of North

1. The descriptions of the tier rankings are based on notes within the "Combined Technical Notes and Memos about the 1999 Academic Study Survey" prepared by Dr. Ivan Katchanovski on September 4, 2004.

Carolina, University of Notre Dame, University of Pennsylvania, University of Rochester, University of Southern California, University of Virginia, Vanderbilt University, Vassar College, Wake Forest University, Washington and Lee University, Washington University, and Whitman College

TIER 2 SCHOOLS

Auburn University–Main Campus, Boston University, Clark University, Florida State University, George Washington University, Gettysburg College, Iowa State University, North Carolina State University at Raleigh, Ohio University–Main Campus, Ohio Wesleyan University, Purdue University–Main Campus, Skidmore College, Southwestern University, Stevens Institute of Technology, University of Texas at Austin, University of Arizona, University of Colorado at Boulder, University of Florida, University of Minnesota–Twin Cities, University of Missouri–Columbia, University of Pittsburgh–Main Campus, University of Tennessee–Knoxville, University of Vermont and State Agriculture, and Wittenberg University

TIER 3 SCHOOLS

Alma College, Brigham Young, Coe College, Florida International University, Guilford College, Hofstra University, Kansas State University of Agriculture, Kansas State University of Agriculture and Applied Science, Oglethorpe University, Oklahoma State University–Main Campus, Saint John's University, University of Idaho, University of Cincinnati–Main Campus, University of Maryland–Baltimore County, University of New Mexico–Main Campus, University of Oklahoma–Norman Campus, University of Oregon, University of Utah, and West Virginia University

TIER 4 SCHOOLS

Ball State University, George Mason University, Louisiana Tech University, Nebraska Wesleyan University, New Mexico State University–Main Campus, Northern Illinois University, Shepherd College, Southern Illinois University–Carbondale, Tennessee State University, University of Texas at Arlington, University of Central Florida, University of Houston–University Park, University of Wisconsin–Milwaukee, Wayne State University, and Wright State University–Main Campus

TIER 5 SCHOOLS

Appalachian State University, California Polytechnic State University–San Luis Obispo, Carson-Newman College, Carthage College, Evergreen State College, Florida Southern College, Lebanon Valley College, Marymount Manhattan College, Messiah College, North Central College, Ohio Northern University, Oklahoma Christian University of Science, Oklahoma Christian University of Science and Arts, Saint Mary's College, Saint Norbert College, Seattle University, Shippensburg University of Pennsylvania, Taylor University–Upland, University of North Carolina at Charlotte, University of St. Thomas, and Valparaiso University

TIER 6 SCHOOLS

Belmont Abbey College, California State University–Stanislaus, College of Our Lady of the Elms, CUNY Brooklyn College, CUNY Hunter College, Elizabeth City State University, Florida Agricultural and Mechanical University, Macmurray College, Northwestern College, Oakland University, Point Loma Nazarene College, Roberts Wesleyan College, Saint Xavier University, SUNY College at Plattsburgh, SUNY College at Potsdam, Tennessee Technological University, Towson State University, University of Montevallo, Ursuline College, and Wingate University

TIER 7 SCHOOLS

Austin Peay State University, Bethany College of the Assemblies of God, California State University–Long Beach, Emporia State University, Jackson State University, Lander University, Mesa State College, Rust College, Saint Leo College, Southern Utah University, University of Southern Colorado, University of Nebraska at Kearney, University of Nebraska at Omaha, University of Wisconsin–Stout, West Texas A&M University, Woodbury University, and Youngstown State University

TIER 8 SCHOOLS

Armstrong Atlantic State University, Augusta State University, Bridgewater State College, Central Connecticut State University, Chaminade University, Colorado Christian University, Columbia College, D'Youville College, Eastern Kentucky University, Hilbert College, La Roche College, Long Island University–Brooklyn Campus, Metropolitan State College of Denver, Northeast Louisiana University, Shawnee State, University of Houston, Virginia State University, Virginia Union, and West Virginia State College

Appendix 4

Models of Trust for Students, Faculty, and Administrators

The results of the regression models in the table illustrate that trust is not merely a function of campus-wide diversity. Indeed, for students and faculty, the best predictor of trust is a respondent's race, with whites expressing more trust in others than nonwhites. Students who attend private schools are generally more trusting than those who attend public schools. Those who attend doctoral institutions are more trusting than those attending either baccalaureate or comprehensive schools. Across students, professors, and administrators, the only variable that consistently predicts trust is campus-wide diversity, with respondents from more diverse campuses expressing less trust than those from more diverse campuses.

It is important to note that trust is, for the most part, rather unpredictable, with the models explaining less than 5 percent of the overall variance. Still, in ascertaining their overall level of trust, campus diversity is a relevant factor.

Regression Models of Trust

	Faculty				Administrators				Students			
Independent Variables	B	*Standard Error*	*Standard Beta*	*Significance*	B	*Standard Error*	*Standard Beta*	*Significance*	B	*Standard Error*	*Standard Beta*	*Significance*
Constant	2.899	2.349		.217	3.524	3.410		.302	2.814	5.777		.626
Institutional traits												
Percent black	−002	.001	−068	.020	−002	.001	−092	.028	−003	.001	−084	.010
Expenditures per student	.000	.000	−075	.015	.000	.000	.003	.936	.000	.000	.043	.202
Doctoral institution?	.039	.025	.046	.111	−032	.026	−048	.224	.074	.032	.075	.021
Baccalaureate institution?	−015	.049	−009	.753	−001	.044	−001	.978	.042	.057	.023	.455
Is school public?	−012	.028	−013	.679	.056	.030	.081	.061	−082	.036	−077	.024
Respondent's traits												
Respondent's age	−001	.001	−027	.327	−001	.002	−032	.420	−001	.003	−012	.670
Is respondent a male?	.013	.026	.013	.618	.044	.027	.061	.101	.013	.026	.013	.630
Is respondent black?	−031	.067	−015	.637	−158	.086	−114	.066	−065	.063	−038	.300
Is respondent white?	.171	.039	.136	.000	.004	.067	.003	.955	.112	.038	.095	.004
Respondent's income	.006	.003	.056	.044	.006	.003	.083	.043	−003	.004	−023	.396
n	1,475				744				1,376			
R^2	0.035				0.039				0.041			

Appendix 5

The Impact of Varying Exclusion Methods on College Satisfaction Results

When researchers construct statistical models in order to study the relationship between independent and dependent variables, they must inevitably decide how to account for gaps in the data. For example, respondents are notoriously hesitant to divulge what they consider to be sensitive information (race, income, sexual orientation, and so on) and thus may participate in a survey but simply refuse to answer what they perceive to be overly personal or intrusive questions. By declining to answer selective questions, respondents often leave holes in the data set with which researchers must contend when building large statistical models. There are a number of ways of coping with missing data, but ultimately there is no perfect solution.

Perhaps the most common method of working with missing data is simply to eliminate survey respondents who failed to answer any part of a questionnaire used in a given statistical model. This exclusion method, known as listwise deletion, is simple in that it makes no assertions about what the missing data might have looked like had the respondent been more forthcoming. Perhaps because of its popularity, listwise deletion has long been the default method of exclusion in SPSS regression models. By contrast, when respondents refuse to answer a question used in a regression analysis, the pairwise deletion retains the usable data, discarding "data only at the level of the variable, not the observation" (McKnight et al. 2007, 147).

Although there is no hard-and-fast rule for when researchers should rely on one particular method of exclusion, McKnight et al. (2007) caution against relying on pairwise exclusion when using a "large" data set. All the regression models presented in this text rely on the listwise method of exclusion.

The table provides general replication of the results of the Rothman et al. (2003) model first reported in the *International Journal of Public Opinion Research*. The regression on the left utilized pairwise exclusion, while the regression on the right utilized listwise exclusion. The results are very similar in that both show academic success and religiosity to be the most important predictors of satisfaction among students. However, the difference in the exclusion method prompts changes in the statistical significance of four variables, including the diversity measure. It is impossible to be certain which method of exclusion best captures the true relationship between diversity and student satisfaction. In either event, the results of the NAASS show either that diversity is unrelated to students' overall assessment of college life or that it is negatively correlated to overall levels of student satisfaction.

Replication of Rothman/Lipset/Nevitte Model Using Varying Methods of Exclusion

	Pairwise Exclusion Method					*Listwise Exclusion Method*					
Coefficients	B	*Standard Error*	*Standardized Beta*	t	*Significance*	B	*Standard Error*	*Standardized Beta*	t	*Significance*	
(Constant)	6.357	.586		10.850	.000	6.622	.644		10.275	.000	
Faculty-to-student ratio	–.114	.079	–.049	–1.444	.149	–.088	.083	–.039	–1.062	.288	
Number of programs	–.003	.002	–.066	–1.670	.095	–.003	.002	–.071	–1.576	.115	
Doctoral	.124	.092	.059	1.344	.179	.113	.099	.055	1.144	.253	
Liberal arts	.127	.102	.042	1.244	.214	.055	.114	.019	.478	.633	
Public university	–.056	.100	–.024	–.560	.575	–.027	.114	–.012	–.241	.810	
Proportion of black students	–1.463	.513	–.094	–2.852	.004	–.455	.752	–.021	–.605	.545	←
Percent of admitted who applied	–.324	.208	–.056	–1.556	.120	–.182	.224	–.031	–.811	.418	
Percent students living on campus	–.172	.215	–.038	–.801	.424	.045	.235	.010	.192	.848	
Number of student organizations	.000	.000	.005	.108	.914	.000	.000	.047	.964	.335	
Age	.006	.007	.032	.890	.373	–.008	.009	–.034	–.884	.377	
Income	.066	.157	.013	.420	.675	.051	.164	.011	.313	.754	
Male	.043	.062	.021	.697	.486	.021	.066	.010	.313	.754	
Married	.115	.106	.035	1.087	.277	.238	.121	.069	1.964	.050	←
U.S. citizen	–.092	.482	–.005	–.190	.849	–.408	.510	–.025	–.799	.425	
Protestant	.116	.076	.055	1.537	.125	.206	.084	.100	2.453	.014	←
Catholic	.004	.083	.002	.053	.958	.093	.091	.040	1.022	.307	
Religious attendance	.231	.064	.111	3.603	.000	.256	.071	.125	3.630	.000	
Gay/lesbian	–.288	.215	–.039	–1.340	.181	–.334	.260	–.041	–1.286	.199	

(continued)

Replication of Rothman/Lipset/Nevitte Model Using Varying Methods of Exclusion (continued)

	Pairwise Exclusion Method					*Listwise Exclusion Method*				
Coefficients	B	*Standard Error*	*Standardized Beta*	t	*Significance*	B	*Standard Error*	*Standardized Beta*	t	*Significance*
White	.093	.077	.036	1.209	.227	.074	.088	.027	.832	.405
Parent with university education	–.019	.067	–.009	–.283	.777	.050	.074	.023	.672	.502
High professional	.059	.087	.025	.681	.496	–.042	.095	–.018	–.448	.655
Low professional	.204	.098	.074	2.084	.037	.156	.106	.057	1.470	.142 ←
Humanities	–.046	.100	–.016	–.456	.648	–.094	.107	–.034	–.883	.377
Science	.032	.095	.012	.336	.737	.039	.102	.015	.383	.702
Academic success	–.199	.039	–.147	–5.104	.000	–.255	.042	–.194	–6.114	.000
Number of years in program	–.036	.028	–.041	–1.306	.192	–.004	.031	–.005	–.131	.895
Paid job	–.005	.062	–.002	–.078	.938	.007	.068	.004	.110	.912
Part-time job	–.058	.084	–.021	–.696	.486	–.103	.092	–.036	–1.118	.264
R^2			.046					.072		
n			1,200					1,024		

Appendix 6

Why Professors Think Academic Tenure Is Important

Based on the regression model listed in the table, a professor's views on the importance of tenure are unrelated to his or her assessment of academic freedom on his or her resident campus. By the estimates of the standardized regression coefficients, the important factors in the support for tenure are a professor's years of teaching experience (with more senior professors expressing greater support for tenure) and their perception that academic freedom is secure overall. Partisanship and social ideology each play an independent role in shaping a professor's support for tenure. Those who teach in the social sciences and humanities are more likely to think that tenure is important than those who teach in other disciplines.

Regression Model: Does Professor Think That Academic Tenure Today Is Important?

Independent Variables (listed in order of importance)	B	*Standard Error*	*Standard Beta*	*Significance*
How many years has professor been teaching at the college/university level?	.086	.022	.160	.000
Does professor think that, in general, academic freedom is secure?	–.209	.044	–.155	.000
Party identification	–.165	.040	–.111	.000
Index of liberal responses to social-ideological questions	.087	.028	.087	.002
Is professor in the social sciences or the humanities?	.173	.053	.085	.001
Is professor a female?	–.132	.061	–.056	.031
Books published or in press	.048	.023	.055	.036
Is professor's school a doctoral institution?	.095	.058	.046	.100
Age	–.004	.004	–.042	.299
Articles, chapters published in past five years	–.022	.018	–.034	.225
Is professor's school a baccalaureate institution?	–.078	.099	–.021	.431
Does professor think that, on his or her campus, academic freedom is secure?	.002	.043	.001	.971
(Constant)	4.199	.231		.000
n			1,523	
Adjusted R^2			.098	

Notes

CHAPTER 1: INTRODUCTION

1. In some instances, like Ohio State, these board members serve as representatives rather than full voting members.

2. Recognizing the importance of transparency and accessibility in debates over social scientific policy, the research team will make the complete NAASS data set available to the public at the Roper Center six months following the publication of the book (http://www.ropercenter.uconn.edu).

CHAPTER 2: VISIONS OF THE UNIVERSITY

1. The AAC&U definition of liberal education is taken from the association's website, February 16, 2009, at http://www.aacu.org/press_room/media_kit/what_is_liberal_education.cfm.

2. Quotes are taken from http://www.aacu.org/leap/what_is_liberal_education.cfm, April 2, 2010.

3. According to the 2007–2008 HERI faculty survey (DeAngelo et al. 2009), 81.5 percent of professors at four-year institutions believe that it is "very important" or "essential" to "prepare students for employment after college." This is an increase in support for this goal since the 1998–1999 survey (Sax et al. 1999), when 67.2 percent of faculty at four-year institutions provided this response.

4. A comparison of HERI surveys of American faculty shows little difference in support for the goal of teaching students "the classic works of Western civilization." In 1999, 30.2 percent of faculty rated this an important or essential goal, compared to 34.7 percent in 2008.

5. The Pearson's correlation coefficient between these two variables is .419 ($p < 0.000$) for faculty and .451 ($p < 0.000$) for administrators.

6. The analysis here is based on fairly small sample sizes when broken down at this level. For example, the NAASS includes only twenty-five professors from liberal arts

colleges. This is simply due to the fact that most professors don't teach at liberal arts colleges, so a representative sample of 1,500 college professors is likely to have relatively few members in this category. However, all three groups of respondents show the same pattern, with those at liberal arts colleges ranking the educational quality higher than those at baccalaureate-general institutions. In addition, the difference in rating between professors at liberal arts and general baccalaureate schools is large enough that it is statistically significant at the 95 percent confidence level, even with the small sample size. The differences in assessments among students and administrators follow the same pattern but are not statistically significant at the 95 percent confidence level.

7. This number combines respondents who reported that "most" students are prepared with respondents who reported that "almost all" students are prepared.

8. The minor differences in findings between the NAASS and the HERI data may be attributed to the fact that the HERI data include community colleges, which the authors of the report find to have the lowest faculty satisfaction with student quality.

CHAPTER 3: PERCEPTIONS OF POWER AND CONTROL IN THE AMERICAN UNIVERSITY

1. It is important to note that neither the ACE nor the AGB formally approved the statement but rather chose to "commend" it.

CHAPTER 4: POLITICS AND CULTURE WARS

1. A Gallup Poll survey of 1,017 national adults, conducted November 22–24, 2002, showed that 58 percent of the general public indicated that they would favor "*invading Iraq with U.S. ground troops in an attempt to remove Saddam Hussein from power*." This survey was conducted within days of the Penn faculty protests mentioned in the following sentence.

2. According to a report in the student newspaper *The Daily Pennsylvanian*, organizers had asked faculty with prowar views to speak, but none of them accepted the invitation. See Courtney Schneider's report, "Faculty Protest War in Iraq," in the November 20, 2002, edition.

3. The minutes from the UCLA Senate meeting are available at www.senate.ucla.edu/SenateVoice/Issue4/Divison%20Minutes%204.14.03%20FINAL.doc. Minutes from the UCSB meeting are available at http://senate.ucsb.edu/meetings/Divisional/2.24%20Minutes%20final%20draft.pdf. The Oregon State University vote was covered in the January 22, 2003, edition of the student newspaper, *The Daily Barometer*: http://media.barometer.orst.edu/media/storage/paper854/news/2003/01/22/News/Faculty.Senate.Makes.AntiWar.Resolution-2295040.shtml. All sources were accessed on August 13, 2008.

4. From Ward Churchill, "Some People Push Back: On the Justice of Roosting Chickens." The essay originally appeared on an obscure Internet Web page (see

original post at http://www.kersplebedeb.com/mystuff/s11/churchill.html, retrieved 8/04/08) but became public after the Hamilton College student newspaper reported on the essay. The editor of the newspaper discovered the essay while researching Churchill, who was scheduled to speak at the college. Conservative pundits picked up on the Hamilton College report.

5. The American Association of University Professors issued a statement on February 3, 2005, calling for restraint in the University of Colorado's response and heralding the "freedom of faculty members to express views, however unpopular or distasteful" as "an essential condition of an institution of higher learning."

6. Results are from the 2000 National Election Study, completed one year after the NAASS faculty survey.

7. National survey results for the cohabitation question come from the 1998 GSS. Although there are slight wording differences between the NAASS faculty survey questions and those posed to the general public through other polls, these minor variations cannot explain the large differences in opinion noted here. Even if different versions of the question produce slightly different survey responses, we would not expect the faculty versions of the questions to consistently produce more liberal responses. In some cases, wording differences may cause the difference between professors and the public to look somewhat inflated, while in others it may cause us to underestimate the difference. For example, on the issue of homosexuality, the question posed to the general population asks if homosexuality is "wrong." By contrast, the survey question posed to faculty sets a higher standard, asking if homosexuality is "as acceptable" as heterosexuality. It is likely that some people would think it not wrong but still not *as* acceptable as heterosexuality. However, note that the faculty version is the one that should produce the more conservative response. In this case, the large difference in opinion between faculty and the public is, if anything, understated.

8. The national survey responses come from the 1998 GSS. The GSS included a response option of "neither agree nor disagree," which was not available to the faculty respondents. However, even if we count all the people who responded neutrally as agreeing with cohabitation (the liberal response), we would still find that the faculty are more likely (76 percent) to support cohabitation than are the general public (65 percent).

9. Whereas the 1998 GSS gave respondents a middle-category label "neither agree nor disagree," the NAASS question did not. It is difficult to make an exact comparison, as respondents had a slightly different set of choices in the two surveys.

10. Again the 1998 GSS gave respondents a middle-category labeled "neither agree nor disagree," while the NAASS question did not. While it is difficult to know the exact differences between the populations, it is clear that there remain vast differences between the views of Republican professors and Republicans in the general population.

11. According to the 2009 report from the Higher Education Research Institute (DeAngelo et al. 2009), 55 percent of professors indicated that their views were liberal or far left, while 16 percent indicated that their views were conservative or far right.

12. A simple correlation between the issues position and their "year in school" reveals that their views on homosexuality do vary as a function of time ($p = 0.032$).

13. Recently, there is an institutional effort on some campuses to promote "sustainability." However, this was less the case at the time of the 1999 NAASS survey.

14. Again, a simple correlation between the issues position and their "year in school" reveals that their views on government "reducing the gap between rich and poor" ($p = 0.003$) and government "ensuring everyone has a job" ($p = 0.004$) also vary as a function of time. As with homosexuality, the finding is consistent with a persuasion hypothesis, but it by no means proves that professors caused these changes in student views.

15. The gender gap for the general population is based on a Pew Research Center report and summarizes the partisan affiliation for men and women from 1997 to 2001. The report, *The 2004 Political Landscape*, was published on November 5, 2003, and retrieved August 11, 2008, at http://people-press.org/report/?pageid=750.

16. While this might suggest that Republicans do tend to be lower achievers in academia, the results are not evidence of their accomplishments elsewhere. It is likely that these partisans are not representative of those in the general population and that Republicans in the general population are less interested in producing "new knowledge" than the average Democrats. Indeed, Woessner and Kelly-Woessner (2009b) find that conservatives tend to steer away from pursuing PhDs in part because they have less of an interest in research and more of a focus on making money and raising a family.

17. The three-part Social Liberalism Index was calculated on the basis of the number of times the faculty member "somewhat agreed" or "strongly agreed" with the following statements: 1) "Homosexuality is as acceptable a lifestyle as heterosexuality," 2) "It is a woman's right to decide whether or not to have an abortion," and 3) "It is alright for a couple to live together without intending to get married."

18. From a statistical standpoint, it is unclear whether a scholar's "time on research" is a measure of productivity or a reflection of the prestige of the academic appointment. More prestigious institutions typically have fewer demands on teaching and thus provide more opportunities for research. Uncertain as to whether "time on research" is the cause or effect, we omitted the variable in models 2, 2a, and 2b.

19. In model 1, the relationship p value for the coefficient "Is Respondent Black?" is .051, placing it just outside of the 95 percent confidence bands. The variable is not flagged as significant because we have only a 94.9 percent confidence in the relationship.

20. It is worth noting that, based on the standardized beta coefficients, it would appear that social-ideological views are the single best predictors of institutional prestige after the various measures of merit. Listed in descending order, the results of model 2's standardized beta coefficients are articles published (.313), liberal social ideology (.129), sex (−.090), U.S. citizen (−0.057), and black (−0.054).

21. The negative relationship, predicting that black professors tend to teach at less prestigious institutions, turns positive, albeit the results are not statistically significant ($p = 0.15$). Since the omission of historically black colleges has the effect of excluding a large portion of the already limited pool of black faculty in the sample, our statistical estimates are imprecise. The results raise the possibility that black faculty who opt to teach outside of historically black colleges tend to hold positions at schools that are more prestigious than their research record might otherwise suggest.

22. It is necessary to eliminate all the merit variables because statistically unimportant factors, such as publishing books or serving on an editorial board, act as proxies for the more important predictors, such as the number of published articles, once the important factors are eliminated from the model.

CHAPTER 5: CAMPUS DIVERSITY

1. It is worth noting that Justice Sandra Day O'Connor and coauthor Stewart J. Schwab (2009) acknowledge the lack of scientific consensus on the educational benefits of diversity. The authors contend that much more research is needed, but warn that diversity studies are "fraught with political implications" and that this must not "prevent us from asking questions whose answers might disappoint us." The authors acknowledge that evidence against diversity must also be considered, citing Putnam's (2007) work on the negative effects that diversity has on social solidarity. Yet even if colleges and universities find no real evidence that racial diversity increases student learning, O'Connor and Schwab suggest that other state interests may be used to justify racial preferences. Specifically, the authors contend that children may achieve more when they have role models of their own race and that the need for positive role models in the African American community may be used, in the future, to justify continuation of affirmative action.

2. Results for Hispanic and Asian students are nearly identical to those for blacks.

3. We cover perceptions of discrimination due to political beliefs in chapter 4.

4. In fact, four heterosexual faculty and three heterosexual students did indicate that they had been treated unfairly on the basis of their sexual orientation; however, given the large sample size, the number of complaints constituted less than 0.5 percent of the total respondents and thus appears in the table as 0 percent.

5. A comparison with the same survey questions from the 1998–1999 HERI survey reveals surprisingly little difference in these measures between the two time periods, with nearly identical responses in the importance assigned to increasing the representation of women and minorities in the faculty.

6. In light of our earlier finding that blacks perceive normal standards to be akin to "affirmative action for whites," the lack of support among blacks for racial preferences is especially noteworthy. One explanation is that blacks may merely desire racial equality, resisting what they perceive to be white privilege, while at the same time rejecting preferences for their own group.

7. This reveals more concern for lowered standards than the similar question on the 2008–2009 HERI survey described earlier. This difference may be due to change over time or to differences in the question wording. Still, the basic conclusion that a sizable minority holds these views is consistent.

8. It is worth noting that performance on these objective indicators also keeps most whites from attending the nation's highest-ranked universities.

9. For a discussion of this limitation as it relates to Gurin's testimony, see Wood and Sherman (2001).

10. http://www.stanford.edu/group/diversity and Antonio et al. (2004).

CHAPTER 6: ACADEMIC FREEDOM, TENURE, AND THE FREE EXCHANGE OF IDEAS

1. As the question about the source of the threat to academic freedom was administered only to respondents who felt that there was a threat, only five hundred professors specifically identified a source. Of those who indicated a threat, only 52 respondents indicated that they were Republicans. The small number of respondents in this category makes it difficult to generalize beyond the sample.

2. Support for tenure is consistent over time. According to the 2008–2009 Higher Education Research Institute survey, only a third of faculty agree with the statement that "tenure is an outmoded concept."

3. Perhaps not surprisingly, of the 260 humanities professors represented in figure 6.2, only 13 identified themselves as Republicans. Subsequently, while the results do indicate that Republicans tend to self-censor at similar rates to their Independent colleagues, the sample is too small to fairly represent the experiences of such Republicans in the humanities disciplines as a whole.

References

Adler, Jerry. 1990. Taking offense. *Newsweek*, December 24.

Allen, Walter R. 1992. The color of success: African-American college student outcomes at predominantly white and historically black public colleges and universities. *Harvard Educational Review* 62, no. 1: 26–44.

American Association of University Professors. 2003. Academic freedom and national security in a time of crisis. *Academe* 89: 34–59.

———. 2005. AAUP releases statement on Professor Ward Churchill controversy. http://www.aaup.org/AAUP/Newsroom/prarchives/2005/Church.htm.

American Council on Education and the American Association of University Professors. 2000. Does diversity matter: Three research studies on diversity in college classrooms. http://www.aaup.org/NR/rdonlyres/97003B7B-055F-4318-B14A-5336321FB742/0/DIVREP.PDF.

American Federation of Teachers. 2007. *Academic freedom in the 21st-century college and university*. Washington, DC: American Federation of Teachers.

Antonio, A. L., M. J. Chang, K. Hakuta, D. A. Kenny, S. Levin, and J. E. Milem. 2004. Effects of racial diversity on complex thinking in college students. *Psychological Science* 15, no. 8: 507–10.

Aronson, Pamela. 2003. Feminists or "postfeminists"? Young women's attitudes toward feminism and gender relations. *Gender and Society* 17: 903–22.

Association of American Colleges and Universities. 2006. Statement on Spellings Commission Report. Statement of the Board of Directors, Association of American Colleges and Universities. http://www.aacu.org/about/statements/Spellings9_26_06.cfm.

Astin, Alexander W. 1993. *What matters in college? Four critical years revised*. San Francisco: Jossey-Bass.

Bacharach, Samuel B., and Edward J. Lawler. 1976. The perception of power. *Social Forces* 55: 123–34.

———. 1980. *Power and politics in organizations: The social psychology of conflict, coalitions, and bargaining*. San Francisco: Jossey-Bass.

Baldridge, J. Victor. 1971. *Power and conflict in the university: Research in the sociology of complex organizations.* New York: Wiley.

Baldridge, J. Victor, David V. Curtis, George P. Ecker, and Gary L. Riley. 1973. The impact of institutional size and complexity on faculty autonomy. *Journal of Higher Education* 44: 532–47.

Bason, James J. 2008. *University system of Georgia survey on student speech and discussion.* Athens: University of Georgia Survey Research Center.

Berkes, Howard. 2008. Cheney speech prompts protests at BYU. NPR Morning Edition. http://www.npr.org/templates/story/story.php?storyId=9371087.

Black, Jim Nelson. 2004. *Freefall of the American university: How our colleges are corrupting the minds and morals of the next generation.* Nashville, TN: Thomas Nelson.

Blackburn, Robert T., and Janet H. Lawrence. 2002. *Faculty at work: Motivation, expectation, satisfaction.* Baltimore: Johns Hopkins University Press.

Black students come up short on the three critical measures used by college admissions officials. 2003. *Journal of Blacks in Higher Education* (Summer): 70–71.

Bloom, Allan. 1987. *The closing of the American mind: How higher education has failed democracy and impoverished the souls of today's students.* New York: Simon and Schuster.

Bok, Derek. 2006. *Our underachieving colleges: A candid look at how much students learn and why they should be learning more.* Princeton, NJ: Princeton University Press.

Bornstein, Rita. 2003. *Legitimacy in the academic presidency: From entrance to exit.* Westport, CT: Praeger.

Bowen, William G., and Derek Bok. 2000. *The shape of the river.* Princeton, NJ: Princeton University Press.

Broadway, R., and S. Broadway Flesch. 2000. Question of integration versus segregation arises on Penn State McKeesport Campus. Penn State McKeesport Collegian. http://psumkcollegian.tripod.com/stories/2000/November/campusnews/question_of_intergration_or_segregation_arises_on_PSUMK_campus.htm.

Brogan, Howard O. 1969. Faculty power: Pretense and reality in academic government. *The Journal of Higher Education* 40: 23–30.

Brown, Christopher M. 2002. Good intentions: Collegiate desegregation and transdemographic enrollments. *Review of Higher Education* 25: 263–80.

Brown, David S. 2006. *Richard Hofstadter: An intellectual biography.* Chicago: University of Chicago Press.

Burgan , Mary. 2006. *What ever happened to the faculty? Drift and decision in higher education.* Baltimore: Johns Hopkins University Press.

Carney, Dana R., John T. Jost, Samuel D. Gosling, and Jeff Potter. 2008. The secret lives of liberals and conservatives: Personality profiles, interaction styles, and the things they leave behind. *Political Psychology* 29, no. 6: 807–40.

Ceci, Stephen J., Wendy M. Williams, and Katrin Mueller-Johnson. 2006. Is tenure justified? An experimental study of faculty beliefs about tenure, promotion, and academic freedom. *Behavioral and Brain Sciences* 29: 553–69

Chamoral, Patrick. 2006. Anti-Europeanism and euroskepticism in the United States. In *Hard power, soft power and the future of transatlantic relations*, edited by Thomas L. Ilgen, 163–92. Burlington, VT: Ashgate.

Chubb, John, and Terry Moe. 1988. Politics, markets, and the organization of schools. *American Political Science Review* 82: 1065–87.

Clark, Veve, Shirley Nelson Garner, Margaret Higonnet, and Ketu H. Katrak. 1996. *Anti-feminism in the academy.* New York: Routledge.

Cohen, Michael D., and James G. March. 1986. *Leadership and ambiguity: The American college president.* 2nd ed. Boston: Harvard Business School Press.

Cole, Stephen, and Elinor G. Barber. 2003. *Increasing faculty diversity: The occupational choices of high-achieving minority students.* Cambridge, MA: Harvard University Press.

Converse, Philip E. 1964. The nature of belief systems in the mass publics. In *Ideology and discontent*, edited by David Apter, 206–61. New York: Free Press.

Cook, P., and R. Frank. 1993. The growing concentration of top students at elite schools. In *Studies of supply and demand in higher education*, edited by C. Clotfelter and M. Rothschild, 121–40. Chicago: University of Chicago Press for the National Bureau of Economic Research.

Crisostomo, L. A. 2001. Neo-segregation occurring on campus. *Badger Herald.* http://badgerherald.com/oped/2001/11/19/neo-segregation_occu.php.

DeAngelo, Linda, Sylvia Hurtado, John H. Pryor, Kimberly R. Kelly, Jose Luis Santos, and William S. Korn. 2009. *The American college teacher: National norms for the 2007–2008 HERI Faculty Survey.* Los Angeles: Higher Education Research Institute, University of California, Los Angeles.

Delta Cost Project. 2009. *Trends in college spending: Where does the money come from? Where does it go?* Washington, DC: Delta Project on Postsecondary Education Costs, Productivity and Accountability.

Delucchi, Michael, and Kathleen Korgen. 2002. We're the customer—We pay the tuition: Student consumerism among undergraduate sociology majors. *Teaching Sociology* 30: 100–107.

Delucchi, Michael, and William Smith. 1997. A postmodern explanation of student consumerism in higher education. *Teaching Sociology* 25: 322–27.

DeNardis, Lawrence. 2001. Shared governance. *The Presidency* 4: 38.

DePalma, Anthony. 1991. In campus debate on new orthodoxy, a counteroffensive. *New York Times*, September 25, A1.

Drago, Robert, Carol L. Colbeck, Kai Dawn Stauffer, Amy Pirretti, Kurt Burkum, Jennifer Fazioli, Gabriela Lazzaro, and Tara Habasevich. 2006. The avoidance of bias against caregiving: The case of academic faculty. *American Behavioral Scientist* 49: 9.

Drummond, Tammerlin. 2000. Black schools go white. *Time*, March 20.

D'Souza, Dinesh. 1991. *Illiberal education: The politics of race and sex on campus.* New York: Free Press.

Dye, Nancy Schrom. 1995. Point of view: On the front lines in the P.C. wars. *Washington Post*, April 2, R20.

Ehrenberg, Ronald G. 2000. *Tuition rising: Why college costs so much*. Cambridge, MA: Harvard University Press.

Flores, Araceli, and Christina M. Rodriguez. 2006. University faculty attitudes on affirmative action: Principles toward faculty and students. *Equity and Excellence in Education* 39: 303–12.

Fong, Bobby. 2005. The economics of higher education. *Liberal Education*. http://eric.ed.gov/ERICDocs/data/ericdocs2sql/content_storage_01/0000019b/80/2a/51/b6.pdf.

Foundation for Individual Rights in Education. 2004. About FIRE. http://www.thefire.org/index.php/article/4851.html.

French, David. 2006. Testimony to the Pennsylvania House of Representatives Select Committee on Student Academic Freedom. http://www.thefire.org/index.php.article/6361.html, http://www.aaup.org/AAUP/GR/state/Academic+Bill+of+Rights-State+Level/frenchtestimony.htm.

Geiger, Roger L. 2005. The ten generations of American higher education. In *American higher education in the twenty-first century: Social, political, and economic challenges*, edited by Philip G. Altbach, Robert O. Berdahl, and Patricia Gumport. Baltimore: Johns Hopkins University Press, 126–45.

Gilovich, Thomas. 1991. *How we know what isn't so: The fallibility of human reason in everyday life*. New York: The Free Press.

Glater, Jonathan D. 2007. Rumsfeld as fellow draws a protest at Stanford. *New York Times*, September 21, A13.

Global Knowledge Economy. Report 06-07. San Jose, CA: National Center for Public Policy and Higher Education.

Goldsmith, Pat Antonio. 2004. Schools' role in shaping race relations: Evidence on friendliness and conflict. *Social Problems* 51: 587–612.

Gross, Neil, and Solon Simmons. 2006. Americans' views of political bias in the academy and academic freedom. Unpublished manuscript.

———. 2007. The social and political views of American professors. Unpublished manuscript.

Grutter v. Bollinger. No 539 U.S. 306. Supreme Court of the United States. June 23, 2003.

Gumport, Patricia J. 2001.Divided we govern? *Peer Review*. Association of American Colleges and Universities. http://www.aacu.org/peerreview/pr-sp01/pr-sp01feature1.cfm.

Gurin, Patricia. 1999. The compelling need for diversity in education. January expert report prepared for the lawsuits *Gratz and Hamacher v. Bollinger*, Duderstadt, the University of Michigan, and the University of Michigan College of LS&A, U.S. District Court, Eastern District of Michigan, Civil Action No. 97-75231, and *Grutter v. Bollinger*, Lehman, Shields, the University of Michigan and the University of Michigan Law School, U.S. District Court, Eastern District of Michigan, Civil Action No. 97-75928. http://www.umich.edu/~urel/admissions/legal/expert/gurintoc.html.

Hart, Jeni. 2006. Women and feminism in higher education scholarship: An analysis of three core journals. *Journal of Higher Education* 77: 40–61.

Haskell, Robert E. 1997. Academic freedom, tenure, and student evaluation of faculty: Galloping polls in the 21st century. *Education Policy Analysis Archive* 5, no. 6: 36–39.

Hayek, Friedrich August. 1976. *The mirage of social justice*, Vol. II of *Law, legislation and liberty*. London: Routledge and Kegan Paul.

Herzog, Serge. 2007. Diversity and Educational Benefits: Moving Beyond Self-Reported Questionnaire Data. Education Working Paper Archive, University of Arkansas. Fayetteville, AR.

Hofstadter, Richard. 1962. *Anti-intellectualism in American life*. New York: Vintage Books.

Hofstadter, Richard, and C. DeWitt Hardy. 1952. *The development and scope of higher education in the United States*. New York: Columbia University Press.

Hofstadter, Richard, and Walter P. Metzger. 1955. *The development of academic freedom in the United States*. New York: Columbia University Press.

Honan, James P., and Damtew Teferra. 2001. The US academic profession: Key policy challenges. *Higher Education* 41: 183–203.

Hoover, Eric. 2007. U. of Delaware abandons sessions on diversity. *Chronicle of Higher Education* 54, no. 12: A1.

Horowitz, David. 2007a. *The professors: The 101 most dangerous academics in America*. Washington, DC: Regnery Press.

———. 2007b. *Indoctrination U: The left's war against academic freedom*. New York: Encounter Books.

———. 2008. Academic Bill of Rights. http://www.studentsforacademicfreedom.org/documents/1925/abor.html.

Hutchins, Robert M. 1951. Freedom of the university ethics. *An International Journal of Social, Political, and Legal Philosophy* 61: 95–104.

Immerwahr, John. 1998. *The price of admission: The growing importance of higher education*. San Jose, CA: National Center for Public Policy and Higher Education.

———. 2002. *The affordability of higher education: A review of recent survey research*. Report 02-04. San Jose, CA: National Center for Public Policy and Higher Education.

———. 2004. *Public attitudes on higher education: A trend analysis, 1993 to 2003*. Report 04-2. San Jose, CA: National Center for Public Policy and Higher Education.

Immerwahr, John, and Tony Foleno. 2000. *Great expectations: How the public and parents—white, African American, and Hispanic—view higher education*. San Jose, CA: National Center for Public Policy and Higher Education.

Immerwahr, John, and Jean Johnson. 2007. *Squeeze play: How parents and the public look at higher education today*. San Jose, CA: National Center for Public Policy and Higher Education.

———. 2009. *Squeeze play 2009: The public's views on college costs today*. San Jose, CA: National Center for Public Policy and Higher Education.

Immerwahr, John, Jean Johnson, and Paul Gasbarra. 2008. *The iron triangle: College presidents talk about costs, access, and quality*. Report 08-2. San Jose, CA: National Center for Public Policy and Higher Education.

Innerst, Carol. 1991. Political correctness gets a presidential chastising. *Washington Times*, May 6, A1.

Institute of Higher Education. 2007. Top 500 world universities (1–99). Institute of Higher Education, Shanghai Jiao Tong University. http://ed.sjtu.edu.cn/rank/2007/ARWU2007_Top100.htm.

Jaschik, Scott. 2005. Redefining liberal education. Insidehighered.com. http://www.insidehighered.com/news/2005/01/28/aacu.

———. 2006. Summers postmortem, beyond Cambridge. Insidehighered.com. http://www.insidehighered.com/layout/set/print/news/2006/02/22/summers.

———. 2007. The liberal (and moderating) professoriate. Insidehighered.com. http://www.insidehighered.com/news/2007/10/08/politics.

Jennings, Kent M. 1992. Ideological thinking among mass publics and political elite. *Public Opinion Quarterly* 56: 419–41.

Johnson, Barbara. 2004. Orientation and colleagues: Making a difference in socialization of Black college faculty. In *Black colleges: New perspectives on publishing and practices*, edited by M. Christopher Brown and Kassie Freeman. Westport, CT: Praeger, 135–48.

Kantrowitz, Mark. 2009. Tuition inflation. FinAid. http://www.finaid.org/savings/tuition-inflation.phtml.

Kelly-Woessner, April, and Matthew Woessner. 2006. My professor is a partisan hack: How perceptions of a professor's political views affect student course evaluations. *PS: Political Science and Politics* 39: 495–501.

Keyishian v. Board of Regents. No 385 U.S. 589. Supreme Court of the United States. January 23, 1967.

Kezar, Adrianna, and Peter D. Eckel. 2004. Meeting today's governance challenges: A synthesis of the literature and examination of a future agenda for scholarship. *Journal of Higher Education* 75: 371–99.

Kimball, Roger. 1990. *Tenured radicals: How politics has corrupted our higher education*. New York: Harper and Row.

Kinder, Donald R., and David Sears. 1981. Prejudice and politics: Symbolic racism versus racial threats to the good life. *Journal of Personality and Social Psychology* 40: 3.

Kissel, Adam. 2008a. Please report to your resident assistant to discuss your sexual identity—It's mandatory! Thought reform at the University of Delaware. Retrieved from Foundation for Individual Rights in Education. http://www.thefire.org/article/9865.html.

Kissel, Adam. 2008b. Sustainability and Indoctrination in the New University of Delaware Plan. http://www.thefire.org/article/9259.html. Retrieved July 24, 2010.

Klein, Daniel, and Charlotta Stern. 2005. Professors and their politics: The policy views of social scientists. *Critical Review* 17: 257–303.

———. 2009. Groupthink in academia: Majoritarian departmental politics and the professional pyramid. In *Reforming the politically correct university*, edited by Robert Maranto, Richard Redding, and Frederick Hess. Washington, DC: American Enterprise Institute Press, 79–98.

Klein, Daniel, and Andrew Western. 2004–2005. Voter registration of Berkeley and Stanford faculty. *Academic Questions* 18: 53–65.

Kolevzon, Michael S. 1981. Grade inflation in higher education: A comparative study. *Research in Higher Education* 15: 195–212.

Kors, Alan Charles, and Harvey A. Silverglate. 1998. *The shadow university: The betrayal of liberty on America's campuses.* New York: Free Press.

Krauthammer, Charles. 1991. Annals of political correctness: On campus, flying the flag is a provocation. *Washington Post*, February 8, A18.

Kreuzer, Terese Lobe. 1993–1994. The bidding war for top black students. *Journal of Blacks in Higher Education*, Winter, 114–18.

Kunda, Ziva. 1990. The case for motivated reasoning. *Psychological Bulletin* 108: 480–98.

Ladd, Everett Carll, and Seymour Martin Lipset. 1975. *The divided academy: Professors and politics*. New York: McGraw-Hill.

Laird, Thomas Nelson. 2005. College students' experiences with diversity and their effects on academic self-confidence, social agency, and disposition toward critical thinking. *Research in Higher Education* 46, no. 4 (June): 365–87.

Latzer, Barry. 2004. The hollow core failure of the general education curriculum. American Council of Trustees and Alumni. https://www.goacta.org/publications/downloads/TheHollowCore.pdf.

Lazarsfeld, Paul F., and Wagner Thielens Jr. 1958. *The academic mind.* Glencoe, IL: Free Press of Glencoe.

Leslie, Larry L., and Gary Rhoades. 1995. Rising administrative costs: Seeking explanations. *Journal of Higher Education* 66: 187–212.

Levinson, Arlene. 2000. As different as day and night. *Black Issues in Higher Education* 16: 30.

Lewin, Tamar. 2006. At colleges, women are leaving men in the dust. *New York Times*. http://www.nytimes.com/2006/07/09/education/09college.html.

Lindholm, J. A., K. Szelényi, S. Hurtado, and W. S. Korn. 2005. *The American college teacher: National norms for the 2004–2005 HERI Faculty Survey.* Los Angeles: Higher Education Research Institute, University of California, Los Angeles.

Lipset, Seymour Martin. 1982. The academic mind at the top: The political behavior and values of faculty elites. *Public Opinion Quarterly* 46: 143–68.

Lord, Charles G., Lee Ross, and Mark R. Lepper. 1979. Biased assimilation and attitude polarization: The effects of prior theories on subsequently considered evidence. *Journal of Personality and Social Psychology* 37: 2098–109.

Lyons, Morgan, and Judith Lyons. 1973. Power and the university: A perspective on the current crisis. *Sociology of Education* 46: 299–314.

Maeroff, Gene I. 1983. College units ask curb on heckling. *New York Times*, March 30, A1.

Maranto, Robert, Richard E. Redding, and Frederick M. Hess. 2009. The PC academy debate: Questions not asked. In *The politically correct university*, edited by R. Maranto, R. Redding, and F. Hess. Washington. DC: AEI Press, 3–14.

Marcus, Ann, Larry C. Mullins, Kimberly P. Brackett, Zongli Tang, Annette M. Allen, and Daniel W. Pruett. 2003. Perceptions of racism on campus. *College Student Journal* 37: 611–26.

Mariani, Mack D., and Gordon J. Hewitt. 2008. Indoctrination U.? Faculty ideology and changes in student political orientation. *PS: Political Science and Politics* 41: 773–83.

Marks, Joseph, and Alicia Diaz. 2007. *SREB Fact Book on higher education*. Atlanta, GA: Southern Regional Educational Board.

Martin, Deanna. 2009. Roll back tuition hike, lawmakers urge colleges. *Indianapolis Star*. http://wap.indystar.com/news.jsp?key=498711&rc=th.

Mason, Mary Ann, and Marc Goulden. 2002. Do babies matter? The effect of family formation on the lifelong careers of academic men and women. Academe Online. http://www.aaup.org/AAUP/pubsres/academe/2002/ND/Feat/Maso.htm.

McClellan, E. Fletcher. 2009. An overview of the assessment movement. In *Assessment in political science*, edited by Michelle D. Deardorff, Kerstin Hamann, and John Ishiyama. Washington, DC: American Political Science Association, 39–58.

McDermott, K. 2002. Thesis raises troubling questions about race at Dartmouth. http://www.southend.wayne.edu/days/may2002/5302002/news/dartmouth/dartmouth.

McKnight, Patrick E., Katherine M. McKnight, Souraya Sidani, and Aurelio José Figueredo. 2007. *Missing data*. New York: Guilford Press.

McNeil, Kristine. 2002. The war on academic freedom. *The Nation*. http://www.thenation.com/doc/20021125/mcneil.

Meacham, Jack, Michelle Mcclellan, Tonia Pearse, and Rashidi Greene. 2003. Student diversity in classes and educational outcomes: Student perceptions. *College Student Journal* 37: 627–42.

Menand, Louis. 2010. *The marketplace of ideas: Reform and resistance in the American University*. New York: Norton.

Miller, David. 1999. *Social justice*. Cambridge, MA: Harvard University Press.

Mincer, Jilian. 2008. State budget cuts push tuition higher. *Wall Street Journal*. http://online.wsj.com/article/SB122427782919745693.html.

Murray, Charles. 2008. For most people, college is a waste of time. *Wall Street Journal*. http://online.wsj.com/article/SB121858688764535107.html.

Myers, Carrie. 2008. Divergence in learning goal priorities between college students and their faculty. *College Teaching* 56, no. 1: 53–58.

National Association of Scholars. 2007. A response to the AAUP's report, Freedom in the Classroom. http://www.nas.org/polArticles.cfm?Doc_Id=32.

National Center for Public Policy and Higher Education. 2008. The bloom is off the rose and the public is jumpy. National Center for Public Policy and Higher Education. http://www.highereducation.org/pa_college_opp/bloom.shtm.

National Education Association. 2003. Why are college prices increasing and what should we do about it? *Update* 9, no. 5.

Neal, Anne, and Jerry Martin. 2002. *Restoring America's legacy*. Washington, DC: American Council of Trustees and Alumni.

Nieli, Russel K. 2004. The changing shape of the river: Affirmative action and recent social science research. *Academic Questions*, Fall, 7–58.

Noel, Barbara, and Alan F. Fontana. 1974. The university as a system with competing constituencies. *Journal of Conflict Resolution* 18: 595–619.

Noelle-Newman, Elizabeth. 1974. The spiral of silence: A theory of public opinion. *Journal of Communication* 24: 43–51.

O'Connor, Sandra Day, and Stewart J. Schwab. 2009. Affirmative action in higher education over the next twenty-five years. In *The next twenty-five years: Affirmative action in higher education in the United States and South Africa*, edited by D. L. Featherman, M. Hall, and M. Krislov. Ann Arbor: University of Michigan Press, 58–73.

Pena, Dely, and Deborah Mitchell. 2000. The American faculty poll. *National Education Association Journal* 6: 3–8.

Peterson, Marvin W., and Theodore H. White. 1992. Faculty and administrator perceptions of their environments: Different views or different models of organization? *Research in Higher Education* 33: 177–204.

Putnam, Robert D. 2007. E pluribus unum: Diversity and community in the twenty-first century: The 2006 Johan Skytte Prize Lecture. *Scandinavian Political Studies* 30: 137–74.

Putten, Jim, Michael McLendon, and Marvin Peterson. 1997. Comparing union and nonunion staff perceptions in the higher education work environment. *Research in Higher Education* 38: 145.

QS World University Rankings 2009—Top Universities. QS. http://www.topuniversities.com/university_rankings/results/2008/overall_rankings/top_100_universities.

Reeves, Thomas C. 2005. Why conservatives should support tenure. History News Network. http://hnn.us/blogs/entries/12076.html.

Renewing the academic presidency: Stronger leadership for tougher times. 1996. Washington, DC: Association of Governing Boards of Universities and Colleges.

Richeson, Jennifer A., Abigail A. Baird, Heather L. Gordon, Todd F. Heatherton, Carrie L. Wyland, Sophie Trawalter, and J. Nicole Shelton. 2003. An FMRI investigation of the impact of interracial contact on executive function. *Nature Neuroscience* 6: 1323–28.

Richeson, Jennifer A ., and J. Nicole Shelton. 2003. When prejudice does not pay: Effects of interracial contact on executive function. *Psychological Science* 14: 287–90.

Richeson, Jennifer A., and Sophie Trawalter. 2005. Why do interracial interactions impair executive function? A resource depletion account. *Journal of Personality and Social Psychology* 88: 934–47.

Rothman, Stanley, and S. Robert Lichter. 2009. The vanishing conservative—Is there a glass ceiling? In *Reforming the politically correct university: Problems, scope and reforms*, edited by R. Maranto, R. Redding, and F. Hess. Washington, DC: AEI Press, 60–76.

Rothman, Stanley, S. Robert Lichter, and Neil Nevitte. 2005. Politics and professional advancement among college faculty. *The Forum* 3, art. 2.

Rothman, Stanley, Seymour Martin Lipset, and Neil Nevitte. 2003. Does enrollment diversity improve university education? *International Journal of Public Opinion Research* 15: 8–26.

Ryan, James J., James A. Anderson, and Allen B. Birchler. 1980. Student evaluation: The faculty responds. *Research in Higher Education* 12: 317–33.

Ryu, Mikyung. *Minorities in higher education 2008: 23rd status report*. Washington, DC: American Council on Education, 2008.

Sax, Linda, Alexander Astin, William Korn, and Shannon Gilmartin. 1999. The American college teacher: National norms for the 1998–1999 HERI Faculty Survey. Los Angeles: Higher Education Research Institute, University of California, Los Angeles.

Schackner, Bill. 2009a. Budget to decide Penn State tuition. *Philadelphia Inquirer*. http://www.philly.com/inquirer/education/20090711_Budget_to_decide_Penn_State_tuition.html.

———. 2009b. No stimulus money for Pitt and Penn State: Rendell delivers big budget blow to four state-related universities. *Pittsburgh Post-Gazette*. http://www.post-gazette.com/pg/09178/980284-298.stm#ixzz0VGD3Z6Rl.

Schatz, Robert T., Ervin Staub, and Howard Lavine. 1999. On the varieties of national attachment: Blind versus constructive patriotism. *Political Psychology* 20: 151–74.

Schulz-Hardt, Stefan, Feliz C. Brodbeck, Andreas Mojzisch, Rudolf Kerschreiter, and Dieter Frey. 2006. Group decision making in hidden profile situations, dissent as a facilitator for decision quality. *Journal of Personality and Social Psychology* 91: 1080–93.

Schulz-Hardt, Stefan, Dieter Frey, Carsten Lüthgens, and Serge Moscovici. 2000. Biased information search in group decision making. *Journal of Personality and Social Psychology* 78: 655–69.

Schuster, Jack H., and Martin J. Finkelstein. 2006. *The American faculty: The restructuring of academic work and careers*. Baltimore: Johns Hopkins University Press.

Scott, Joanna V. 1996. The profession: The strange death of faculty governance. *Political Science and Politics*, December, 724–26.

Sears, David, and Jack Citrin. 1982. *Tax revolt*. Cambridge, MA: Harvard University Press.

Shapiro, Ben. 2004. *Brainwashed: How universities indoctrinate America's youth*. Nashville, TN: Thomas Nelson.

Shrecker, Ellen. 1986. *No ivory tower: McCarthyism and the universities*. New York: Oxford University Press.

Sidanius, Jim, Shana Levin, Colette van Laar, and David O. Sears. 2008. *The diversity challenge: Social identity and intergroup relations on the college campus*. New York: Russell Sage Foundation.

Sidanius, Jim, Colette van Laar, Shana Levin, and Stacey Sinclair. 2004. Ethnic enclaves and the dynamics of social identity on the college campus: The good the bad and the ugly. *Journal of Personality and Social Psychology* 87: 96–110.

Smith, Bruce L. R., Jeremy D. Mayer, and A. Lee Fritschler. 2008. *Closed minds? Politics and ideology in American universities*. Washington, DC: Brookings Institution.

Sniderman, P. M., & P. E. Tetlock. 1986a. Reflections on American racism. *Journal of Social Issues* 42: 173–88.

———. 1986b. Symbolic racism: Problems of motive attribution in political analysis. *Journal of Social Issues*. 42: 129-150.

Sniderman, Paul M., and Thomas Piazza. 1995. *The scar of race*. Cambridge, MA: Harvard University Press.

Sommers, Christina Hoff. 2000. The war against boys: How misguided feminism is harming our young men. *The Atlantic*. http://www.theatlantic.com/doc/200005/war-against-boys.

Stouffer, Samuel Andrew. 1992. *Communism, conformity and civil liberties: A cross section of the nation speaks its mind*. New Brunswick, NJ: Transaction.

Superson, Anita M., and Ann E. Cudd. 2002. *Theorizing backlash: Philosophical reflections on the resistance to feminism*. Lanham, MD: Rowman & Littlefield.

Sweezy v. New Hampshire. No. 354 U.S. 234. Supreme Court of the United States. June 17, 1957.

Taylor, Paul. 2008. Republicans: Still happy campers. Pew Research Center. http://pewresearch.org/pubs/1005/republicans-happier.

Taylor, P., C. Funk, and P. Craighill. 2006. Are we happy yet? Pew Research Center. http://pewresearch.org/assets/social/pdf/AreWeHappyYet.pdf.

Tetlock, Philip E. 1994. Political psychology or politicized psychology: Is the road to scientific hell paved with good moral intentions? *Political Psychology* 15: 509–29.

Thelin, John. 2004. *A history of American higher education*. Baltimore: Johns Hopkins University Press.

The state of black student freshman enrollments at the nation's highest-ranked colleges and universities. 2008. *Journal of Blacks in Higher Education*, Autumn, 44.

Tierney, William G., and Vicente M. Lechuga. 2005. Academic freedom in the 21st century. *Thought and Action*, Fall, 7–22

Tierney, William G., and James T. Minor. 2003. *Challenges for governance: A national report*. Los Angeles: Center for Higher Education Analysis, University of Southern California.

Trawalter, Sophie, and Jennifer A. Richeson. 2006. Regulatory focus and executive function after interracial interactions. *Journal of Experimental Social Psychology* 42: 406–12.

Trower, Cathy. 2001. Negotiating the non-tenure track. *Chronicle of Higher Education*. http://chronicle.com/jobs/news/2001/07/2001070601c.htm.

Usher, Alex, and Amy Cervenan. 2005. *Global higher education rankings 2005*. Toronto: Educational Policy Institute.

US News & World Report. 2007. A history of controversial campus speakers. http://www.usnews.com/articles/news/national/2007/10/01/a-history-of-controversial-campus-speakers.html.

Vobeda, Barbara. 1986. Education group warns of censorship dangers. *Washington Post*, October 10, A12.

Wagner, Alan. 2006. *Measuring up internationally: Developing skills and knowledge for the global knowledge economy*. San Jose, CA: National Center for Public Policy and Higher Education.

Waugh, William L., Jr. 2003. Issues in university governance: More "professional" and less academic. *Annals of the American Academy of Political and Social Science* 585: 84–96.

Welch, Susan. 1985. The more for less paradox: Public attitudes on taxing and spending. *Public Opinion Quarterly* 49: 310–16.

Whaples, Robert. 1995. Changes in attitudes among college economics students about the fairness of the market. *Journal of Economic Education* 26: 308–13.

Whitt, Elizabeth J., Marcia I. Edison, Earnest T. Pascarella, Patrick T. Terenzini, and Amaury Nora. 2001. Influences on Students' Openness to Diversity and Challenge in the Second and Third Years of College. *Journal of Higher Education* 72, no. 2: 172–204.

Williams, Don, William Gore, Charles Broches, and Cynthia Lostoski. 1987. One faculty's perceptions of its governance role. *Journal of Higher Education* 58: 629–57.

Wilson, John K. 1995. *The myth of political correctness: The conservative attack on higher education.* Durham, NC: Duke University Press.

———. 2005. Academic freedom in America after 9/11. *Thought and Action: The NEA Higher Education Journal*, Fall, 119–31.

Wilson, Robin. 2003. The unintended consequences of affirmative action. *Chronicle of Higher Education* 49: A10.

———. 2007. The AAUP, 92 and ailing. *Chronicle of Higher Education* 53: A8.

Woessner, Matthew, and April Kelly-Woessner. 2009a. I think my professor is a democrat: Considering whether students recognize and react to faculty politics. *PS: Political Science and Politics* 42: 343–52.

———. 2009b. Left pipeline: Why conservatives don't get doctorates. In *Reforming the politically correct university,* edited by R. Maranto, R. Redding, and F. Hess. Washington, DC: AEI Press, 38–55.

Wood, Thomas E., and Malcolm J. Sherman. 2001. Race and higher education: Is campus racial diversity correlated with educational benefits? Part IV of the National Association of Scholars Report: Race and higher education: Why Justice Powell's diversity rationale for racial preferences in higher education must be rejected. http://www.nas.org/polimage.cfm?doc_Id=89&size_code=Doc.

Index

About the Authors

Stanley Rothman is the Mary Huggins Gamble Professor of Government Emeritus at Smith College and the director of the Center for the Study of Social and Political Change. He received his PhD in government from Harvard University. He is the author or coauthor of twenty books, including *European Society and Politics* (1970), *Roots of Radicalism* (1982), and *The Media Elite* (1986). His more recent books include *American Elites* (1996), *Hollywood's America: Social and Political Themes in Motion Pictures* (1996), *Environmental Cancer: A Political Disease?* (1999), and *The Least Dangerous Branch? The Consequences of Judicial Activism* (2002).

He is also the author or coauthor of over 120 articles in professional and popular journals, and he has written reviews and articles for such magazines as *Commentary*, *The National Review*, *The Public Interest*, *The American Spectator*, *The New Leader*, and *The Columbia Journalism Review*. His research has been covered by, among other outlets, *The New York Times, The Washington Post,* and *The Chronicle of Higher Education.*

Professor Rothman has received grants from, among others, the Ford Foundation, the Smith Richardson Foundation, The Olin Foundation, the National Science Foundation, The Scaife Foundation, and the Social Science Research Council. He has served on a number of committees of the American Political Science Association and as a member of the board of editors of *Political Psychology*.

April Kelly-Woessner is associate professor of political science at Elizabethtown College. She received her PhD in political science from The Ohio State University in 2001, where she specialized in public opinion, mass political behavior, and political psychology. Professor Kelly-Woessner has published articles on politics and policy, including recent work on politics in higher education. Professor Kelly-Woessner's previous research on politics in the academy has been featured in *The Christian Science Monitor*, *The Chronicle of Higher Education*, *The Guardian*, *The New York Times*, *The New York Times Magazine*, *Science Magazine*, *The Wall Street Journal*, and *The Washington Post*.

Matthew Woessner is associate professor of political science and public policy at Penn State University at Harrisburg. He received his PhD in political science in 2001 from The Ohio State University, where he specialized in public opinion, mass political behavior, and political psychology. He has published articles on policing, constitutional law, public opinion, voting, and ethics. His recent work has been devoted almost exclusively to politics in higher education. Professor Woessner's work on views within higher education has been featured in *The Christian Science Monitor*, *The Chronicle of Higher Education*, *The Guardian*, *The New York Times*, *The New York Times Magazine*, *Science Magazine*, *The Wall Street Journal*, and *The Washington Post*.